R. Bilsborrow
NYU, 7/69

Population Dilemma
in Latin America

"Es nuestro problema"—ALBERTO LLERAS CAMARGO
Cali, Colombia, August 1965

D1248626

WASHINGTON, D.C.

POTOMAC BOOKS, INC. PUBLISHERS

1966

© 1966 by The American Assembly, Columbia University

Copyright under International and Pan American Copyright Conventions

All Rights Reserved
No part of this book may be reproduced in any form, by mimeograph or
any other means, without permission in writing from the Publisher.

Library of Congress Catalog Card No.: 66-18575

Printed in the United States of America for the Publisher
By the George Banta Company, Menasha, Wisconsin

To Gabriel Velasquez

Contents

Preface

On August 11, 1965, a group of persons prominent in North, Central, and South America in business, education, government, medicine, communications, the Church, and other pursuits gathered in Cali, Colombia, for the Pan-American Assembly on Population. The Assembly was sponsored by Universidad del Valle, the Association of Colombian Medical Schools, and The American Assembly of Columbia University, with the cooperation and financial support of The Population Council, Inc.

In addition to serving as Chairman of the Assembly, Dr. Alberto Lleras Camargo, former President of Colombia, delivered a formal address. Other addresses were given by Dr. Frank W. Notestein, President of The Population Council, and Dr. Manuel San Miguel, Executive Director of the International Bank for Reconstruction and Development. These have been published in a pamphlet entitled *Three Talks on Population,* available from The American Assembly, Columbia University.

The directors of the Pan-American Assembly were Dean Gabriel Velazquez Palau and Dr. Ramiro Delgado Garcia of the Faculty of Medicine, Universidad del Valle.

For three days participants engaged in small group discussions at separate tables. On the fourth day in plenary session they approved a final report of findings and recommendations, which has been printed separately and may be obtained from The American Assembly.

Under the editorial supervision of Dr. J. Mayone Stycos of Cornell University and Dr. Jorge Arias, Rector, University of San Carlos, Guatemala, the papers which follow were designed as background reading for the Pan-American Assembly on Population as well as for the general reader. A Spanish edition is being published by Universidad del Valle for circulation in Central and South America.

The views found in the chapters which follow are the authors' own and not those of the sponsoring institutions, which take no official position.

Clifford C. Nelson
President
The American Assembly

Introduction

J. MAYONE STYCOS,
Cornell University

JORGE ARIAS,
University of San Carlos

Latin America is a demographer's paradise. In a region with so many significant historic, cultural, and linguistic similarities, the demographic variations and changes are truly remarkable. A few examples:

. . . whereas the developed countries of the world grew by 40% between 1920 and 1960, and the less developed regions grew by 70%, Latin America grew by 138%.

. . . Mexico probably established a world's record by adding a year to its average citizen's life expectancy every year for the past 25 years.

. . . Brazil, which had 20 cities of over 50,000 population in 1940, had 71 such cities in 1960.

. . . Venezuela advanced as much in urbanization in the past quarter century as the United States did in 90 years.

. . . the difference in birth rate between Argentina and Costa Rica is probably greater than the difference in birth rate between pre-industrial and contemporary England.

But the demographer's dream can be the social planner's nightmare. The planner, seeking to introduce changes which will improve health, education, housing, agriculture, etc., must face the stark fact that by the end of the century Latin America's current population of 240 million will almost certainly be doubled, and may even be tripled. Shorter-run forecasts are more certain but no more reassuring. Thus, between 1960 and 1970 Latin America will have to construct 1,800,000 houses per year to keep the housing situation from continually deteriorating. Every year for the next 15 years, Latin America will have to supply 28,000 additional hospital beds, 530 additional out-patient health units, and 4,800 additional doctors just to *maintain* the present admittedly inadequate ratio of medical resources to population. To surpass population growth and achieve improvement in *per capita* welfare will often require Herculean efforts. As an extreme example, in order to enroll only 30% of its 15-19 year age group in school by 1980, Haiti will require *twelve times* the number of secondary school seats available in 1960. Even providing employment for such massive increments of people becomes a problem. Over the past decade in Central America, for every death or retirement from the labor force there were three or four new job applicants in rural areas and two or three in urban areas. In the next decade additions to the labor force will be even greater. Can this many jobs be created, and, more importantly, can the present level and productivity of employment be improved? This kind of question must be faced in most of the important fields of national activity—agriculture, industry, health, education, etc. —for improvements in such areas are at the very heart of the modernization process.

There are no easy and truly satisfactory answers to these questions, but solutions to such a range of problems may require efforts not only directly to stimulate economic development, but to slow down the current rates of population growth.

During the period of its agricultural and industrial transformation, Europe offset its high rates of natural increase by massive emigration to the Western Hemisphere. Today Latin America looks at a world of nations no longer eager for heavy doses of immigrants, while the very number of people involved makes migration an unlikely solution. For example, every four years Brazil increases by the size of the population of Portugal, and every five years Latin America by the population of Spain.

European death rates, moreover, declined slowly. Latin America's mortality has declined rapidly, but in most instances still has not reached modern levels. Thus, 42 of every 100 deaths occur to pre-school age children, as contrasted with 7 in the United States. Since it is both desirable and likely that mortality will decline even further in the future, the only remaining avenue of attack is to retard the high rate of fertility characteristic of most Latin American nations. It may be, as Dr. Lleras Camargo pointed out in his speech to the Pan-American Assembly, that "For us, the human solution, the Christian solution, the economic and politically sound solution is birth control." Certainly birth control and development complement rather than contradict one another. Reasonable as this may seem, it is still the case that Latin America has evidenced the least concern of any major world region with population problems and "unlike mortality, there are no comparable programs designed to influence fertility." (Miró) This is the basic population dilemma in Latin America.

good quote

We have, then, the fact of population growth and change, the problems occasioned by this growth, and the demographic solutions likely to alleviate the population problem. We have organized this volume accordingly.

FACTS

If there is any truth to the adage that facts speak for themselves, it is demonstrated by the first three articles in this book, which deal with the demographic situation in Latin America generally, in Brazil, and in the English-speaking Caribbean. In describing the past and projecting the future components of population change, Miró's paper documents the remarkable gap between fertility and mortality characteristic of most Latin American countries, a gap so large that if it continues there will be 740 million Latin Americans by the year 2000. Those who take comfort in the imminent and inexorable decline of fertility as a result of modernization may be startled by Roberts' data on rising birth rates in some parts of the Caribbean, where a larger proportion of women are bearing children, possibly as a result of the improvement in public health. The power of facts emerges clearly from Neiva's discussion of the continual and frightening upward revisions of Brazil's estimated rate of growth.

PROBLEMS

Refuting a number of current misconceptions concerning population, Notestein considers the basic question of the relation between population size, growth, density, and the wealth, power, and well-being of nations. Based on short-run economic and demographic data, Cabello finds that the relation between population growth and economic development in Latin America is not clear, and concludes that programs of fertility control alone would not contribute significantly to economic development. At the same time, he shows how difficult it will be to achieve improvement in the housing situation in the face of sustained population growth. Similarly, Arévalo, while showing the primary need for increasing the rate of school attendance, demonstrates the difficulty of achieving this in the face of a rapidly increasing population.

SOLUTIONS

Direct solutions to the problem of high fertility in Latin America are considered from several points of view. Father Pérez analyzes the strains which result from discrepancies between norms and behavior, and expresses the hope that the Church will clarify its position on family planning in a way which will reduce these strains. Delgado presents evidence from public opinion surveys and from current organization activities sufficient to make him cautiously optimistic about the possibilities for future national family planning programs in Latin America. Stycos contrasts the lack of concern about population problems among Latin American intellectuals with the average woman's great interest in family planning. He stresses the need to strengthen the development of professional demography on the one hand, and to service the needs and the demands of the public on the other.

CONCLUSION

The 75 delegates to the Pan-American Assembly on Population utilized the papers of this volume as background for their three days of discussion in Cali, Colombia, in August 1965. The conclusions reached by the participants are eloquent testimony to the deep concern with the population problems which are emerging in Latin America. The objective basis for this concern can be found in the following papers. The broader goals on which this concern is based were aptly phrased in the Final Report:

> In all instances, whether or not the approach be demographic, the ultimate ends of improvement in the cultural, economic, and physical well-being of the individual human being must be kept in view. Our recommendations are intended as means to these ends, as ways of further liberating man in his pursuit of higher goals.

1. The Population of Twentieth Century Latin America

CARMEN A. MIRÓ

This paper presents quantitative data concerning (a) the evolution of the Latin American population since the beginning of this century, (b) the principal demographic characteristics around 1965, and (c) the prospects for its evolution up to the end of this century. The data refer to the 20 republics of Latin America and to Puerto Rico. It is hoped that studies like this will help call attention to the accelerated growth of the Latin American population and its inevitable consequences.

EVOLUTION OF THE POPULATION, 1900-1960

Growth

The predominant feature of Latin American population is its speed of growth. This becomes dramatically clear if we note that at the beginning of this century the area had a population just over 60 million, and that by the middle of 1960 the population had reached more than 207 million; that is, it almost tripled in the short period of sixty years. Data for the early part of this century are sparse and only relatively trustworthy. General estimates for the whole area, including the population of territories that are generally not considered as part of Latin America (Surinam, Jamaica, the Guianas, etc.), indicate a total of 63 million inhabitants for 1900.

Perhaps the simplest way of illustrating how the growth rate has been accelerating is to show the number of years the population took or should take to double during different

1

TABLE 1.

Latin America.
Population 1900–1980.
(in thousands)

	1900	1920	1930	1940	1950	1960	1965	1970	1980
All Latin America	—	86,907	104,451	126,325	158,125	207,379	238,310	274,170	364,398
Tropical South America	—	45,188	53,985	66,200	83,337	111,571	128,749	148,597	197,745
Brazil	17,318	27,554	33,718	41,525	52,328	70,459	81,450	93,902	123,716
Colombia	3,825	6,089	7,280	9,097	11,679	15,468	17,787	20,514	27,691
Peru	3,791	5,313	5,752	6,784	8,036	10,199	11,611	13,275	17,500
Venezuela	2,344	2,438	2,980	3,740	5,004	7,394	8,752	10,429	14,857
Ecuador		1,930	2,102	2,546	3,277	4,355	5,013	5,819	7,981
Bolivia	1,696	1,864	2,153	2,508	3,013	3,696	4,136	4,658	6,000
Continental Central America	—	19,369	22,380	26,776	34,585	46,686	55,183	65,408	92,933
Mexico	13,607	14,500	16,589	19,815	25,826	34,988	41,460	49,282	70,581
Guatemala		1,450	1,771	2,201	2,805	3,765	4,343	5,033	6,878
El Salvador		1,168	1,350	1,550	1,868	2,442	2,859	3,346	4,585
Honduras	443	783	948	1,146	1,428	1,838	2,182	2,592	3,656
Nicaragua	448	600	700	825	1,060	1,403	1,666	1,979	2,791
Costa Rica	285	421	499	619	801	1,171	1,424	1,718	2,419
Panama	323	447	523	620	797	1,079	1,249	1,458	2,023
Temperate South America	—	14,824	18,875	22,317	26,854	32,794	36,065	39,572	47,483
Argentina	4,743	8,861	11,896	14,169	17,189	20,956	22,841	24,784	28,998
Chile	2,904	3,785	4,365	5,063	6,073	7,627	8,625	9,753	12,378
Uruguay	809	1,479	1,734	1,974	2,195	2,491	2,647	2,802	3,126
Paraguay		699	880	1,111	1,397	1,720	1,952	2,233	2,981
Caribbean	—	7,526	9,211	11,032	13,349	16,328	18,313	20,593	26,237
Cuba	1,573*	2,950	3,837	4,566	5,508	6,797	7,523	8,307	10,034
Haiti		2,124	2,422	2,827	3,380	4,140	4,645	5,255	6,912
Dominican Republic		1,140	1,400	1,759	2,243	3,030	3,588	4,277	6,174
Puerto Rico	953*	1,312	1,552	1,880	2,218	2,361	2,557	2,754	3,117

* 1899 census.

Source: 1900: Brazil, Bolivia, Mexico, Cuba, and Puerto Rico, census data; other countries, estimates made by CELADE. 1920–1980: UN St/SOA/SER.R/7 Provisional Report on World Population Prospects, as assessed in 1963.

periods. While the population of 1900 took 40 years to double, that of 1950, according to present estimates, will double in the short period of only 25 years:

Estimated Population In	Doubled by	Number of years necessary to double
1900	1940	40
1920	1954	34
1930	1960	30
1940	1967	27
1950	1975	25

Of course, the rate of growth has varied among the different nations and sub-regions of Latin America.

TABLE 2.

Latin America.

Per cent of population growth 1900–1980. *

	1900–20	1920–30	1930–40	1940–50	1950–60	1960–65	1965–70	1970–80
All Latin America	—	20.4	20.9	25.2	31.1	14.9	15.0	32.9
Tropical South America	—	19.7	22.6	25.9	33.9	15.4	15.4	33.1
Brazil	59.1	22.4	23.2	26.0	34.6	15.6	15.3	31.8
Colombia	59.2	19.6	25.0	28.4	32.4	15.0	15.3	35.0
Peru	40.1	8.3	17.9	19.3	26.0	13.8	14.3	31.8
Venezuela	4.0	22.2	25.5	33.8	47.8	18.4	19.2	42.5
Ecuador	—	8.9	21.1	28.7	32.9	15.1	16.1	37.2
Bolivia	9.9	15.5	16.5	20.1	22.7	11.9	12.6	28.8
Continental Central America	—	15.5	19.6	29.2	35.0	18.2	18.5	42.1
Mexico	6.6	14.4	19.4	30.3	35.5	18.5	18.9	43.2
Guatemala	—	22.1	24.3	27.4	34.2	15.4	15.9	36.7
El Salvador	—	15.6	14.8	20.5	30.7	17.1	17.1	37.0
Honduras	76.7	21.1	20.9	24.6	28.7	18.8	18.8	41.0
Nicaragua	33.9	16.7	17.9	28.5	32.4	18.8	18.8	41.0
Costa Rica	47.7	18.5	24.0	29.4	46.2	21.6	20.6	40.8
Panama	38.4	17.0	18.5	28.5	35.4	15.8	16.7	38.8
Temperate South America	—	27.3	18.2	20.3	22.1	10.0	9.7	20.0
Argentina	86.8	34.3	19.1	21.3	21.9	9.0	8.5	17.0
Chile	30.3	15.3	16.0	19.9	25.6	13.1	13.1	26.9
Uruguay	82.8	17.2	13.8	11.2	13.5	6.3	5.9	11.6
Paraguay	—	25.9	26.2	25.7	23.1	13.5	14.4	33.5
Caribbean	—	22.4	19.8	21.0	22.3	12.2	12.5	27.4
Cuba	87.5	30.1	19.0	20.6	23.4	10.7	10.4	20.8
Haiti	—	14.0	16.7	19.6	22.5	12.2	13.1	31.5
Dominican Republic	—	22.8	25.6	27.5	35.1	18.4	19.2	44.4
Puerto Rico	37.7	18.3	21.1	18.0	6.4	8.3	7.7	13.2

* Based on the figures in Table 1.

The preceding Table gives the percentages of population growth for the different periods considered in Table 1. Temperate South America shows the greatest growth during 1900-1930, considerably greater than that of the other regions. This is due in part to a moderately high rate of natural increase (the balance of births and deaths) and to a significant immigration. (Landry gives the following estimates for gross immigration in the period 1900-1930 into three countries of this sub-region: Argentina, 2,400,000; Uruguay, 402,000; Chile, 102,000. *Traité de Démographie,* Payot, Paris, 1949, p. 421.)

National data indicate that those with the most rapid growth between 1900 and 1930 were Argentina, Uruguay, Cuba, and Brazil. Again, we must point out the important contribution of immigration to the growth of Brazil and Cuba. Landry estimates the total immigration to Brazil was almost 2,500,000 during this period; and Carr Saunders notes that 857,000 immigrants entered Cuba in 1901-1932.[1]

In the decade 1930-40 the other three sub-regions surpassed temperate South America in population growth, and in the period 1940-60 continental Central America occupied first place, closely followed by tropical South America. The

TABLE 3.

Latin America.

Annual per cent of regional population growth (1920–1980). *

	1920– 30	1930– 40	1940– 50	1950– 60	1960– 65	1965– 70	1970– 80
All Latin America	1.8	1.9	2.2	2.7	2.8	2.8	2.8
Tropical South America	1.8	2.0	2.3	2.9	2.9	2.9	2.8
Continental Central America	1.4	1.8	2.5	3.0	3.3	3.4	3.5
Temperate South America	2.4	1.7	1.8	2.0	1.9	1.9	1.8
Caribbean	2.0	1.8	1.9	2.0	2.3	2.3	2.4

* Calculated on the basis of the figures in Table 1.

TABLE 4.

Latin America.

Crude birth rates for indicated periods.

	Period	Rate (per M)	Source
Tropical South America			
Brazil	1940–45	43	(1)
	1945–50	43–47	(2)
	1955–60	43–47	(2)
Colombia	1900–04	43	(3)
	1905–09	44	(3)
	1910–14	44	(3)
	1915–19	44.1	(3)
	1920–24	44.6	(3)
	1925–29	44.9	(3)
	1941–46	44	(1)
	1945–50	44–47	(2)
	1955–60	43–46	(2)
Peru	1930–35	46	(1)
	1945–50	42–48	(2)
	1955–60	42–48	(2)
Venezuela	1945–50	44–48	(2)
	1955–60	45–50	(2)
Ecuador	1940–45	47	(1)
	1945–50	45–50	(2)
	1955–60	45–50	(2)
Bolivia	1940–45	43	(1)
	1945–50	41–45	(2)
	1955–60	41–45	(2)
Continental Central America			
Mexico	1900–04	46.5	(3)
	1905–09	46.0	(3)
	1910–14	43.2	(3)
	1915–19	40.6	(3)
	1920–24	45.3	(3)
	1925–29	44.3	(3)
	1930–34	44.5	(1)
	1935–39	43.5	(1)
	1940–44	44.2	(1)
	1945–49	44.4	(1)
	1950–54	44.9	(1)
	1955–59	45.9	(1)
	1960	46.0	(1)
Guatemala	1930–34	51.6	(1)
	1935–39	47.7	(1)
	1940–44	47.2	(1)
	1945–49	50.6	(1)
	1950–54	51.4	(1)
	1955–59	49.1	(1)
	1960	49.5	(1)
El Salvador	1920–24	45.9	(4)
	1930–34	43.3	(1)
	1935–39	42.7	(1)
	1940–44	43.3	(1)
	1945–49	44.4	(1)
	1950–54	49.4	(1)
	1955–59	50.0	(1)
	1960	49.9	(1)
Honduras	1945–50	45–50	(2)
	1955–60	45–50	(2)
Nicaragua	1945–50	45–52	(2)
	1955–60	45–52	(2)
Costa Rica	1900–04	46.9	(3)
	1905–09	48.2	(3)
	1910–14	48.9	(3)
	1915–19	44.7	(3)
	1920–24	44.9	(3)
	1925–29	46.2	(3)
	1930–34	45.7	(1)
	1935–39	45.0	(1)
	1940–44	44.9	(1)
	1945–49	45.1	(1)
	1950–54	49.2	(1)
	1955–59	50.0	(1)
	1960	50.2	(1)
Panama	1920–24	37.4	(4)
	1930–34	36.5	(1)
	1935–39	36.4	(1)
	1940–44	37.5	(1)
	1945–49	36.0	(1)
	1950–54	35.9	(1)
	1955–59	39.9	(1)
	1960	41.0	(1)
Temperate South America			
Argentina	1900–04	41.0	(3)
	1905–09	40.0	(3)
	1910–14	40.3	(3)
	1915–19	36.1	(3)
	1920–24	34.3	(3)
	1925–29	32.4	(3)
	1930–34	26.8	(1)
	1935–39	24.0	(1)
	1940–44	24.1	(1)
	1945–49	25.1	(1)
	1950–54	25.1	(1)
	1955–59	24.0	(1)
	1960–62	22.3	(1)
Chile	1900–04	44.7	(3)
	1905–09	44.6	(3)
	1910–14	44.4	(3)
	1915–19	43.3	(3)
	1920–24	42.2	(3)
	1925–29	43.8	(3)
	1930–34	40.5	(1)
	1935–39	36.6	(1)
	1940–44	36.4	(1)
	1945–49	35.7	(1)
	1950–54	33.8	(1)
	1955–59	36.0	(1)
	1960–62	34.8	(1)
Uruguay	1910–14	36.8	(5)
	1915–19	31.9	(5)
	1920–24	30.0	(5)
	1925–29	28.6	(5)
	1930–34	25.9	(5)
	1935–39	22.5	(5)
	1940–44	21.6	(5)
	1945–49	21.1	(5)
	1950–54	22.3	(5)
	1955–59	22.2	(5)
	1960	22.0	(5)
	1961	21.8	(5)
	1962	21.7	(5)
	1963	21.5	(5)
Paraguay	1945–50	45–50	(2)
	1955–60	45–50	(2)
Caribbean			
Cuba	1931	32.9	(6)
	1943	31.0	(6)
	1945–49	30.5	(6)
	1950–54	28.1	(6)
	1955–59	25.4	(6)

TABLE 4.—(*Continued*)

	Period	Rate (per M)	Source		Period	Rate (per M)	Source
	1960	29.6	(6)		1920–30	39.3	(7)
	1961	32.2	(6)		1930–34	40.6	(1)
	1962	35.1	(6)		1935–39	39.1	(1)
Haiti	1945–50	42–50	(2)		1940–44	39.6	(1)
	1955–60	42–50	(2)		1945–49	41.0	(1)
Dominican	1945–50	48–54	(2)		1950–54	36.6	(1)
Republic	1955–60	48–54	(2)		1955–59	33.7	(1)
Puerto Rico	1899–1910	40.5	(7)		1960	31.7	(1)
	1910–20	40.4	(7)		1961	31.0	(1)
					1962	31.1	(1)

(1) *Provisional Report on World Population Prospects as Assessed in 1963*, UN ST/SOA/SER.R/7.
(2) *Economic Bulletin for Latin America*. Vol. VII No. 1 Statistical Supplement. Santiago, Chile, 1962.
(3) Kingsley Davis, "Posición de América Latina en la Historia Demográfica Mundial" en *Demografía y Salud Pública en América Latina*, Traducción de la Publicación Trimestral de la Fundación Milbank Memorial, Vol. XLII, No. 2, April 1964, Part 2, New York.
(4) Naciones Unidas. América Latina, Seminario sobre Población ST/TAA/SER.C/33 ST/SOA/36.
(5) Uruguay. Dirección General de Estadística. *Tasas Demográficas Estimadas para el Período 1910–1984*. Doc. Trabajo No. 3, Estimación No. 1, 13-XII-64. Mimeographed.
(6) Central Planning Committee. Bureau of Statistics. *Statistical data on the principal characteristics of the Cuban population*, Havana, May 1965.
(7) *The Demographic Evolution of Puerto Rico*. Jose L. Vasquez, Chicago, Illinois, 1964. Mimeographed.

same picture emerges if we observe annual growth rates instead of the growth percentages.

As the volume of international immigration decreased, the differences in rates of growth depended primarily on variations of fertility and mortality.

Birth and Death Rates

Information on births and deaths for the beginning of this century is very unreliable. Nevertheless, the little knowledge we have permits us to construct a general picture of the situation, a picture which explains why the population of the region grew at an annual rate of less than 2%during this period. With the possible exception of Uruguay, all countries showed high birth rates of more than 40 per 1000, with some probably closer to 50. Mortality rates were also generally high—over 25 per 1000, and reaching 30 per 1000 in several countries.

Tables 4 and 5 show birth and death rates since 1900. Birth rates are probably more reliable than death rates, the latter being generally based on official registers which are known to be imperfect.[2] Figures for Chile and Puerto Rico seem the most accurate. Argentina and Uruguay show them-

TABLE 5.

Latin America.

Crude death rates for indicated periods.

Period		Rate (per M)	Source	Period		Rate (per M)	Source
Tropical South America				**Temperate South America**			
Brazil	1945–50	17–23	(1)	Argentina	1911–13	16.8	(2)
	1955–60	11–16	(1)		1921–25	14.4	(2)
Colombia	1945–50	17–21	(1)		1926–30	13.3	(2)
	1955–60	14–17	(1)		1930–34	11.6	(4)
Peru	1945–50	18–24	(1)		1935–39	11.6	(4)
	1955–60	13–18	(1)		1940–44	10.3	(4)
Venezuela	1911–13	22.0	(2)		1945–49	9.6	(4)
	1920–24	21.7	(3)		1950–54	8.7	(4)
	1926–30	18.9	(2)		1955–59	8.6	(4)
	1945–50	16–20	(1)		1960–62	8.1	(4)
	1955–60	10–15	(1)	Chile	1905–09	32.5	(2)
Ecuador	1945–50	20–25	(1)		1911–13	31.0	(2)
	1955–60	15–20	(1)		1921–25	30.3	(2)
Bolivia	1945–50	23–27	(1)		1926–30	25.8	(2)
	1955–60	20–25	(1)		1930–34	23.9	(4)
Continental Central America					1935–39	23.3	(4)
Mexico	1921–25	25.5	(2)		1940–44	19.8	(4)
	1926–30	25.6	(2)		1945–49	17.2	(4)
	1930–34	25.6	(4)		1950–54	13.6	(4)
	1935–39	23.3	(4)		1955–59	12.6	(4)
	1940–44	22.1	(4)		1960–62	12.0	(4)
	1945–49	17.8	(4)	Uruguay	1910–14	13.6	(5)
	1950–54	15.5	(4)		1915–19	14.1	(5)
	1955–59	12.5	(4)		1920–24	12.5	(5)
	1960	11.5	(4)		1925–29	11.9	(5)
Guatemala	1930–34	26.1	(4)		1930–34	11.6	(5)
	1935–39	26.5	(4)		1935–39	11.1	(5)
	1940–44	27.8	(4)		1940–44	10.3	(5)
	1945–49	23.8	(4)		1945–49	9.1	(5)
	1950–54	21.4	(4)		1950–54	8.5	(5)
	1955–59	19.9	(4)		1955–59	8.8	(5)
	1960	17.5	(4)		1960	8.8	(5)
El Salvador	1905–09	24.7	(2)		1961	8.6	(5)
	1911–13	25.0	(2)		1962	8.7	(5)
	1921–25	23.9	(2)		1963	8.6	(5)
	1926–30	23.7	(2)	Paraguay	1945–50	15–20	(1)
	1930–34	23.0	(4)		1955–60	12–16	(1)
	1935–39	21.1	(4)	**Caribbean**			
	1940–44	20.5	(4)	Cuba	1930–34	11.3	(3)
	1945–49	17.1	(4)		1939	9.8	(6)
	1950–54	15.2	(4)		1943	10.6	(6)
	1955–59	13.2	(4)		1945–49	8.3	(6)
	1960	11.0	(4)		1950–54	6.7	(6)
Honduras	1945–50	18–24	(1)		1955–59	6.4	(6)
	1955–60	15–20	(1)		1960–62	6.8	(6)
Nicaragua	1945–50	16–20	(1)	Haiti	1945–50	25–30	(1)
	1955–60	12–17	(1)		1955–60	20–28	(1)
Costa Rica	1911–13	25.0	(2)	Dominican	1945–50	20–25	(1)
	1921–25	23.1	(2)	Republic	1955–60	16–20	(1)
	1926–30	21.1	(2)	Puerto Rico	1899–1909	28.0	(7)
	1930–34	22.1	(4)		1910–1919	23.9	(7)
	1935–39	20.0	(4)		1920–29	22.2	(7)
	1940–44	18.3	(4)		1930–39	19.7	(7)
	1945–49	14.0	(4)		1940–49	14.5	(7)
	1950–54	11.6	(4)		1950–59	8.0	(7)
	1955–59	9.6	(4)		1960	6.7	(7)
	1960	8.6	(4)		1961	6.7	(4)
Panama	1945–50	14–17	(1)		1962	6.7	(4)
	1955–60	9–13	(1)				

(1) *Economic Bulletin for Latin America.* Vol. VII No. 1 Statistical Supplement. Santiago, Chile, 1962.
(2) United Nations: *Population Bulletin of the United Nations,* No. 6, 1962. Table III-10, p. 32.
(3) Naciones Unidas. América Latina. Seminario sobre Población, ST/TAA/SER.C/33 ST/SOA/36.
(4) *Provisional Report on World Population Prospects as Assessed in 1963.* UN ST/SOA/SER.R/7.
(5) Uruguay. Dirección General de Estadística. *Tasas Demográficas Estimadas para el Período 1910–1984.* Doc Trabajo No. 3, Estimac. No. 1, 13-XII-64. Mimeographed.
(6) Junta Central de Planificación. Dirección General de Estadística. *Datos Estadísticos sobre las Principales Características de la Población de Cuba,* La Habana, Mayo, 1965.
(7) Vásquez, José L., *The Demographic Evolution of Puerto Rico.* Chicago, Illinois, 1964. Mimeographed.

selves to have been in a more advanced stage of the demographic cycle. By the beginning of the century, these two countries show lower birth and death rates than those in the majority of Latin American countries in 1960.

Despite their limitations, these data allow us an approximate judgement of the evolution of mortality rates. This evolution is characterized by a continual decline, gradual in the first years of the century, but gathering momentum, especially since 1930. In several countries, the decline reduced 1960 mortality rates to levels less than half of those of 1900.

Based on the figures in Table 5, the percentage declines in the rates for different periods are presented in Table 6.

For eight countries, somewhat representative of the four sub-regions of Latin America, it is possible to compare the evolution of the rates prior to 1930. For age groups between 15 and 21 years, decreases in mortality rates fluctuated between 4 and 21%. On the other hand, between 1930 and 1962, the percentage decline in mortality was between 26 and 66% for those 28 to 31 years of age. Argentina and Uruguay, which already had moderate mortality rates in 1930, registered the smallest declines (30 and 26%, respectively). For 11 countries, it was only possible to calculate the percentage of decrease for the periods 1945-50 and 1955-60. For these countries, the decline in the mortality rate either began later or took place more slowly than elsewhere, for the levels reached in the period 1945-50 are comparable to those which had been reached 15 years earlier in the eight countries previously mentioned. Two extreme cases are Bolivia, which in ten years reduced its mortality rate by only 10%, and Brazil, which reduced it by 33% in the same period.

While death registration has generally been incomplete, it is reasonable to suppose that records have gradually improved, resulting in an increase in registered deaths that does not precisely reflect actual changes in mortality rates. Thus, any reduction in the death rate deduced only from a comparison of official mortality figures over a given period probably is an underestimate.

TABLE 6.

Latin America.

Reduction in death rates for indicated periods.

	Initial period		Final period		Percentage decrease from initial period	No. of years between periods
	Date	Rate (per M.)	Date	Rate (per M.)		
Tropical South America						
Brazil	1945–50	20.0	1955–60	13.5	32.5	10
Colombia	1945–50	19.0	1955–60	15.5	18.4	10
Peru	1945–50	21.0	1955–60	15.5	26.2	10
Venezuela	1911–13	22.0	1926–30	18.9	14.1	16
	1926–30	18.9	1955–60	12.5	33.9	29
Ecuador	1945–50	22.5	1955–60	17.5	22.2	10
Bolivia	1945–50	25.0	1955–60	22.5	10.0	10
Continental Central America						
Mexico	1921–25	25.5	1926–30	25.6	+0.4	5
	1930–34	25.6	1960	11.5	55.1	28
Guatemala	1930–34	26.1	1960	17.5	33.0	28
El Salvador	1905–09	24.7	1926–30	23.7	4.0	21
	1930–34	23.0	1960	11.0	52.2	28
Honduras	1945–50	21.0	1955–60	17.5	16.7	10
Nicaragua	1945–50	18.0	1955–60	14.5	19.4	10
Costa Rica	1911–13	25.0	1926–30	21.1	15.6	16
	1930–34	22.1	1960	8.6	61.1	28
Panama	1945–50	15.5	1955–60	11.0	29.0	10
Temperate South America						
Argentina	1911–13	16.8	1926–30	13.3	20.8	16
	1930–34	11.6	1960–62	8.1	30.2	29
Chile	1905–09	32.5	1926–30	25.8	20.6	21
	1930–34	23.9	1960–62	12.0	49.8	29
Uruguay	1910–14	13.6	1925–29	11.9	12.5	15
	1930–34	11.6	1963	8.6	25.9	31
Paraguay	1945–50	17.5	1955–60	14.0	20.0	10
Caribbean						
Cuba	1930–34	11.3	1960–62	7.0	38.1	30
Haiti	1945–50	27.5	1955–60	24.0	13.7	10
Dominican Republic	1945–50	22.5	1955–60	18.0	20.0	10
Puerto Rico	1899–1909	28.0	1920–29	22.2	20.7	20.5
	1930–34	19.7	1962	6.7	66.0	29

Source: Table 5.

When we compare the trend of mortality between 1900 and 1960 with that of the birth rate for the period, we can see why in Latin America—which has not received substantial immigration since the 1930's—the annual growth rate of the population has risen from 1.8% in 1920-30 to 2.8% in 1960-65.

Birth rate statistics have also been deficient owing to incomplete birth registration in most countries, making the levels appear lower than they actually are. Moreover, improved registration would in time mask any actual decrease in birth rates.

The previously mentioned obstacles do not preclude the following conclusions, based on the data of Tables 4 and 7:

1. Except for Argentina, Uruguay, Puerto Rico, Chile, and Cuba, the countries we are considering have very high birth rates, over 4%, and in some cases reaching 5%.
2. Throughout this century, except for the aforementioned countries, significant reductions in birth rates have not been registered.
3. The increases which have been registered in the birth rate can be generally attributed to improvements in record-keeping, although in a few cases they could reflect small rises in fertility.

Various hypotheses have been advanced to explain the reduction of the birth rate in Argentina, Uruguay, Chile, and Cuba: e.g., the impact of immigration, the ethnic and cultural origin of the immigrants, and the degree of urbanization. However, we lack sufficiently detailed data to establish a causal relationship between any or all of these factors and the birth rate.

Urbanization

A relationship seems to exist between the level of urbanization and the birth rate. Like other variables, data on urbanization in the beginning of this century are extremely scarce. Moreover, the historical study of urbanization is made difficult by the different criteria which have been used to define a city in different countries and within the same

TABLE 7.

Latin America.

Variation in birth rates for indicated periods.

	Initial period	Rate (per M.)	Final period	Rate (per M.)	Total no. of years in period	Variation (in percentages)
Tropical South America						
Brazil	1940–45	43.0	1955–60	45.0	15	+ 4.6
Colombia	1900–04	43.0	1925–29	44.9	25	+ 4.4
	1925–29	44.9	1955–60	43–46	30.5	− 0.9
Peru	1930–35	46.0	1955–60	43.0	25	− 2.2
Venezuela	1945–50	46.0	1955–60	47.5	10	+ 3.3
Ecuador	1940–45	47.0	1955–60	47.5	15	+ 1.1
Bolivia	1940–45	43.0	1955–60	43.0	15	0
Continental Central America						
Mexico	1900–04	46.5	1925–29	44.3	25	− 4.7
	1930–34	44.5	1960	46.0	28	+ 3.4
El Salvador	1920–24	45.9	1960	49.9	38	+ 8.7
Honduras	1945–50	47.5	1955–60	47.5	10	0
Nicaragua	1945–50	48.5	1955–60	48.5	10	0
Costa Rica	1900–04	46.9	1925–29	46.2	25	− 1.5
	1930–34	45.7	1960	50.2	28	+ 9.8
Panama	1920–24	37.4	1960	41.0	38	+ 9.6
Temperate South America						
Argentina	1900–04	41.0	1925–29	32.4	25	−21.0
	1930–34	26.8	1960–62	22.3	29	−16.8
Chile	1900–04	44.7	1925–29	43.8	25	− 2.0
	1930–34	40.5	1960–62	34.8	29	−14.1
Uruguay	1910–14	36.8	1925–29	28.6	15	−22.3
	1930–34	25.9	1963	21.5	31	−17.0
Paraguay	1945–50	47.5	1955–60	47.5	10	0
Caribbean						
Cuba	1931	32.9	1955–59	25.4	26	−22.8
Haiti	1945–50	46.0	1955–60	46.0	10	0
Dominican Republic	1945–50	51.0	1955–60	51.0	10	0
Puerto Rico	1899–1910	40.5	1920–30	39.3	20.5	− 3.0
	1930–34	40.6	1962	31.1	30	−23.4

Source: Table 4.

country. Despite these limitations, it is possible to establish the degree of urbanization before 1930 in nine Latin American countries. Three sizes of inhabited localities are considered: (1) less than 20,000 inhabitants (generally identified for purposes of international comparison as "rural"); (2) cities of 20,000 to 99,999 inhabitants; and (3) cities of 100,000 inhabitants and more.

Table 8 shows that in Argentina, Chile, and Cuba the urbanization process must have been initiated in the nineteenth century. By the beginning of the twentieth century, the percentage of the population in cities was relatively high, as is proved by the following figures:

		Percentage of total population in cities of	
	Date	20,000 inhabitants or less	20,000– 99,999 inhabitants	100,000 or more inhabitants
Argentina	1914	40.5	7.9	32.6
Chile	1907	27.7	10.6	17.1
Cuba	1919	24.3	9.6	14.7

From what we know about contemporary Uruguay (46% of the total population is concentrated in Montevideo) we can suppose that here also a similar phenomenon occurred. But in the other countries for which information for 1920 is available, urbanization lagged far behind.

	Percentage of the total population in cities of:		
	20,000 or less	20,000–99,999 inhabitants	100,000 or more
Brazil	11.3	2.6	8.7
Puerto Rico	9.2	9.2	—
Nicaragua	4.4	—	4.4
Dominican Republic	3.5	3.5	—

It is appropriate to investigate the conditions that favored early urbanization in Argentina, Uruguay, Chile, and Cuba, and discover, if possible, how urbanization contributed to lowering their birth rates. Even more important would be to discover why the present accelerated urbanization in most of

Latin America does not seem to be clearly associated with changes in the birth rate. Countries such as Venezuela, that since 1950 have had a high level of urbanization (32% of the population in cities of over 20,000), show birth rates which not only continue high but which are tending to rise still further. Robert O. Carleton has shown that while there are urban-rural differences in fertility, accelerated urbanization has produced only a slight change in the national rate.[3] Thus, we may conclude that in the four countries mentioned previously a reduction of the birth rate must have occurred not only in cities, but in less urbanized areas. If so, urbanization must not only have originated restrictive fertility practices, but served to stimulate these practices among diverse social groups. How? In conjunction with what other socio-economic factors? Enlightenment on these questions could contribute to a better understanding of the actual demographic situation in most of the countries with which we are concerned.

THE DEMOGRAPHIC SITUATION IN THE 1960's

Other than in Argentina and Venezuela, international immigration does not seem to have contributed greatly to population growth. While some emigrants have left Paraguay, Chile, El Salvador, and Cuba, their loss has had little effect on the birth or death rates.[4]

The present demographic situation in Latin America is generally the result of the interaction of the birth and death rates. In the section that follows we shall examine the consequences of high and stationary birth rates, combined with moderate and declining death rates.

Demographic Consequences

The Latin American population is characterized today by: a high and progressively increasing growth rate; an age structure in which young people predominate; and, heavy migration from rural to urban areas.

High and progressively increasing growth rate: It is sufficient here to point out that it is estimated that between

TABLE 8.

Latin America.

Percentage of population by size of city.

Country	Year of census	Rural areas	Populated places over 20,000	20,000 to 100,000	More than 100,000 inhabitants
Tropical South America					
Brazil	1920	88.7	11.3	2.6	8.7
	1940	84.7	15.3	4.6	10.7
	1950	79.8	20.2	7.0	13.2
	1960	71.9	28.1	9.3	18.8
Colombia	1938	87.1	12.9	5.7	7.2
	1951	77.8	22.2	7.5	14.7
Peru	1940	85.8	14.2	5.8	8.4
	1961	71.1	28.9	10.4	18.5
Venezuela	1936	83.8	16.2	5.9	10.3
	1941	81.9	18.1	6.3	11.8
	1950	68.1	31.9	11.6	20.3
	1961	52.8	47.2	17.2	30.0
Ecuador	1950	82.2	17.8	3.2	14.6
	1962	73.1	26.9	8.0	18.9
Bolivia	1900*	91.4	8.6	5.5	3.1
	1950	80.4	19.6	9.0	10.6
Continental Central America					
Mexico	1940	81.9	18.1	7.9	10.2
	1950	75.9	24.1	8.9	15.2
	1960	70.4	29.6	11.0	18.6
Guatemala	1950	88.8	11.2	1.0	10.2
El Salvador	1930	91.0	9.0	9.0	—
	1950	87.1	12.9	4.2	8.7
	1961	82.3	17.7	7.5	10.2
Honduras	1940	93.9	6.1	6.1	—
	1950	93.1	6.9	6.9	—
	1961	88.4	11.6	4.4	7.2
Nicaragua	1920*	95.6	4.4	—	4.4
	1940*	92.5	7.5	—	7.5
	1950	84.8	15.2	4.9	10.3
	1963	77.0	23.0	7.8	15.2
Costa Rica	1927	80.7	19.3	19.3	—
	1950	77.7	22.3	—	22.3
	1963	76.0	24.0	—	24.0

TABLE 8.—(Continued)

Country	Year of census	Rural areas	Populated places over 20,000	20,000 to 100,000	More than 100,000 inhabitants
Panama	1930	77.1	22.9	22.9	—
	1940	73.4	26.6	7.1	19.5
	1950	73.2	26.8	6.5	20.3
	1960	66.9	33.1	7.7	25.4
Temperate South America					
Argentina	1914*	59.5	40.5	7.9	32.6
	1947	51.7	48.3	11.2	37.1
	1960	42.5	57.5	12.0	45.5
Chile	1907*	72.3	27.7	10.6	17.1
	1920	72.0	28.0	9.5	18.5
	1930	67.5	32.5	11.7	20.8
	1940	63.6	36.4	13.3	23.1
	1952	57.2	42.8	14.3	28.5
	1960	45.3	54.7	21.4	33.3
Uruguay	1963	—	—	—	—
Paraguay	1937*	88.8	11.2	—	11.2
	1950	83.5	16.5	—	16.5
	1962	—	—	—	16.8
Caribbean					
Cuba	1919	75.7	24.3	9.6	14.7
	1931	72.4	27.6	9.1	18.5
	1943	69.3	30.7	10.8	19.9
	1953	64.5	35.5	12.5	23.0
Haiti	1950	94.9	5.1	0.8	4.3
Dominican Republic	1920	96.5	3.5	3.5	—
	1935	92.9	7.1	7.1	—
	1950	88.9	11.1	2.6	8.5
	1960	81.3	18.7	6.5	12.2
Puerto Rico	1920	90.8	9.2	9.2	—
	1930	85.9	14.1	5.8	8.3
	1940	81.2	18.8	8.7	10.1
	1950	73.0	27.0	10.9	16.1
	1960	72.0	28.0	4.7	23.3

* "Demographic aspects of urbanization in Latin America," by Division of Population, Department of Social Affairs, United Nations, published in *The Urbanization in Latin America*, UNESCO, 1962.

Source: Excluding above exception, John D. Durand and César Peláez, "Patterns of Urbanization in Latin America," document submitted to the Milbank Memorial Foundation's Conference, New York, 1965.

1960 and 1965 the Latin American population grew by 31 million, or more than 6 million per year (Table 1). This indicates an annual rate of growth of 2.8% (Table 3), one-and-a-half times faster than the growth rate for 1920-30. At this rate, the total population of Latin America will surpass 238 million by the middle of 1965.

The countries that have contributed to creating this situation are chiefly those of continental Central America and tropical South America. In 12 of the 13 countries that make up these two sub-regions, and which contain 72% of the region's population, it is estimated that the growth between 1960 and 1965 was more than 15%, or stated in another way, at an average annual rate between 2.9 and 3.9% (Table 9).

Only in Argentina, Uruguay, and Puerto Rico was growth for this period less than 10%. The populations of Bolivia, Haiti, and Cuba probably increased by between 10.7 and 12.2% (average annual rate of 2.2%). In Cuba, the relatively low rate of growth reflects a moderate birth rate. For the other two the growth percentages reflect high mortality rates —more than 22 per 1000 annually.

Of Peru, Chile, and Paraguay, whose populations increased by about 13.5% during the 1960-65 period (average annual rate of 2.5%), only Chile shows a declining birth rate (34.8% in 1960-62). The mortality rate is high in these three countries, although Chile's is the lowest.

In most Latin American countries there still exists a considerable potential for reducing mortality. In all of them health campaigns are being planned and carried out, which will necessarily bring about further reductions in the mortality rate.

The birth rate, with the exceptions mentioned, has remained stationary during the first 60 years of this century. We may conclude that the already high growth rate will continue unless a drastic change occurs in the birth rate. This seems improbable, since, unlike mortality, there are no programs in Latin America designed to influence fertility.

Age structures in which young people predominate: By means of theoretical models, demographers have shown[5] that

TABLE 9.

Latin America.
Population increases.
1960–65.

	Average annual increase 1960–65	Total increase 1960–65	Total population 1965	Per cent of total Latin America
Argentina Puerto Rico Uruguay	1.7%	8.5%	28,100,000	11.8%
Bolivia Cuba Haiti	2.2%	10.1%	16,300,000	6.8%
Chile Paraguay Peru	2.5%	12.5%	22,200,000	9.3%
Brazil Colombia Ecuador El Salvador Guatemala Panama	2.9%	14.5%	112,700,000	47.3%
Dominican Republic Honduras Mexico Nicaragua Venezuela	3.4%	17.0%	57,600,000	24.2%
Costa Rica	3.9%	19.5%	1,400,000	.6%
Latin America as a whole	2.8%	14.0%	238,300,000	100.0%

Source: Table 1.

in a population not affected by international migration the age structure is principally determined by the past birth rate. This can be seen by comparing the age structures of two populations that have had differing levels of fecundity for prolonged periods. A high birth rate generates a population with a high proportion of children and young adults. A low birth rate for a long period results in a decreasing proportion of children and more old people. This can be illustrated by the cases of Argentina and Mexico. Argentina's birth rate dropped from 41 per 1000 in 1900-04 to 22.3 per 1000 in 1960-62. Mexico's remained nearly constant, dropping only from 46.5 to 46.0 during the same period. The percentage age structure of their populations in 1960 stood as follows:

Age Group	Argentina	Mexico
0–14	31.0	44.4
15–19	8.4	10.2
20–49	42.3	34.5
over 50	18.3	10.9

While in Argentina persons less than 20 years old made up only 39% of the total population, in Mexico this same group constitutes 55%. Mexico's is typical of the present Latin American age structure. In 17 Latin American countries the proportion of minors exceeds 40%, while that of people of 60 years or over is usually less than 6%.

That the already high proportion of minors had tended to increase can be seen in Table 10, where age structures at the last two censuses are compared for 21 countries. As we cannot affirm categorically that there has been any general increase in the birth rate, we must suppose that the changes occurring in the age structure are associated with the evolution of the mortality rate. In the case of Latin American populations, the effect of declining mortality has been to lower the average age of the population. This is so because the improvement of public health has a disproportionate effect on the rate of disease and death among the youngest groups of the population.

Heavy emigration from rural to urban areas: We noted earlier that urbanization had very little significance during the first decades of this century, except in Argentina, Cuba, Chile, and Uruguay. Taking the percentage of the population in cities of over 20,000 as an index of the degree of urbanization, in 1940 most Latin American countries were less

TABLE 10.

Latin America

Age structure of the population (in per cent).

	Year	0–14 yrs.	15–19 yrs.	20–49 yrs.	50–59 yrs.	60–64 yrs.	Over 65
Tropical South America							
Brazil	1950	41.9	10.6	38.1	5.1	1.8	2.5
	1960	42.7	10.2	36.8	5.4	2.1	2.8
Colombia	1951	42.6	10.2	37.0	5.1	2.0	3.1
Peru	1940	42.1	9.5	36.9	5.1	2.1	4.3
	1961	43.3	9.9	35.7	5.2	2.1	3.8
Venezuela	1950	42.0	9.9	38.3	5.3	1.8	2.7
	1961	44.8	9.4	36.0	5.2	1.8	2.8
Ecuador	1950	42.5	9.9	36.4	5.5	2.2	3.5
	1962	45.1	9.7	34.7	5.0	2.2	3.3
Bolivia	1950	39.6	9.9	37.8	5.5	2.9	4.3
Continental Central America							
Mexico	1950	41.8	10.2	37.2	5.3	2.1	3.4
	1960	44.4	10.2	34.5	5.4	2.1	3.4
Guatemala	1950	42.3	11.0	37.2	5.1	1.9	2.5
El Salvador	1950	41.2	10.7	37.8	5.4	2.0	2.9
	1961	44.8	9.5	35.1	5.1	2.3	3.2
Honduras	1950	40.6	10.1	36.9	6.1	2.3	4.0
	1961	48.1	9.9	33.1	4.5	1.8	2.6
Nicaragua	1950	43.3	10.4	36.6	4.9	1.9	2.9
	1963	48.3	9.7	32.7	4.4	2.0	2.9
Costa Rica	1950	42.9	10.5	36.9	5.0	1.8	2.9
	1963	47.6	9.5	32.6	5.1	2.0	3.2
Panama	1950	41.6	9.6	37.9	5.4	2.3	3.2
	1960	43.2	10.0	35.8	5.4	2.0	3.6
Temperate South America							
Argentina	1947	30.9	9.9	44.6	8.1	2.6	3.9
	1960	31.0	8.4	42.3	9.4	3.3	5.6
Chile	1952	37.3	9.7	39.9	6.6	2.5	4.0
	1960	39.8	9.9	37.0	6.6	2.5	4.2
Uruguay	1963 (To June 30th)	28.3	7.9	42.4	9.8	3.9	7.7
Paraguay	1950	43.8	9.7	35.2	5.3	2.3	3.7
	1962	45.2	10.0	34.0	5.1	1.8	3.9
Caribbean							
Cuba	1953	36.3	9.6	41.2	6.0	2.6	4.3
Haiti	1950	38.0	10.0	40.6	5.1	2.3	4.0
Dominican Republic	1950	44.5	10.6	35.8	4.5	1.8	2.8
	1960	44.6	10.6	35.6	4.5	1.8	2.9
Puerto Rico	1950	43.2	10.0	35.4	5.3	2.2	3.9
	1960	42.7	10.5	33.1	6.0	2.5	5.2

Source: 1947, 1950, 1951, 1952 and 1953. *America in Numbers*, 1961, Vol. I and *Demographic Year-book of the United Nations*, 1955. 1960, 1961, 1962 and 1963(except Uruguay), News of IASI.

than 20% urbanized. The exceptions are the aforementioned countries and Panama. The situation has changed substantially since then (Table 8). We have spectacular cases, such as Venezuela, in which an index of 18% in 1940 soars to more than 47% in 1961. The less urbanized countries are found in Central America and the Caribbean region. But even in these, except for Honduras and Haiti, the proportion of inhabitants in cities of over 20,000 ranges from 20 to 25%. An important characteristic of urbanization has been the heavy concentration of people in the large cities, which have grown as a result of a heavy influx from rural areas and small cities. Table 8 shows how the percentage of population in cities of over 100,000 has changed in the last few decades. In general, such cities have grown faster than cities in the 20-100,000 range. But even this comparison does not fully make clear the way in which the populations of major cities, especially the capitals, have grown. According to calculations made by Juan C. Elizaga, these centers absorbed an important part of the total population growth around 1950-60, ranging from 55 and 41% in Buenos Aires and Santiago to 13 and 12% in San Salvador and Tegucigalpa, respectively.[6]

The great city of more than a million inhabitants is no longer exceptional in Latin America. While there were only four cities of this size in 1940, there were ten by 1960, of which nine are national capitals. Among these, the most impressive example of concentration is Montevideo, which contains 46% of the total population of Uruguay. If we limit our comparison to the urban population, the strong attraction exerted by the capital city is even more evident, and occurs with even greater force in small, less-urbanized countries. (Table 11).

In modern times, the growth of cities has generally been associated with the process of economic development. As industrial activity was intensified and agricultural productivity rose, a displacement of the population from rural to urban areas occurred, in adaptation to the new needs of a changing economic system.

In Latin America, however, the accelerated growth of

TABLE 11.

Latin America.
Population and growth of the capitals.[1]

City	Country	Year	Population	Percentage of Total population	Percentage of Urban population	Est. growth in last inter-census per (%) Cap.	Coun.
Buenos Aires	Argentina	1960	6,763,000	33.8	58.8	2.9	1.7
Mexico City	México	1960	4,666,000	13.4	26.4	4.9	3.0
Río de Janeiro[2]	Brazil	1960	3,233,000	4.5	16.2	4.3	3.0
Santiago	Chile	1960	1,907,000	25.9	47.3	4.2	2.5
Havana	Cuba	1960	1,460,000	21.8	—	2.7	—
Lima	Peru	1961	1,436,000	14.5	50.2	4.9	2.4
Caracas	Venezuela	1961	1,333,000	17.7	37.6	6.8	3.9
Bogotá	Colombia	1964	1,329,000	—	—	6.8	—
Montevideo	Uruguay	1963	1,173,000	45.9	—	—	—
Quito	Ecuador	1962	511,000	11.2	41.4	5.2	3.1
San Juan	Puerto Rico	1960	432,000	18.4	65.6	1.9	0.6
Santo Domingo	Dominican Republic	1960	367,000	12.2	65.1	7.3	3.4
San José	Costa Rica	1963	318,000	24.0	100.0	4.6	3.8
Asuncion	Paraguay	1962	305,000	16.8	—	3.3	2.6
Panama City	Panama	1960	273,000	25.4	76.7	5.2	2.9
San Salvador	El Salvador	1961	256,000	10.2	57.6	4.3	2.8
Managua	Nicaragua	1963	226,000	15.3	66.3	5.4	3.3
Tegucigalpa	Honduras	1961	134,000	7.1	61.5	5.9	2.8

[1] Excluding Guatemala, where census results are unknown (1964); also Bolivia and Haiti, which have not had a census since 1950. The information covers, in general, the metropolitan area of the city.
[2] Included, as Rio was the capital until recently.
Sources: John D. Durand and César Peláez, *op. cit.:* Carmen Miró, etc. The figures on Havana were obtained from "Statistical Data on the Main Characteristics of the Cuban Population," Central Planning Board, General Office of Statistics, Havana, May, 1965.

urban populations is in great measure a consequence of the patterns of fecundity and mortality that have already been described. Since rural fertility is significantly higher than urban, the rate of natural increase is greater in rural areas.[7] On the other hand, the low productivity of agriculture and the excess of population in relation to effectively exploited resources have created conditions which impel rural inhabitants to seek better opportunities elsewhere. This movement could have led to the settling of uncolonized areas, but it gravitated instead toward the cities. Nevertheless, the movement of population has no clear and direct relationship to the level of economic development and modernization.[8]

Non-demographic Consequences

In addition to the demographic consequences already described, consequences of an essentially economic, social and political nature are being produced by factors not exclusively demographic. The fact that they are so evident today is due to an ever more generalized acceptance of the right of each member of the community to claim for himself adequate working, housing, health, and educational conditions, as well as adequate nourishment. While this implies a level of personal income consonant with these necessities, most Latin Americans have insufficient income for these purposes.

The populations of the countries we are considering, with a few exceptions, have not reached disproportionate size in relation to their living area and potential resources. Although the low population density in most Latin American countries is frequently cited as justifying a need for continued population growth, those who advocate this fail to take into account the problems resulting from a phenomenon which until now has been totally unknown, relating not to the size of the population, but to the high and progressively rising rate of its growth. Both Venezuela and Chile had, in 1960, populations equal to that of Sweden. What makes the Swedish situation completely different is that Sweden's rate of natural increase is about 0.4% a year and decreasing, while those of Venezuela and Chile are 3.9 and 2.5 respectively, and still rising.

An increasing rate of population growth will inevitably produce greater need for capital investment in order to achieve a pre-determined level of *per capita* production. But nothing inherent in a high rate of population growth automatically generates a greater availability of capital funds. Instead, the present growth rate of Latin America is causing an increasing scarcity in the funds available for promoting economic development. Joseph J. Spengler has estimated that 4% of the national income is needed by a developed country to create the necessities needed by a population growing at an annual rate of 1%.[9] More would necessarily be needed in Latin America. By limiting the availability of capital, rapid population growth impedes the opening and developing of new areas and causes instead the displacement of the population toward urban areas which already have social services.

We do not propose to over-simplify the solution to Latin America's underdevelopment by suggesting that a reduction in the growth rate of the population would suffice to over-come all problems. It is only one of the necessary steps, to which would have to be added others of an economic, social, and political nature. Such measures, falling outside the scope of this paper, will not be discussed here.

The age structure peculiar to Latin America's population has consequences of a different type; the necessity, for example, of increasing investment to fulfill the needs of children and adolescents, especially their education. The number of dependents grows in proportion to the number of persons able to work, creating a situation in which the urgency of attending to the needs of minors and the aged reduces the availability of capital for directly productive ends. It also makes it difficult to meet the demands for jobs of a growing number of young adults who enter the labor force. Positive aspects of the age structure in most Latin American countries include great geographical and occupational mobility of an essentially young labor force disposed to adapt itself to change, and a growing number of potential consumers able to contribute toward creating a greater demand for investment.

Finally, heavy migration to large cities presents complex economic, social, and political problems. Since people move to great cities with little concern for the existing labor market in them, many migrants must live in marginal circumstances with regard to employment, housing, education, and health. The city, unable to give adequate attention to the needs of its new immigrants, must bear the growth of slums on its periphery; the ranks of its unemployed and under-employed grow ever larger; its transportation services deteriorate; and the problems connected with the administration of public services multiply. In part, this explains why the city, usually a seat of political power, is the focus of social movements seeking to modify the present unfavorable conditions.

At the other extreme, emigration to large cities aggravates already unsatisfactory conditions in rural areas and small cities. Because emigrants are generally persons of working age, with a better education and more receptive toward change and progress, the more backward rural communities see themselves increasingly deprived of their more dynamic and enterprising elements. At the same time, the proportion of rural minors and aged becomes greater.

PROSPECTS FOR DEVELOPMENT UP TO THE END OF THE TWENTIETH CENTURY

Growth

Table 1 contains population projections for Latin American countries up to 1980. These predictions, most of which have been prepared by the Latin American Demographic Center (CELADE), and the Economic Commission for Latin America (CEPAL) of the United Nations, involve assumptions as to future birth and mortality rates. Although based on a study of recent growth tendencies in the respective countries, the assumptions are not strictly comparable because they depend somewhat on their author's subjective interpretation of the future. Nevertheless, in approximate terms, we can expect that by 1980 the population of Latin America will exceed 364 million, a population which will be one-and-a-half times larger than the projected population of the United States, although the population of Latin America exceeded that of the United States by only 6 million in 1950.

In Table 12 four different estimates involving different assumptions are presented, one assuming a continuation of present tendencies, the others based on high, medium, and low projected growth.[10] The first estimate assumes that in the four sub-regions of Latin America the 1960 birth rate will be maintained. However, it is assumed that the mortality rate will continue to drop approximately at the same rate as in recent years, and that by about 2000 it will be comparable to the level reached by Sweden in 1960 (a life expectancy of 73 years). In the Caribbean zone it is expected that the mortality rate will descend more slowly, and that by the end of the century it will be comparable to that of the United States in 1960 (a life expectancy of 70 years). If these assumptions are correct, it is calculated that the population of Latin America in the year 2000 will surpass 740 million, triple the present population.

TABLE 12:

Latin America.
Population projection by regions.

Region and year	Estimates* (in millions)			
	Continuation of present growth	High	Med.	Low
All Latin America				
1990	526.4	507.0	478.6	421.0
2000	740.4	660.1	612.4	504.7
Tropical South America				
1990	297.7	286.4	268.9	229.8
2000	427.8	371.1	347.0	273.9
Continental Central America				
1990	133.0	130.0	124.5	114.0
2000	194.4	180.3	165.6	144.8
Temperate South America				
1990	56.6	56.5	53.2	49.5
2000	67.8	66.8	60.5	54.6
Caribbean				
1990	37.1	34.1	32.0	27.7
2000	50.4	41.9	39.3	31.4

* As explained in the text.

This projection implies that the mortality rate will continue to drop without reference to socio-economic conditions, a dubious assumption in some cases;[11] or, alternatively, that living standards will improve in spite of a persistently high birth rate, an achievement which history has never witnessed. Thus, any of the other three hypotheses seems more plausible. The "high estimate" is based on similar assumptions with respect to mortality, although a generally slower drop in mortality is foreseen. It is presumed that the birth rate will remain stationary until 1980 in tropical South America, the Caribbean zone, and continental Central America, at which time it will begin to drop at different rates, more rapidly in the first two sub-regions. For temperate South America, it is assumed that the 1960 levels will be maintained until the end of the century. If these assumptions prove true, Latin America's population will number 660 million in the year 2000, a figure which exceeds by 23 million the highest estimate for the same year made by the United Nations in 1957. Although we have had no indication thus far that the national birth rates for the majority of Latin American countries have begun to fall, it is generally accepted that in all the countries certain classes, particularly educated city dwellers, practice birth control. It seems unduly pessimistic to assume that these practices will not be adopted by other groups to an extent that national birth rates will change. For this reason the "high growth" hypothesis cannot be accepted as very likely.

We can largely discount the "low growth" hypothesis also, because it is based on the assumption that in tropical South America, the Caribbean, and continental Central America, the birth rate would begin to drop in 1960, and that it would be halved in the first two sub-regions within 30 years, and within 45 years in the last sub-region. For temperate South America it is estimated that the birth rate will have dropped to 18.9 per 1000 by 1975, remaining at this level until the end of the century. Recent data, however, indicate that, contrary to the assumptions of this hypothesis, the birth rate in the majority of the countries under consideration does not yet appear to be changing significantly.

This leaves the "medium growth" hypothesis as the most plausible. According to this projection, the birth rate will take 60 years from 1960 to drop to half its present level in tropical South America and the Caribbean; and 45 years, from 1970, to half in continental Central America. In temperate South America it is assumed that the birth rate will be 21.6 per 1000 by 1985, remaining stationary until the end of the century. Estimates as to mortality figures are similar to those for the "high growth" prediction. If the above estimates are correct, in the year 2000 Latin America will have more than 612 million inhabitants, or two-and-a-half times its present population.

Of course, none of these projections pretends to be exact.

However, they permit us to appreciate the order of magnitude of the probable figures. If we can count on substantial modifications of the birth rate in the near future, the figure will be around 505 million. If present tendencies of birth and mortality rates continue, it will rise to more than 740 million. Between these two extremes, which in the light of actual conditions seem implausible, we have the two other possibilities represented by the "high growth" and "medium growth" hypotheses, which set the probable figure between 612 and 660 million. On the basis of these figures we can judge the magnitude of the population problem facing Latin America in the next 35 years.

Age Structure of the Population

In any consideration of the population problem the effect of the age structure of the population must be considered, for, although we assume a decreased birth rate, 15 years after initiation of the decline the population will continue to have an important percentage of minors (over 40%).[12] The new persons seeking work between 1966 and 1980 will be the non-migratory survivors of the births between 1951 and 1965. No action taken to reduce the future birth rate can alter their number, which will be increased if the mortality rate is lowered. The same is the case with children hoping to start school between 1966 and 1973. These will be the survivors of those born during the previous seven years. If the proportion of minors is not expected to vary substantially for the next 15 years, then even with a reduced birth rate important problems connected with education and the incorporation of adolescents into the labor force will continue for some decades to exert pressure on available capital resources, a pressure that will grow along with Latin Americans' aspirations for a higher standard of living.

Urbanization

To predict the course of urbanization in Latin America is a task so difficult that it has not been seriously attempted by any demographer. The behavior of this variable depends on

the interaction of a complex group of demographic, economic, social, and political factors whose trends would be risky to
predict.

Nevertheless, we can point out some limits within which
we may expect urbanization to occur. Assuming the potential growth referred to in the previous paragraphs, Latin
America would have between 204 and 220 million people
residing in cities of 20,000 or more by the year 2000.[13]

We must also consider that in the future numerous Latin
American countries will not need to employ more than 25-
30% of their labor force in agriculture, although the present
proportion is two to three times greater. This presupposes an
increase in agricultural productivity, a development to
which agrarian reform programs would necessarily contribute. If such changes occur, a larger proportion of the
rural population will seek urban occupations. The pattern of
settlement will depend on the programs that are adopted to
balance urban and rural development; e.g., programs leading to decentralization of the industrial and politico-adminis-
trative functions of the cities, as well as to the economic development of rural areas.

In summary, if present conditions in Latin America continue, three times the urban population of 1960 will concentrate in cities by the end of the century. On the other hand,
if the marked differences in present-day Latin America between traditional rural societies and modern urban societies
can be diminished through the adoption of specific programs, it is probable that the urbanization pattern will be
modified.

Latin America and the World

Until now we have examined the demographic evolution
of Latin America without reference to the rest of the world.
In the following section we shall briefly look at Latin America in its world context.

The United Nations estimated that the world population
in 1920 was 1,862,000,000, of which 1,256,000,000 people
lived in regions which are considered underdeveloped.[14]

Among these was Latin America, which had the smallest population among the less developed areas (87 million). Forty years later in 1960, according to the same source, the world population had grown to 2,990,000,000 and the developed regions had increased by 40%, but the underdeveloped regions had grown by 70%. The Latin American population, however, grew by 138%. Thus, it grew at a rate triple that of the more advanced regions and more than twice the rate registered by other underdeveloped regions.

TABLE 13.

Percentage rates of world population growth, 1920–2000.

	1920–30	1930–40	1940–50	1950–60	1960–70	1970–80	1980–90	1990–2000
Total World	1.1	1.0	0.9	1.7	1.8	1.8	1.7	1.6
More developed areas	1.1	0.7	0.3	1.3	1.0	1.0	1.0	0.9
Europe	0.8	0.7	0.3	0.8	0.7	0.5	0.5	0.5
U.S.S.R.	1.4	0.9	−0.8	1.7	1.4	1.2	1.3	1.1
United States	1.4	0.7	1.4	1.8	1.3	1.4	1.6	1.5
Oceania	1.6	1.0	1.3	2.1	1.7	1.9	1.8	1.7
Less developed areas	1.0	1.2	1.2	1.9	2.1	2.0	1.9	1.8
Eastern Asia	0.7	0.7	0.8	1.5	1.4	1.3	1.1	1.0
Southern Asia	1.2	1.4	1.3	2.1	2.4	2.3	2.0	1.9
Africa	1.4	1.5	1.5	2.1	2.4	2.6	2.7	2.7
Latin America	1.8	1.9	2.2	2.7	2.8	2.8	2.7	2.5

Table 13 permits us to compare annual population growth rates in Latin America for 1920-60 with those in other parts of the world. In the periods considered, while the rate of growth for all underdeveloped areas has been rising, Latin America's has risen the most, followed by Africa and South Asia. Estimates for the last four decades suggest that Latin America will continue to have the most rapid growth until 1970-80. By the following decade it will be equaled by Africa, and in the last decade of the century it is presumed that there will be a reduction in the birth rate, in accordance with the aforementioned estimate that it should have fallen to half its present level sometime between 2015 and 2020.

It should be noted that for the present decade the annual population growth of Latin America will exceed that of the world by one-and-a-half times, and that of the most advanced regions by almost three times.

While Latin America's proportion of the world population has risen from 4.7% in 1920 to 6.9% in 1960, its total population is still small, exceeding only North America and Oceania in 1960. Nevertheless, according to the "medium growth" hypothesis, by the year 2000 Latin America will also exceed Europe and the Soviet Union, and will constitute 10.3% of an estimated world population of 5,965,000,000.

The age structure of Latin America's population is very similar to those of Africa and Asia and, as in those continents, is not expected substantially to change during the next 15 years.

On the other hand, as can be seen in the figures below, Latin America has achieved a higher degree of urbanization than the majority of the countries of Africa and Asia, and even of southern Europe. Indeed, the degree of urbanization of Argentina, Uruguay, and Chile in 1960 surpassed that of every other region of the world except Australia and New Zealand.

	Per cent of the population living in cities of more than 20,000
World Total	24–25
Underdeveloped Regions	17–18
Africa	13
North Africa	26
Africa (south of the Sahara)	9
Asia	16–18
Excluding Mainland China	19
China	10–15
Latin America	32
Argentina, Chile, Uruguay	56
Other	28

Developed Regions	41
North America	46
Europe (excluding USSR)	40
Northwest	54
Central	40
Meridional	27
USSR	36
Oceania	53
Australia and New Zealand	65
Remainder of Oceania	3

Source: United Nations, *World Survey of Urban and Rural Population Growth,* E/Cn. 9/187 (Data for 1960).

The foregoing comments help to place Latin America within the general framework of world demographic growth. Three major points emerge:

1. Latin America has the most rapid rate of population growth in the world. Given certain assumptions about future birth and death rates, and international migration, it is likely to maintain this rate until the end of this century.
2. The age structure of the majority of its population is very like those of present-day Africa and Asia.
3. The degree of urbanization in Latin America is higher than that of any other underdeveloped region in the world, and surpasses even that of some of the more developed regions.

FOOTNOTES

1. A. M. Carr Saunders, *World Population,* Oxford, Clarendon Press, 1936, 49.
2. In the provisional report of the prospects for future world population, published by the United Nations in 1964 (St/SOA/SER.R/7), referring to the tendencies of the mortality rate in the countries making up tropical South America, it is pointed out that "at the beginning of the twentieth century the mortality rate ought to have been about 30-35 per thousand, having descended gradually to the level of 20-25 per thousand by the end of 1930."
3. Robert O. Carleton, "Tendencias y diferencias de la fecundidad en la América Latina," Series D E/Cn. CELADE. D. 13 Santiago, Chile, 1965.
4. Puerto Rico has lost population through heavy emigration, and to this fact is attributed a reduction of the birth rate in this territory.

José L. Vasquez gives evidence tending to demonstrate that "the radical change observed in the gross birth rate during the last decade was in great part a result of the heavy emigration."

5. F. Lorimer, "Dynamics of Age Structure in a Population with Initially High Fertility and Mortality," *United Nations Population Bulletin No. 4,* December 1951; "The Cause of the Aging of Populations: Declining Mortality or Declining Fertility?" *United Nations Bulletin No. 4,* December 1954; United Nations, "The Aging of Populations and its Economic and Social Implications," ST/SOA/Series A.26, New York, 1956.

6. Juan C. Elizaga, "Urban-Rural Pattern of Population in Latin America, and Changes in this Pattern During the Last Few Decades," CELADE, Santiago, Chile, 1964.

7. Carleton, *loc. cit.*

8. United Nations, *Conclusiones del Informe Provisional del Seminario sobre Problemas de Urbanización en América Latina,* E/CN.12/URB.26, Santiago, Chile, 1959, p. 75.

9. Joseph J. Spengler, "Population and Economic Growth," *Population: The Vital Revolution,* ed. by Ronald Freedman, Anchor Books, Garden City, New York, 1964.

10. United Nations, *Provisional Report on World Population Prospects, as Assessed in 1963.* ST/SOA/SER.R/7.

11. Hugo Behm Rosas, *Mortalidad Infantil y Nivel de Vida,* Ediciones de la Universidad de Chile, Santiago, 1962.

12. An illustration of this, in the case of Mexico, can be found in Ansley J. Coale and Edgar M. Hoover, *Population Growth and Economic Development in Low Income Countries,* Princeton University Press, Princeton, New Jersey, 1958, Table 41, p. 301.

13. This figure has been obtained by applying the proportion of city dwellers in 1960—estimated to be 68.7 million, or almost a third of the total population for this date—to the "high growth" predictions for the year 2000. See United Nations, *World Survey of Urban and Rural Population Growth,* E/CN. 9/187, Chart No. 2, p. 21.

14. United Nations, *Provisional Report of World Population Prospects, as Assessed in 1963,* ST/SOA/SER.R/7.

2. The Population of Brazil

ARTUR HEHL NEIVA

NON-DEMOGRAPHIC FACTORS

While this study attempts to present the outstanding facts and implications concerning the current population of Brazil, the present situation has been conditioned by many non-demographic factors. This background section covers some of the pertinent general aspects necessary for an understanding of the contemporary situation.

Geographic

Brazil, with its 3,286,473 sq. miles, has about half the area of South America, and extends over 38 degrees of latitude. North to south, and east to west, it extends for over 2,700 miles. The sea coast is around 4,400 miles, and the international boundaries extend for 10,000 miles.

Brazil is a plateau country, interrupted only by the lowlands of the Amazon basin in the north and by the *Pantanal* (swamp) region in the extreme southwest. Bordering the ocean, there is a rather narrow low coastal strip, whose width fluctuates. The transition to the plateau, whose height is about 2,400 ft., is always sufficiently steep to create rapids or cataracts in the rivers, thus rendering navigation difficult. (The Amazon and the lower reaches of its tributaries are exceptions.) All other major rivers, except for the São Francisco, flow inland to either the Amazon or Rio de la Plata basins. This had important demographic consequences, for it made colonial exploration and occupation of the hinterland more difficult, thus providing the basic pattern for today's population distribution.

So varied is Brazil's geography that about 16 natural regions and subregions have been recognized. For brevity, however, 5 general regions may be mentioned: the hot, humid, equatorial forest region, covering some 970,000 sq. miles; *Caatinga,* the hot, semi-arid northeastern zone, with an area of about 386,100 sq. miles; *Cerrado,* the savanna country occupying most of the central plateau for some 970,000 sq. miles of wide rolling plains. Here lies the *Pantanal,* flooded yearly by the Paraguay river; then the tropical forest region, along the coast beginning in the Northeast and widening as it continues southward until the northern part of the state of Rio Grande do Sul, and comprising Brazil's best agricultural soil.

Brazil is a Federated Republic composed of 22 states, 4 territories, and a Federal District. Each is divided into municipalities, of which there were 2,767 in 1960. The seat of the municipality is defined as a city, whatever its population, while the seat of each district, the smallest administrative subdivision of a municipality, is defined as a *vila* (borough). There were 6,586 *vilas* in 1960. The states and territories are grouped into five great regions: *North* (states of Acre, Amazonas, and Pará; territories of Rondônia, Roraima, and Amapá); *Northeast* (states of Maranhão, Piauí, Ceará, Rio Grande do Norte, Paraíba, and Pernambuco; territory of Fernando de Noronha (an island); *East* (states of Sergipe, Bahía, Minas Gerais, Espírito Santo, Rio de Janeiro, and Ghanabara); *South* (states of São Paulo, Paraná, Santa Catarina, and Rio Grande do Sul); and *Central-West* (states of Mato Grosso, Goiás, and the Federal District with the nation's capital, Brasília).

Historical

When discovered by the Portuguese in 1500, Brazil contained between 1 and 1.1 million aborigines, all of mongoloid stock. By the end of the sixteenth century the Portuguese occupied the coastline, although not continuously, from Natal in the Northeast to Cananeia in the South. A general government was established in Bahía in 1549. The economic basis of the country was sugar cane plantations, for

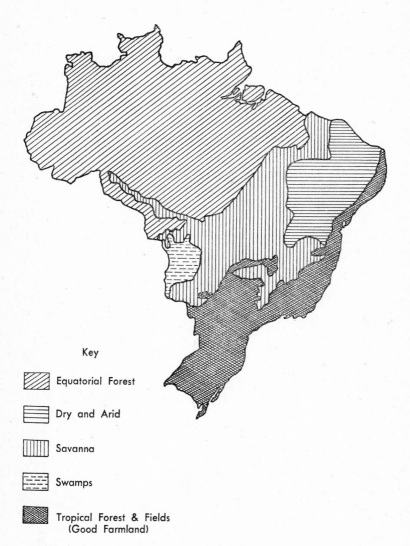

Key

Equatorial Forest

Dry and Arid

Savanna

Swamps

Tropical Forest & Fields
(Good Farmland)

Figure 1. Brazil: Natural regions.

which Negro slaves were introduced from Africa on a substantial scale beginning in 1559. Defeat of the Dutch, who occupied the Northeast from 1624 to 1654, allowed exploration of the Northeast hinterland and its occupation by the Portuguese, with penetration of the South via the São Francisco River, the northern coastline, and the Amazon River. The seventeenth century also saw the apogee of exploration by the *bandeirantes* (for the flag they carried), who passed far beyond the *Tordesillas Line* in their search for precious metals, gems, and Indian slaves. Around 1690 gold and diamonds were discovered, provoking a rush to the central states of Minas Gerais, Goiás, and Mato Grosso in the eighteenth century, which represented the take-off of Brazilian demographic growth.

In 1750 the Treaty of Madrid was signed, fixing the boundaries between the Spanish and the Portuguese crowns in South America.

As is seen in Figure 2, the Brazilian boundaries approximated the present ones. (Indeed, one year after the United States declared their independence while still limited to thirteen eastern seacoast colonies, Brazil had already practically its present limits.) Since the Treaty of Madrid was based on the principle of *uti possidetis*—the land should belong to those who occupied it—the existing human resources of Portugal and Brazil were overextended. Since the frontier had to be occupied to avoid Spanish incursions, the interior was neglected, as it is still today. In 1808 the Portuguese court transferred to Rio de Janeiro, fleeing from the Napoleonic occupation of Portugal, and Brazil became the first and only seat of European monarchy. Elevated to a kingdom in 1815, Brazil proclaimed its independence in 1822, establishing an empire which lasted until 1889.

The settlement of non-Portuguese Europeans was encouraged beginning in 1820. From the mid-nineteenth century onward, with the development of railroads, migration penetrated the southern plateau. Germans predominated until the 1860's, then Italians, closely followed by Portuguese and Spaniards. Slavic migration began in the seventies, but was

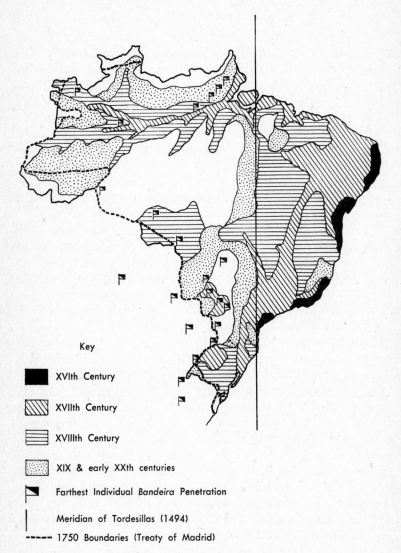

Key

◼ XVIth Century

▨ XVIIth Century

▤ XVIIIth Century

⬚ XIX & early XXth centuries

⚑ Farthest Individual *Bandeira* Penetration

| Meridian of Tordesillas (1494)

----- 1750 Boundaries (Treaty of Madrid)

Figure 2. Brazil: Territorial occupation.

minor. The Japanese first arrived in 1908. Practically all foreign immigrants went to the South, mostly to the state of
São Paulo. The peak of foreign immigration was reached between 1889 and 1914. The 1929 depression and the 1930 revolution increased restrictive immigration policies and immigration declined to the current trickle, less than 24,000 in
1963.

Economic and Social

Economic activity in Brazil has been intimately connected
with demographic changes since the sixteenth century. Since
population was generally scarce in the huge country, people
moved freely toward the most currently profitable activity.
These population shifts often caused prosperity or depression, and originated a series of economic cycles: brazilwood
extraction in the sixteenth century, followed by a sugar cane
cycle concentrated mostly in the Northeast; a cycle of extensive cattle breeding based on the São Francisco River; a
cycle of drugs in the Amazon valley; the great cycle of gold
and diamonds in the seventeenth century; the coffee cycle in
the states of Rio de Janeiro, São Paulo, and Paraná in the
nineteenth and twentieth centuries; and the rubber cycle
which enriched the great northern region before it collapsed
around World War I. Until 1930, Brazil was just another
underdeveloped country, exporting basic crops and import-
ing manufactured articles. The next 20 years saw the establishment of the bases for the transition to a more developed
economy, especially in the South. From the early Fifties onward the economy was off on a spurt of industrialization.
By then, basic industries already existed and the whole economy was changing from a semi-colonial to an urbanized one.
The next step in development took place from 1956 to 1961,
mainly through inflation, which resulted in a stoppage of development by 1962. This has now been corrected by the revolution. Inflation is being controlled, basic reforms have
been promulgated, and economic planning on a massive
scale is being consistently executed. The southern part of the
country is by far the most developed. In 1960, income *per
capita* in the great southern region reached U.S. $390 (in the

state of São Paulo, $475), and in the Northeast only $130 (in the state of Piauí, $77). The national average was then $267.

Brazil has always been a vast melting pot. Miscegenation between Europeans, Indians, and Negroes has existed since the early sixteenth century and continues unabated. There is an almost total lack of racial—as opposed to social—prejudice in Brazil. With miscegenation, acculturation and the exchange of cultural traits between groups belonging to different cultures continues. Brazil is today a pluralistic society, with a noticeable social stratification tempered by a large amount of vertical mobility which contributes to the reduction of social tensions. The country is now in transition, moving from a mainly rural to an urban society. An interesting example are the *favelas* (slums) around the large cities where the social patterns and values are still rural, an aspect which distinguishes them sharply from slums. Another is the emergence of a new and powerful elite representing urban and industrial mentality and interest, as opposed to the traditional ruling class of landowners and their clients. Here again, family alliances through marriage diminish social and even political tensions.[1]

THE STRUCTURE OF BRAZILIAN POPULATION

Demography, as every science, is based on facts. Demographic facts, the raw material of population studies, are primarily numbers obtained through censuses. A census can thus be compared to a photograph taken of the population of a certain region of the earth at an instant in time. Census figures are elicited through technically formulated questionnaires, whose answers can be subjected to rigorous and refined statistical treatment.

Demographic data have a two-fold character. Either they describe the population at a given point in time, according to such categories as age and sex, family status, ethnic composition, residence, and territorial distribution, or they describe the evolution of a population through time. If the first category of data can be compared to a still photograph, the second may be compared to a moving picture whose plot revolves around the themes of birth, death, and migration.

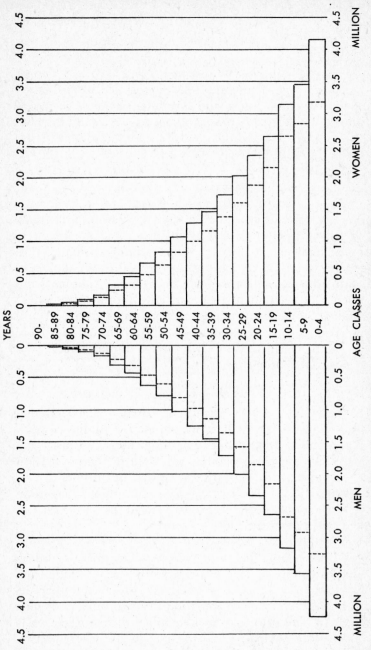

Figure 3. Brazil: Population age groups, 1950. (millions).

Just as a movie film strip is composed of still frames, the study of population dynamics compares data from a series of successive censuses. We shall deal first with Brazilian population structure, then with its dynamics.

Age and Sex

Demographers represent the basic structure of a population by means of the "population pyramid," a graphic technique which allows us to see at a glance the total sex and age distribution of a given population. In countries such as Brazil, the base is wide because of high fertility, and the pyramid narrows quickly because of high mortality. In countries such as Sweden, the pyramid is characteristically pear-shaped, the base being narrower because of low fertility, the body wider because of lower mortality.

Corrected 1950 data for Brazil are represented in the pyramid shown in Figure 3.

The most noticeable characteristic of Brazil's population is its extreme youth: a full 42% of its total population is composed of children under 14 years of age, while only 4% are over 60. Over half of the population is less than 20 years old. As usual, males outnumber females in the age group up to 14 years, and females outnumber males thereafter.[2]

Ethnic Composition

Brazil's ethnic composition is summarized below.

TABLE 1.

Brazil.
Racial composition—1940 and 1950.

Color	1940	1950
White	63%	62%
Black	15%	11%
Pardos (mixed)	21%	26%
Yellow	1%	1%

Source: IBGE, CNG, SNR, *Censo Demográfico* (July 1, 1950), *Estados Unidos do Brazil, Seleção dos Principais Dados*, Table I, p. 1.

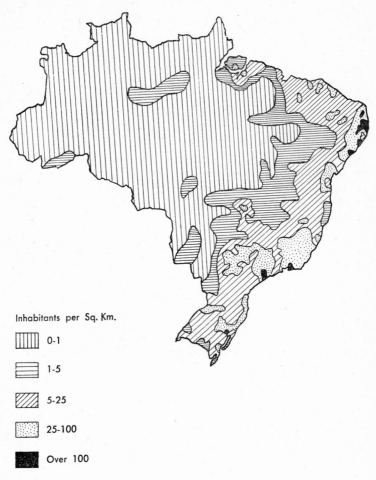

Inhabitants per Sq. Km.

▥	0-1
▤	1-5
▨	5-25
▦	25-100
■	Over 100

Figure 4. Brazil: Population density, 1960.

Between 1940 and 1950 the proportion of both whites and blacks declined, while that of the *pardos* (literally, browns) increased, suggesting a higher rate of natural increase or that miscegenation is continuing. Moreover, the population is whitening; the reduction of blacks is double that of whites. Of course, since the figures are based on individual declarations, the number of whites may be somewhat exaggerated, and a number of lighter blacks may also swell the reported numbers of mulattoes, but the figures generally are accurate.[3]

Territorial distribution

Brazilian population density increased from 2.88 inhabitants per sq. km. in 1940 to 6.14 in 1950 and to 8.39 in 1960 (respectively, 12.6, 15.9, and 21.7 persons per sq. mile). Due to the geographical, climatic, economic, and historical factors outlined above, however, the population is very unevenly distributed.

As seen in Figure 4, the major concentration is along the coast, with one-third of the territory containing 93% of the population. Variation by states is also considerable. In 1960, the highest density was reached in the state of Guanabara, practically a city-state, containing Rio de Janeiro, with 2,824 persons per sq. km. (7,075 per sq. mile), and the lowest was that of Roraima with 0.13 persons per sq. km. (0.34 per sq. mile). Regional densities are given below.

The accelerating trend in Brazilian urbanization over the

TABLE 2.

Brazil.
Regional population density—1960.

Great Regions	Inhabitants per	
	Square kilometer	Square mile
North	1	2
Northeast	16	42
East	20	51
South	31	79
Central-West	2	3
Total Brazil	8.4	21.7

Source: Table III, p. 6, of IBGE, SNR, VII Recenseamento Geral do Brazil, 1960. *Sinopse Preliminar do Censo Demográfico*, Rio de Janeiro, 1962. (Densities concentrated on the net land surface of the country, deducting all interior water bodies and 11 sq. km. of uninhabited rocks and islands; Brazil's net area is then 8,457,591 sq. km, or 3,265,479 sq. miles.)

TABLE 3.

Brazil.

Urban area population by region (1940–1960).

	1940	1950	1960
North	28%	31%	38%
Northeast	23%	26%	34%
East	33%	39%	49%
South	37%	42%	51%
Central-West	22%	24%	35%
Total Brazil	31%	36%	45%

Source: Table VII, p. 11, of IBGE, SNR, VII Recenseamento Geral do Brazil, 1960. *Sinopse Preliminar do Censo Demográfico*, Rio de Janeiro, 1962.

past three decades is seen in Table 3, and is especially notice-able in the Central-West region. Suburban population is in-cluded in the urban category. While data for 1960 are still unpublished, in 1950 the Brazilian over-all figure of 36% could be broken down into 25% urban and 11% suburban. The latter figure varied from 15% in the North to 7% in the Central-West.

Nationality

In 1920, 5% of the total population were foreigners and naturalized Brazilians; by 1950, the figure had declined to 2%. These figures show the effect of declining migration and the small demographic influence of the foreign-born. In ab-solute numbers, the foreign-born and naturalized declined from 1,565,961 in 1920, to 1,406,568 in 1940 and 1,214,184 in 1950. In the latter year, 867,118 lived in the South, and 296,870 in the East. Twenty-eight per cent were Portuguese, 20% Italian, 11% Spaniards, 11% Japanese, 7% Germans and Austrians, 4% Poles, 4% Russians and Balts, and 4% Syrians and Lebanese.[4]

Marital Status

In 1950, 39% of the population 15 years of age and over was classified as single, 54% married, and 7% widowed. However, because of defects in registration, these figures reveal only part of the situation. Moreover, since there is no divorce in Brazil, many married people live separately, and others declare themselves married when living in common law unions. This is apparent from the different number of men and women who declared themselves ever married and with a living spouse: in 1940, 6,093,724 men and 6,204,511 women (a difference of 110,787): in 1950, 8,100,537 men and 8,310,930 women (a difference of 210,393). These differences are obviously too great to be *bona fide*.[5]

Economic Activity

Brazil's economically active population is defined as those who take part in the production of economic goods and services, including unpaid family workers in an economic enterprise. (Housewives, students, retired workers, and children under ten years of age are excluded.) The active population is divided into three basic sectors of economic activity: the primary sector (agriculture, animal husbandry, forestry, and extractive industries such as mining, fishing, etc.); the secondary sector (industries of transformation); and the tertiary sector (trade services, public administration, defense, and the professions).

Between 1940 and 1950 the decrease in primary sector activities and the increase in the other sectors, especially the tertiary, indicate clearly the trend toward development in Brazil (Table 4).

TABLE 4.

Brazil.

Population distribution by type of activity.

	1940	1950
Primary Sector	70%	61%
Secondary Sector	10%	13%
Tertiary Sector	20%	26%

Source: José Francisco de Camargo, *Exodo Rural no Brasil*, Universidade de São Paulo, Faculdade de Ciencias Economicas e Administrativas, Boletin no. 1, São Paulo, 1957, *cf*, Table 3, Vol. I, p. 143.

Literacy

In 1940, 43% of the population over ten years old was literate (48% for males and 38% for females). By 1950, the rate had increased to 48%, with males at 53% and females at 44%. Urban areas were 79% literate, as opposed to 62% in the suburban areas and 32% in the rural.

The most interesting breakdown is by state. In Guanabara (still the Federal District at the time of the 1950 census), the literacy rate was 85% in 1950. In the South, Rio Grande do Sul, São Paulo, Santa Catarina, and Paraná had rates of 66%, 65%, 64%, and 53%. At the other extreme we find 29% in Paraíba, 26% in Piauí, 25% in Maranhão, and 24% in Alagoas, *all in the Northeast,* the other three states of this great region (Ceará, Rio Grande do Norte, and Pernambuco) each having rates of about 32%.[6]

When the 1960 data are published, it is probable that literacy rates across the country will have been considerably improved, due to the unceasing efforts being made in this regard. For example, for the first time in Brazil's history, one state—Guanabara—has enough primary and secondary schools to be able to enforce compulsory education up to 14 years of age (decree of January, 1965). Further, a concentrated effort to eradicate illiteracy is being made in the problem region of the Northeast, through Sudene and the Alliance for Progress.

POPULATION DYNAMICS

Like life itself, population is never static. Its fluctuations can best be described by a simple formula which relates a population at two points in time. If we call P_o the earlier population (at a given census date) and P the population at the next census date, their relationship is expressed by: $P = P_o + (B - D) + (I - E)$, where B represents the number of births, D that of deaths, and I the immigration and E the emigration that occurred between the dates of the earlier and the later census.

It will be noticed that B and D are purely biological phenomena, although with large socio-cultural consequences, while *I* and *E* are essentially socio-cultural, but with biological consequences. *B* and *I,* the positive factors, increase population, while the negative ones, *D* and *E,* decrease it. The difference between *B* and *D, B-D,* is the balance of births and deaths and is called *natural increase. I-E* is correspondingly called the balance of migration, or *net migration. I-E* can be subsumed under the term *migration (M),* which can be either positive or negative according to whether the influx of people (*I*) or the outflow (*E*) prevails. Thus, for simplicity's sake, the equation can be rewritten:

$$P = P_0 + (B - D) + M$$

This has the advantage of pinpointing the three sole factors whose complex interaction is responsible for changes in the number of any population—fertility, mortality and migration.

While vital statistics can often give the absolute numbers of these phenomena during the time between P_0 and *P,* demographers usually measure these happenings through *rates,* indicating the relative frequency of the events. Birth, death, and other rates which tell us how many of these events occurred per 1,000 people in a population are crude rates; many other more refined rates are used, but will not be mentioned here.

Fertility

Fertility depends partly on fecundity, the biological capacity to procreate. In women, the child-bearing period lasts from menarche at puberty to menopause in middle age, roughly from 15 to 49 years of age. But fecundity does not guarantee that a woman will be fertile. For example, she may remain a virgin or choose not to have children. Human fecundity is probably about the same everywhere in the world, while fertility varies greatly, indicating different sets of socio-cultural values and customs among different types of populations.

Brazil's high fertility is characteristic of countries with very young populations, and which are generally underdeveloped economically. Unfortunately, the registration of births in Brazil is woefully incomplete, so that exact birth rates cannot be computed. However, according to Giorgio Mortara's estimates[7] the crude birth rate was 43 in 1950, meaning that 43 live children were born for each 1,000 inhabitants. Expressed otherwise, 174 children were born to every 1,000 women aged 15-49 years in Brazil in 1950. The average number of children born alive by the end of the child-bearing period was 5.8.[8] This figure varied according to ethnic group, from 6.3 for the *pardos* and 6.0 for the whites, to only 5.6 for the blacks.[9] The differences are also apparent among women of proved fertility (about 60% of all women). In 1950, every 100 prolific white women had 513 children, while *pardos* and black women had 551 and 532 respectively.[10]

Efforts are being made by the Ministry of Justice to improve the inadequate birth registration statistics. During 1964, tables for vital statistics for 1959-61 were published, and those for 1962-64 are expected shortly. The information on *registered* births is broken down by municipalities, states, and regions. Each breakdown gives the number of male and female live births and stillbirths occurring in the current year, as well as live births from former years which were registered in the current year. In 1960 and 1961, 94% of the country's *cartórios* reported the vital facts on births and marriages. Of the missing 6.0%, 3.5% gave incomplete information and 2.5% were completely absent. Since incomplete or absent data are indicated in the tables, we at least know where the remaining blanks are. The total number of live registered births in Brazil in 1960, not including those born in former years but only those registered in 1960, was 1,517,647 and the corresponding figure for 1961 was 1,511,142.[11]

In short, Brazil's high fertility patterns are due to women who begin their reproductive activities early and continue them intensively during their childbearing period. Also, they reflect the traditional attitude and the Catholic socio-cultural values toward childbearing. There probably is a fertility differential according to race, but more needs to be known. Saunders writes that "highest fertility is to be found in the most rural portions of the nation's territory, and lowest fertility in the most urban ones," as would be expected.

Mortality

As with fertility, the registration of deaths is very deficient in Brazil. Thus, it is impossible accurately to determine the death rate, life expectancy, infant mortality, and many other related measurements of phenomena affecting population. Here, again, indirect methods for computation have to be resorted to,[12] and Mortara in 1962 made a preliminary estimate of 17 deaths per 1,000 population.[13] Again, this over-all rate conceals great variation. Thus, there is a definitely lower mortality in the South and especially in the great urban areas of Rio de Janeiro and São Paulo. Life expectancy at birth between 1940 and 1950, as estimated by Mortara, was 43.7 years (41.5 for men, 46.0 for women) for the whole of Brazil, while it was 54.2 (52.4 and 56.0 for men and women) in the state of São Paulo in 1949-51. In the period 1951-60 there is no doubt that the death rate fell and that life expectancy increased, but only the publication of the 1960 census data allows us to tell by how much.[14] In any case, life expectancy should by now have reached a median level of 45 to 55, while in Rio de Janeiro, São Paulo, and the Southern states, it may exceed this. As elsewhere in Latin America, the levels of mortality, when compared with those in more developed countries, show differences which are exceptionally high in the lower age groups, lower in middle age, and rather moderate in old age. Although women average 4.5 years longer life expectancy than men, the mortality differences between Brazil and more developed countries are larger for women than for men.[15]

Death and birth registration has been improving. Data are broken down in a fashion similar to fertility breakdowns, but in addition there are breakdowns by cause of death, according to month, and state of occurrence. It is still too early for detailed studies on these new data, but a few indications may be given. In 1960, for instance, the total number of *registered* deaths was 636,398, although data are entirely lacking for the Territory of Roraima, where the total population is small (29,489 in 1960) and from the Federal District (141,742 in 1960). If we assume that the 6% of the *cartórios* that did not report or reported incompletely had the same number of deaths as the average reporting *cartório,* we would add 38,452 deaths to those registered, raising the total to 674,850. If we add 2,410 for Brasília (based on an estimated rate of 17 per 1,000), and round out our result, we have an estimate of 700,000 deaths.

Since the population indicated in the census is 70,967,185, the crude death rate for Brazil works out at 9.8 per 1,000, which is of course too low because of the *unregistered* deaths. Even if we raise it to 11 per 1,000 to include the unregistered deaths, it is clear that the decline in the death rate has primarily been responsible for recent population growth. Thus, we can see that in the last 15 years the death rate in Brazil decreased substantially, from about 20 per 1,000 in the early Fifties to some 11 per 1,000 ten years later, and is still declining, perhaps to 10 per 1,000. This is not so improbable as it may seem. Something of the sort happened in Ceylon between 1946 and 1954, when the crude death rate dropped from 20.3 per 1,000 to 10.4.[16] The same reasons—better public health measures and campaigns—were also operative in Brazil during 1950-65.

Infant mortality is defined as the deaths of children under one year of age, and the infant mortality rate is this number per 1,000 live births during the same year. Because of their dependence on adequate registration of births and deaths, rates of infant mortality in Brazil should be interpreted with care. Smith, whose section on Infant Mortality should be read in connection with these comments, gives some ludicrous examples.[17] Almost all that can be said is that it is so high as to constitute a national scandal. For 1940-50, Mortara estimated it to be about 171—meaning that of every 1,000 children born alive, 171 died before reaching their first birthday. But he also indicated that it was declining, perhaps coming down to 160 in the early Fifties.[18] As noted earlier, however, this average rate is misleading. While the 1961 infant mortality rate was 77 in the state of São Paulo and 124 in Guanabara, it reached 465 in Rio Grande do Norte in the Northeast, one of the very few states where all *cartórios* reported to the Ministry of Justice.[19] It is of interest that the rate for Natal, the capital of Rio Grande do Norte, was only 242.

As development gradually reaches the hitherto underdeveloped areas of the country and the concerted action of the authorities, backed by an aroused public opinion, raises the standards of public health, mortality will continue to decline. However, as these positive results are attained, the much larger number of surviving children will be a major factor in increasing the rate of Brazil's demographic growth, as they become adults and their reproductive cycle begins.

Migration

A distinction should be made between intercontinental, intracontinental and internal migration. Each has its own characteristics and raises different problems.

Intercontinental: The importance of intercontinental migration is dwindling for Brazil, as it is for all Latin America. Brazil's population is a product of a long history of migration, miscegenation, diffusion, and acculturation. In the prehistoric period, Indian migrations established the ethnic substratum encountered in Brazil by the Portuguese conquerors. From the sixteenth to the eighteenth centuries, Negroes and Europeans, through their interaction with each other and with the Indian population, established Brazil's distinctive socio-cultural patterns. In the imperial and first republican period, 1820-30, European migration dominated, especially between 1880 and 1930. Japanese immigration began in 1908 and reached its peak in 1933. From 1840 to 1940, immigrants contributed about 8% of the total population increase. Following the second World War immigration declined considerably. After increasing from 13,039 in 1946 to 88,150 in 1952, it has been steadily decreasing, and in 1963 it was only 23,850. Of course, the problem has changed completely. Today Brazil does not demographically need foreign immigration, since its population growth rate is extremely high, but it still desperately needs a highly selective immigration of qualified people to supply some of the skills needed for its development. However, such people are exceedingly difficult to find anywhere, due to the boom conditions promoted by the European Common Market. This is a principal reason for the decline in intercontinental migration.

Intracontinental: Rather small in numbers, intracontinental migration is generally due either to political or economic change. Thus, conditions of political unrest somewhere in Latin America may cause an inflow of refugees from Paraguay, Bolivia, Peru, or Cuba, or alternately cause an outflow, as occurred after the 1964 Brazilian revolution. Economic reasons also cause a small exchange of numbers along the frontiers, especially with Argentina, Uruguay, Paraguay, Bolivia, and Peru. These movements should increase in importance as South American countries begin drawing together within common market organizations, such as ALALC. Finally, there is also a small amount of re-emigration, as, for instance, some Portuguese leaving Brazil for Venezuela.[20]

Internal: Brazil owes to internal migration her territorial expansion, economic development and, in a sense, her underlying socio-cultural unity and basic political integration. Internal migration continues to be a principal factor in miscegenation, and one means of ensuring the dissemination and diffusion of ideas and cultural traits, thus providing the vital elements of interaction essential in an ethnically and culturally pluralistic society. At the same time, migration is one of Brazil's most pressing problems.

While the phenomenon is still inadequately studied and researched, Figure 5 suggests the complexity of current internal migration.

The main fact indicated is the flow of migrants from the Northeast. For economic reasons, northeasterners are attracted to the more developed South (Rio de Janeiro, São Paulo, and even further to Paraná) and to the new capital, Brasília in the Central-West; the northward current to the Amazon basin is traditional. Northeasterners contributed much to the opening of the Amazon area. We also note the spilling over, as it were, of some states such as Rio Grande do Sul into new demographic frontiers in the states of Santa Catarina, Paraná, and Mato Grosso, and of northeasterners

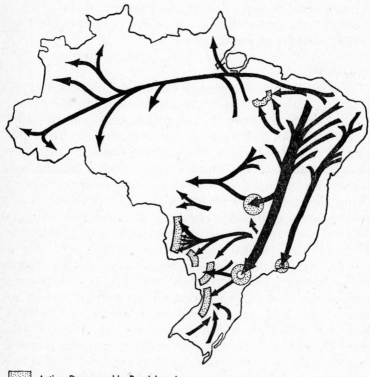

Active Demographic Receiving Areas
(Width of arrow indicates general volume of migration)

Figure 5. Brazil: Internal Migration—up to 1960.

into the active demographic frontiers of the state of Maranhão. Settlement is also occurring along the new roads radiating
from Brasília, although this is not revealed on the map.

While data are very deficient, a few facts about the migration currents are known. First, the numbers involved are
substantial, probably around a quarter of a million people
per year. Further, analysis of census data indicates a rather
strong return flow to the Northeast of about one-third to
one-half of the migrants. The characteristics of these migrants, who arrive by river, railroad, auto, or foot, is also
of interest. There are about three times as many men as

women, and between three and four times as many adults as
children, creating many social problems at their destinations
and in the areas they have left.

Growth

Brazilian population growth has been conditioned by the
rambling path of its history. When discovered in 1500, Brazil
was inhabited by about a million Indians, according to the
recent estimates of Rosenblat and Steward. For three centuries after 1559, African slaves were imported in large numbers. Estimates of the number range from 2,300,000 to a
highly exaggerated 16,000,000, a reasonable approximation
being about 4,700,000 for the three centuries. Peopling of
the country was initially very slow; current estimates suggest
15,000 Europeans and their slaves by 1550; around 57,600 by
1585; perhaps 100,000 by 1600; and by 1690—the year of
the discovery of the first gold placers—close to 300,000. In
the eighteenth century, with the gold rush, the population
grew twelve-fold. This was due not only to migration, but
to the increased area of settlement which included considerable numbers of Indians. These factors speeded up
the processes of miscegenation and acculturation. Mortara
estimates Brazil's population as 2,500,000 in 1770-71, and
3,660,000 by 1800-01. Almost certainly these figures should
be revised downward, since when they were computed the
1920 census data had not been corrected. But even if the
population increase in the eighteenth century was ten-fold
rather than twelve-fold, this was certainly the take-off century for Brazilian population growth. Half a century later, in
1851, the population is estimated to have been 7,340,000.[21]

In 1872, the first Brazilian census was taken. The results of
the succeeding censuses are given in Table 5. The adjusted
figures, corrected by Mortara and his students, should be accepted instead of the official figures.

As is seen, the censuses were of unequal value. Those of
1872, 1900, and 1950 underestimated, and the remaining three
overestimated, population size. The census of 1920 missed the
mark by around 10%, while those of 1940 and 1950 were

TABLE 5.

Brazil.

Population growth (1872–1960).

Year	Census results	Corrected results
1872	9,930,478	10,099,000
1890	14,333,915	14,199,000
1900	17,438,434	17,984,000
1920	30,635,605	27,404,000
1940	41,236,315	41,114,000
1950	51,944,397	51,976,000
1960	70,967,185	—

Source: For census results, Table I, pp. 2–3, of Brazil: *Sinopose Preliminar de Censo Demográfico*, IBGE, SNR, Rio de Janeiro, 1962. For corrected results, Table 1, p. 29, of *Anuário Estatístico do Brasil, 1961*, IBGE, CNE, Rio de Janeiro, 1961, and the sources indicated therein.

judged quite accurate. The data from the 1960 census are still preliminary, and no correction has yet been attempted, but a population of about 71 million is a reasonable assumption.

This figure shocked Brazilian demographers, who as late as 1960 were estimating the total population to be between 65,700,000 and 66,300,000.[22] The mean annual rate of population increase in Brazil between 1940 and 1950 had been 2.4%. Due to continuing declines in mortality, it was thought that this rate would increase slowly during the Fifties, from 2.4% to 2.6% or 2.7% a year by 1960. When the 1960 census results showed an increase of roughly 5 million *above* the projection, the whole painfully built structure of estimates was shattered, as the mean annual rate for 1950-60 was now set at 3.12%.[23] Whereas the population had increased by 26% between 1940 and 1950, it increased by 37% between 1950 and 1960. By state, the increase varied from 102% in Paraná to 18% in Sergipe.[24] More than two-fifths of the increase occurred in the three states of São Paulo, Paraná, and Minas Gerais.

Controversy over the value of the mean annual rate of increase is still raging. Officially, the projections for the annual rate for 1960-70 were placed at 3.2%. Thus, in September

1964, Brazil would have reached 80 million. But some, like myself, regard this rate as still too low. Because of declining mortality I suspect the correct rate should be at least 3.3%, and still increasing. Recently, government sources have even mentioned 3.5%.

Even if we accept the more conservative 3.2% rate, in 1970 Brazil will have 95,262,000 inhabitants. At that rate, population doubles every 22 years. Starting from the 1964 estimated 80 million, this would mean that by 1986 Brazil would have a population of 160 million—*if,* and this is a big *if*—the factors affecting population growth are unchanged. This is a matter of educated guesswork. My view is that there will be about 96 million by 1970. During the Seventies, contradictory influences will be felt. On the one hand, accelerating urbanization will tend to reduce fertility. On the other hand, increasing life expectancy will expand the number of women who live through the entire childbearing period, as well as the absolute number of people who reach the reproductive ages. On balance, and considering that it takes time to change ingrained socio-cultural patterns, I believe that the peak mean annual rate of growth increase will not be reached until the late 1970's. If fertility falls slowly at first, Brazil should reach 140 million in the early 1980's and somewhat more than 200 million by the year 2000. In any case, the best-calculated population projections, like those prepared by the United Nations, appear too low, even when the high assumptions are used. More accurate should be Grauman's estimates made for ECLA, which suggest Brazil's population in 1970 as 96,700,000, in 1975 as 111,400,000, and in 1980 as 126,800,000.

However rapid the increase in total population, urban growth has been even more spectacular in recent years. From 1940 to 1950 the urban (including suburban) population increased 46%, or over 5,900,000 persons, while the rural only increased about 17%, or 3,800,000 people. From 1950 to 1960, the urban increase was 13,208,047, or 70%, and the rural 5,814,741, or 18%. The urban increase was thus 69% of the total. This enormously enhanced the number and importance of cities. For instance, Rio de Janeiro and São Paulo in

1920 had some 1,250,000 and 579,000 inhabitants respectively. The metropolitan area of each one today comprises more than five million inhabitants, a fact which is not apparent from the census data (because of their spillover of population into neighboring municipalities or even states). Furthermore, this mushrooming urban growth is by no means limited to the metropolises: Belo Horizonte, the capital of Minas Gerais state, almost tripled from 1940 to 1960, while Recife more than doubled. Both should be near the million mark by now, while the municipalities of Salvador (Bahía), Pôrto Alegre (Rio Grande do Sul), and Fortaleza (Ceará) had passed

TABLE 6.

Brazil.
Size of cities (1940–1960).

Number of inhabitants	1940	1950	1960
25,000– 50,000	18	44	80
50,000– 100,000	12	19	42
100,000– 250,000	5	8	21
250,000– 500,000	3	3	4
500,000–1,000,000	0	1	4

the half-million mark by 1960, and should now be nearing three-fourths of a million. Belém (Pará), Curitiba (Paraná), and Niterói (Rio de Janeiro) should be almost 500,000; and other state capitals—Natal, Manaus, Maceió, João Pessoa, Goiânia, São Luis, Aracajú, Teresina, together with the Federal capital, Brasília—are on their way to the 200,000 mark.

The number of cities of all sizes has grown markedly in the past two decades. In 1940 there were only 166 cities with 10,000 or more inhabitants, and in 1960 there were 405. Table 6 illustrates this phenomenal growth.[25]

CONCLUSION

What will Brazil look like 15 years from now? Prophesying, always very risky, has fallen into disrepute, and crystal balls are notoriously cloudy. But as an innocent pastime, it can be indulged for the sake of catching a few fleeting glimpses of the results of some trends we examined.

Demographically, Brazil should have a population around

125 million. This population will be young, but probably not so young as in 1965. It will also be lighter in hue, with some 60% whites, 33% *pardos*, 5% blacks and 2% yellow or undeclared. Life expectancy will be higher, possibly around 70. The population distribution will be much more urban than today; probably agriculture will be more developed, having reached a higher productivity, and the size of farms will be economically more sensible, as in the United States today. The number of people employed in the primary sector will be definitely less, and more people than today will be active in the tertiary sector, that of services. Fertility will be reduced—but not too much, the birth rate hovering around 35 per 1,000. The death rate may be down around 8 per 1,000. The annual rate of natural increase will be about 2.7%.

What this population's *per capita* income will be I do not know. But I know that it will depend on the economic policy decisions of 1965 to 1970. These five years will be decisive for Brazil. If education, health, and economic development problems are either solved or, at least, realistically faced and tackled, Brazil will be on the threshold of greatness by 1980. If not, the rate of population growth alone will create more difficult problems, especially in the political and social field, and the high hopes for greatness of a free and happy people will dissolve as the morning mists.

FOOTNOTES

1. Fundamental: Gilberto Freyre, *The Masters and the Slaves; A Study in the Development of Brazilian Civilization*. Tr. Samuel Puthan, Alfred A. Knopf, New York, 1946; T. Lynn Smith, *Brazil: People and Institutions*. rev. ed., Louisiana State University Press, 1963. Social classes: Thales de Azevedo, "Classes Sociais e Grupos de Prestígio," *Ensaios de Antropologia Social,* Livraria Progresso Editora, Salvador, Bahía, 1959, pp. 103-20. Favelas: Louis J. Lebret, José Arthur Rios, Carlos Alberto de Medina, and Helio Modesto, "Aspectos Humanos de Favela Carioca," Special Supplement of *O Estado de São Paulo,* Parts I and II, São Paulo, April 13, 15, 1960.
2. Giorgio Mortara, "Retificação da Distribuição por Idade de População do Brasil em 1º de julho de 1950," IBGE, CNE, Laboratório de Estatística, *Contribuicões para o Estudo de Demografia no Brasil,* Rio de Janeiro, 1961, pp. 158-60.
3. Darcy Ribeiro, *Linguas e Culturas Indígenas do Brasil,* Centro

Brasileiro de Pesquisas Educacionais, Rio de Janeiro, 1957 *cf.* Table IV, p. 39, and pp. 34-43.

4. Romulo Coelbo, "Distribuição Territorial dos Estrangeiros e Brasileiros Naturalizados Presentes no Brasil em 1950," CEDB, pp. 213-218.

5. Giorgio Mortara, "A Composição da População do Brasil segundo o Estado Conjugal em 1950," CEDB, pp. 207-12 for more details; T. Lynn Smith *op. cit.*, ch. XVIII, pp. 459-83.

6. Alcou Vicente W. Carvalho, "A Alfabetização nas Diversas Unidades da Federação em 1940 e 1950," and Giorgio Mortara and Ernani Thimoteo de Barros, "A Alfabetização das Populações Urbanas, Suburbanas e Rurais do Brasil"; CEDB, pp. 401-07 and 408-13.

7. Giorgio Mortara, *Natalidade, Fecundidade e Prolificidade na América Latina*, IBGE, CNG, Laboratório de Estatística, *Estudos Demográficos N° 264* (mimeographed), Rio de Janeiro, January 5, 1962, *cf.* Table I, p. 4; on deficiencies of Brazil's birth registration see T. Lynn Smith, *op. cit.*, pp. 98-100.

8. Mortara, *op. cit.*, p. 23.

9. Giorgio Mortara, "A Fecundidade da mulher no Brasil e a sobrevivência dos filhos nos diversos grupos de cor," *A Fecundidade da mulher no Brasil*, IBGE, Rio de Janeiro, 1957, quoted in Alcou V. W. Carvalho, *op. cit.*, p. 24, note 14.

10. Giorgio Mortara, *A Fecundidade da mulher no Brasil segundo as Unidades da Federação*, IBGE, CNE, Laboratório de Estatística, Estudos Demográficos, no. 267 (mimeographed), Rio de Janeiro, May 8, 1962, *cf.*, p. 2; Data on differential fertility, in Giorgio Mortara, *op. cit. Estudos Demográficos N° 268* (mimeograph), Rio de Janeiro, May 7, 1962 *cf.* Table VI, p. 18, and pp. 17-19. Only the yellow group increased its corresponding cumulative prolificity rates from 449 in 1940 to 499 in 1950. *But* see also J.V.D. Saunders, *Differential Fertility in Brazil*, University of Florida Press, Gainesville, 1958. cf. especially pp. 84-85 *pass.*, who concludes, I believe correctly, that there is a true racial differential fertility for Negroes, due to a handicap in mating for Negro women.

11. Brazil: *Ministério da Justiça e Negócios Interiores*, Serviço do Estatística Demográfica, Moral e Politica, *Registro Civil, Ano 1959; Registro Civil Ano 1960; Registro Civil, Ano 1961.*

12. Giorgio Mortara, "Conjeturas sôbre a Mortalidade no Brasil," *Pesquisas sôbre a Mortalidade no Brasil*, 4th series pp. 24-32.

13. *A mortalidade na América Latina, op. cit.*, Table I, p. 3.

14. *Ibid.*, pp. 28-29, note 17, Table XII on p. 30.

15. *Ibid.*, pp. 18-29.

16. Marcel Reinhard and André Armengaud, *Histoire Générale de la Population Mondiale*, Editions Montchrestien, Paris, 1961, *cf.* p. 570.

17. T. Lynn Smith, *op. cit.*, pp. 115-17.

18. Giorgio Mortara, "Dados e Conjeturas sôbre a Mortalidade Infantil no Brasil," in *Pesquisas sôbre a Mortalidade no Brasil*, pp. 7-12, 1954, *cf.* p. 10.

19. Rates computed from data in publications mentioned in note (7).

20. T. Lynn Smith, "Migration from One Latin-American Country to Another," in *International Population Conference, Vienna, 1959*, pp. 695-702, *cf.* pp. 700-701, Union Internationale pour l'Étude Scien-

tifique de la Population, Vienna, 1959; and Bureau International du Travail (ILO), *Les Migrations Internationales 1945-1957*, Genève 1959. (cf., Table 57, p. 173.)

21. Indian population estimates: in 1492, Ángel Rosenblat, *La Población Indígena y el Mestizaje en América*, 2 cols., Editorial Nova, Buenos Aires, 1954, *cf.* I, p. 102; in 1500, "The Native Population of South America," Julian H. Steward, *ed. Handbook of South American Indians*, Smithsonian Institution, Bureau of American Ethnology, *Bulletin 143*, 5, pp. 655-68, Washington, D.C., 1949, *cf.* p. 666. Estimates during the colonial period: F. Contreiras Rodrigues, *Traços da Economia Social e Política do Brasil Colonial*, Ariel Editora, Rio de Janeiro, 1935, *cf.* pp. 31-35. Negroes: discussion in Artur Hehl Nieva, *International Migrations Affecting Latin America*. XVIIIth century: see Artur Hehl Neiva, "Povoamento do Brasil no Século XVIII," in *Revista de História*, III, 10, pp. 379-86, São Paulo, April-June 1952. Historic demographic projections: Giorgio Mortara, "Estudos sôbre a utilização do censo demográfico para a reconstrução das estatísticas do movimento da população do Brasil, V, in *Revista Brasileira de Estatística*, II, 5, pp. 39-89, Rio de Janeiro, Jan.-March 1941, cf. Table II, p. 43. Estimate in 1851: *Anuário Estatístico do Brasil 1960*, IBGE, CNE, Rio de Janeiro, 1960, cf. Table I, p. 21.

22. Both estimates are found in the *Anuário Estatístico do Brasil 1960*, IBGE, CNE, Rio de Janeiro, 1960; the lower in Table I, 1, p. 21, and the higher in Table I, 3., p. 22.

23. Data on 1940/1950 and 1950/1960 rates in IBGE, Censo Demográfico, *População do censos de 1940, 1950, e 1960, por situação do domicilio, segundo as regiões fisiográficas e as Unidades da Federação* (mimeograph), Rio de Janeiro, n.d.

24. T. Lynn Smith, "The Growth of Population in Central and South America," Committee on the Judiciary, Subcommittee No. 1, House of Representatives, *Study of Population and Immigration Problems*, Western Hemisphere (II), U.S. Government Printing Office n. 95042, Washington D.C., 1963, pp. 151-76 (hereafter CJHR), cf. Table II, p. 155. See also Alfred Sauvy, "La Population des Pays d'Amérique Latine," in *Population*, 18th year, 1, pp. 49-64, Paris, Jan.-March 1963.

25. Best and most recent analyses are T. Lynn Smith's in CJHR, quoted in note (24).

3. Populations of the Non-Spanish-Speaking Caribbean

G. W. ROBERTS

The non-Spanish-speaking Caribbean forms part of a wider region with well defined social characteristics. Some writers, in fact, identify a group of territories as "Plantation America," which includes Spanish-speaking, English-speaking, French-speaking, and Dutch-speaking peoples. For instance, C. Wagley recognizes several factors conferring a degree of unity on the countries of this region. In the first place, they were developed for the production of export crops—principally sugar—which could be most efficiently grown with the aid of a large labor supply recruited and employed under conditions of slavery. Secondly, because of the nature of the slave system there developed a deep cleavage between the planter class, comprising the original slave owners, and the workers and peasants who evolved from the original slave population. An integral part of the plantation system was the importation of labor, at first slaves, and later indentured workers. In these processes, the descendants of African slaves, the original white element, the indigenous inhabitants, and other ethnic groups introduced during the period of indenture, came to constitute a multi-racial society, which further emphasized the division into rigid classes. Another feature associated with the region has been the generally underdeveloped community structure, most noticeable in weak social links at a local level. Again, a complex peasantry emerged after slavery in most of these plantation societies, as ex-slaves acquired holdings and began small-scale farming under a wide range of conditions. Finally, throughout these societies the family often developed with weak

bonds between the spouses and distinct emphasis or matri-
lineage.

Some writers envisage Plantation America as spreading
from Brazil to the South of the United States. Usually, however, this region is considered to cover the Caribbean islands
and the mainland territories which have been under colonial
domination until recently. The latter are, from the standpoint of population, small, although by comparison with the
Caribbean islands they cover a large area. In sum, the plantation area comprises the Caribbean republics—Cuba, the
Dominican Republic, and Haiti—Puerto Rico, together with
the English-speaking, Dutch-speaking, and French-speaking
islands recently under, or just emerging from, colonial status,
as well as the three Guianas and British Honduras.

Table 1 below gives the population of the territories con-
stituting this Caribbean region from 1841 to 1960. It will be
seen that, although a long series of censuses are available for
the English-speaking territories and Cuba, the data for other
countries do not go back very far. The Caribbean region
supported a population of 21,100,000 in 1960. By far the
largest country is Cuba which, with 6,800,000 people in
1960, accounts for nearly one-third of the total population of
the area. Haiti, with 4,200,000, is next, followed by the Dominican Republic, with 3 million, and the Commonwealth
of Puerto Rico, which in 1960 had a population of 2,400,000.
These four countries contain more than three-quarters of the
population of the Caribbean region, although they comprise
only 29% of its area of 268,400 square miles.

It is therefore apparent that the territories which this
paper discusses comprise a small portion of the total Caribbean region. For present purposes language constitutes a
convenient, but not altogether satisfactory, method of di-
viding the region. Because of its checkered history, language
is only a rough indication of cultural differentiation. The
Spanish-speaking population totals 12,100,000, or 57% of the
region's total. Largely because of the size of Haiti, the
French-speaking group numbers 4,200,000, or 20% of the
total. Just under one-fifth (18%) of the population of the re-

TABLE 1.

Populations of the Caribbean (1841–1960).

Territory	1841-48	1851	1861-63	1871	1877-81	1887-91	1899-1901	1907-11	1919-21	1930-31	1935-50	1960
Cuba	1,007,600	—	1,396,500	—	1,521,700	1,631,700	1,572,800	2,049,000	2,889,000	3,962,300	4,778,600	6,797,000
Dominican Republic	—	—	—	—	—	—	—	—	894,700	—	1,479,400	2,994,000
Haiti	—	—	—	—	731,600	798,600	953,200	1,118,000	1,299,800	1,543,900	3,097,300	4,156,000
Puerto Rico	447,900	—	—	—	—	—	—	—	—	—	1,869,300	2,350,000
Jamaica	377,400	—	441,300	506,200	580,800	639,500	—	831,400	858,200	—	1,321,100	1,609,800
Trinidad and Tobago	73,000	83,000	99,800	126,700	171,200	218,400	273,900	333,600	365,900	412,800	558,000	828,000
Barbados	122,200	135,900	152,700	162,000	171,900	182,900	—	172,300	156,800	—	192,800	232,300
Grenada	28,900	32,700	31,900	37,700	42,400	53,200	63,400	66,700	66,300	—	72,400	88,700
St. Lucia	21,000	24,300	26,700	31,600	38,600	42,200	49,900	48,600	51,500	—	70,100	86,100
St. Vincent	27,200	30,100	31,800	35,700	40,500	41,100	—	41,900	44,400	48,000	61,600	79,900
Dominica	22,500	—	25,100	27,200	28,200	26,800	28,900	33,900	37,100	—	47,600	59,900
St. Kitts-Nevis	32,700	20,700	34,100	42,600	44,200	47,700	46,400	43,300	38,200	—	46,200	56,700
Antigua	36,700	37,800	37,100	35,200	35,000	36,900	35,000	32,300	29,800	—	41,800	54,100
Montserrat	7,400	7,100	7,600	8,700	10,100	11,800	12,200	12,200	12,100	—	14,300	12,200
British Virgin Islands	6,700	—	—	6,700	5,300	4,600	4,900	5,600	5,100	—	6,500	7,900
Netherland Antilles	—	—	—	—	—	—	—	—	54,000	71,800	143,500	190,000
Martinique	123,400	—	—	—	—	158,700	203,800	184,000	—	234,500	246,700	277,000
Guadeloupe	—	—	—	—	—	—	182,100	212,400	—	267,400	278,500	270,000
British Honduras	10,000	—	25,600	24,700	27,500	31,500	37,500	40,600	45,300	51,300	59,200	90,500
British Guiana	98,100	125,700	148,000	193,500	244,500	270,900	—	289,100	288,500	302,600	359,400	560,400
French Guiana	—	—	—	—	—	—	—	—	—	—	28,500	31,000
Dutch Guiana	—	—	50,000	—	—	—	—	—	108,000	132,000	169,000	308,000

Note: Populations for 1960 are estimates from the *United Nations Demographic Yearbook* (1963) and from censuses for that year. With three exceptions, earlier populations are from censuses taken within the intervals indicated. The exceptions are the Netherlands and Dutch Guiana (Caribbean Commission, 1957); Martinique, Guadeloupe and French Guiana (Pellier, 1958), Haiti (Census, 1950).

gion speaks English. Dutch speakers total no more than half a million, about 2% of the region's total. Although the English-speaking group is only a small portion of the total population discussed here, the relative paucity of data on the other groups has necessitated an emphasis on analysis of population movements in the English-speaking islands and mainland territories.

GROWTH OF THE POPULATION

British Caribbean

Population growth in these territories can conveniently be divided into five phases. The first phase, from the period of settlement to the late eighteenth century, was characterized mainly by reliance on immigration. While an effort was made to increase the number of white settlers, more emphasis was placed on building up the Negro population by the slave trade in order to provide a labor force for the plantations. The low price of slaves and their ready availability through the slave trade made this a highly economical and practical policy. In Jamaica, where data on slave population movements are more adequate than those for other territories, this influx of slaves resulted in an annual rate of growth of 2% during most of the eighteenth century. Fragmentary data on other territories suggest that their slave populations also increased during this period.

The second phase, also falling during the slave period, covers the years from 1790 to emancipation. It was no longer practical to rely on immigration alone. Opposition to slavery and the slave trade was rising. Some contended that a halt in the trade would induce the Negro slaves to reproduce more rapidly. Sugar interests in the West Indies had to face growing competition from sugar produced elsewhere, while at the same time mounting demand for slaves in North America forced up their price on the slave market. After the Negro uprisings in Santo Domingo, the wisdom of building up vast populations of African slaves was questioned. These factors made acquiring slaves difficult, and the abolition of the slave trade in 1807 made a change in the policy and methods of recruiting plantation labor inevitable. It became essential to stimulate slave reproduction and policies to this end were devised in the late eighteenth and early nineteenth centuries. Still, the evidence is that the end of the slave trade marked a decline in slave reproduction. Slave registration, introduced in 1816, provided the first reliable figures on population growth among slaves. These show that during the period 1816-34 the slave population declined, the sole exception being Barbados. In 1816 slaves of the British Caribbean colonies totalled 728,400. By 1826 they numbered 690,200, and in 1834, 651,900, a decline of 10%. In Barbados, however, the number of slaves increased 7% (77,500-83,100). This is in marked contrast to declines in other territories, which in some cases exceeded 20%.

The third phase of demographic development in the British Caribbean, extending from the end of slavery to the late nineteenth century, witnessed a reappearance of immigration. This was again promoted in order to augment the plantation working force. Two forms developed. The more important, from the political and demographic standpoint, was indenture immigration, which commenced in the 1830's and continued up to 1917. East Indians, Africans, Chinese, Madeirans, and Europeans were brought in under different schemes to work on the plantations. Table 2 below shows the race or ethnic origin of the approximately 536,000 individuals who thus entered the area. 430,000 (80%) were East Indians. Africans numbered 39,000 (7% of the total). British Guiana took the largest proportion (56%), while Trinidad absorbed 29% and Jamaica, 10%. The shortage of plantation labor in British Guiana and Trinidad was also responsible for the second characteristic of migration during this period—the shift of population from the older and more densely settled islands to the newer and more sparsely settled colonies. Emigrants from Barbados to British Guiana and Trinidad during the nineteenth century totalled at least 50,000, in addition to many from the Windward and Leeward Islands.

These currents of migration were the dominant factor in population growth during the nineteenth century. Their

TABLE 2.

Race and destination of immigrants entering the British Caribbean, mainly under indenture (1838–1977).

Race or ethnic origin	Destination									
	British Guiana	Trinidad	Jamaica	Grenada	St. Lucia	St. Vincent	St. Kitts	Dominica	British Honduras	Total
East Indian	238,909	143,939	36,412	5,932	4,354	2,472	337	—	—	432,355
African	14,060	8,854	11,391	2,406	730	1,036	455	400	—	39,332
Chinese	13,533	2,645	1,152	—	—	—	—	—	474	17,804
Portuguese	28,946	897	379	—	—	—	—	—	—	30,222
Other Europeans	—	—	3,736	—	—	—	—	—	—	3,736
Other	1,531*	1,301†	258†	—	—	—	—	—	178†	3,268
Total	296,979	157,636	53,328	8,338	5,084	3,508	792	400	652	526,717

* Includes 345 from Dutch Guiana.
† From United States.
Note: This table is compiled from a forthcoming paper by the author on indenture immigration into the British Caribbean.

influence can be measured, since this period coincided with the development of reliable censuses throughout the region. Such migration determined the high rates of growth in Trinidad and Tobago, and British Guiana, and retarded population growth in the home islands of the emigrant workers. Between 1841 and 1861 the population of British Guiana increased from 98,000 to 148,000; by 1881 it was 244,000. Trinidad and Tobago showed slower initial increases, from 73,000 in 1841 to 100,000 in 1861. Then the rate of growth accelerated. By 1881 the population stood at 171,000. Between 1841 and 1861 the average annual growth rate in British Guiana ranged from 1.7% to 2.7%; in Trinidad the range was from 1.8% to 3.1%. No other country in the region experienced comparable growth. The smaller islands at no time showed growth rates exceeding 1.4%. In the majority of cases their annual rates were well under 1%. Jamaica, which had little immigration, still exhibited a steady and appreciable growth rate, ranging from 0.9% to 1.4% per year. Between 1841 and 1881 its population increased from 377,000 to 581,000.

A fourth demographic phase extended from the 1880's to about 1920, and was marked by a decline in indenture immigration and a net outflow from the region. Depression in the sugar industry resulted in a lessened need for plantation workers and reduced indenture immigration, which ended in 1917. Work on the Panama Canal gave employment to a number of West Indian laborers, while work on Cuban sugar plantations and jobs in the United States attracted other people of the region, principally from Jamaica, Barbados, and the Windward Islands. It is estimated that between 1881 and 1921 net Jamaican emigration to the United States totalled 46,000, to Panama 45,000, to Cuba 22,000, and to other areas 33,000.

Since increased emigration was not accompanied by any decline in the death rate, throughout the region there was a notable decline in growth rates, the only exception being Trinidad, which at least until 1911 experienced an annual growth rate exceeding 2%, a consequence, no doubt, of continued immigration from Barbados and the Windward Islands. Many territories such as Barbados, British Guiana, and some of the smaller islands actually witnessed a population decline during this period. The population of Barbados, for example, fell from 183,000 in 1891 to 172,000 in 1911, and to 157,000 in 1921.

In many fundamental respects, the fifth demographic phase differs from all previous ones. From the early 1920's the region saw a continuous decline in mortality which, coupled with high levels of fertility, accelerated population growth. Accompanying these changes has been a decline in immigration. After the termination of the indenture movement in 1917, no alternative source of immigration appeared until the 1950's. Some emigration continued in the 1920's but the passing of legislation restricting entry into the United States around this time, together with the growing restrictions on entry into many Latin American countries, meant the end of this outflow. The fact that, despite the cessation of immigration, growth rates in general exceeded those of the past decades attests to the magnitude of the declines in mortality.

The total population of the British Caribbean, which rose from 1,400,000 in 1881 to 2,000,000 in 1921, amounted to 2,900,000 in 1946 and 3,800,000 in 1960. This movement was entirely due to the natural increase which the control of mortality made possible. Increases in excess of 2% per year have been general. An important development, noted since 1954, has added a new dimension to the pattern of growth. This has been emigration to the United Kingdom which, until its control in 1962, markedly reduced growth. In Jamaica, for instance, the total natural increase between 1943 and 1960 was 568,000, but because of the net outward movement of 190,000 the island had an actual increase of only 378,000. With the exception of Trinidad and Tobago and British Honduras, such reductions from emigration were general. For the region as a whole, the natural increase between 1946 and 1960 amounted to 1,180,000, but because of a net outward movement of about 248,000 the population grew by only 932,000. These gains remain formidable despite significant levels of emigration. In fact, the region's total gain exceeds the population of its second largest unit—Trinidad and Tobago—which in 1960 was 834,000. To place emigration to the United Kingdom in perspective it may be noted that the net loss of 248,000 exceeded the population of Barbados, which in 1960 was 233,000.

With the passing by the United Kingdom of the Commonwealth Immigration Act of 1962, West Indian emigration was drastically reduced. If, as seems the case, the closing of this outlet marks the end of ready avenues for large-scale emigration, a powerful curb to growth has been removed and a new phase of population increase may be imminent. This may, in the absence of fertility declines, amount to an annual growth of between 3 and 4%.

French-Speaking Territories

Information on population growth in the largest of the non-Spanish-speaking populations of the Caribbean—Haiti —remains fragmentary. An estimate made in 1791 placed the population of the republic at 519,000, while according to a census of 1805 the population was 389,000; but J. G. Leyburn describes both of these as "mere guesses." The increase to over 3 million in 1950 implies appreciable rates of natural increase, especially as the population remained a closed one. In view of the unsettled conditions in Haiti after 1790, the decline in its agriculture after 1805, and its continued extremely low level of production, we should expect that the patterns of low reproduction in the slave population would continue into the nineteenth century.

Two other units—Martinique and Guadeloupe—showed sequences of population growth paralleling those of their English-speaking counterparts. Developed largely for the production of plantation crops, these two islands were also under slave systems in the early period of their exploitation. At the time of the abolition of slavery in these territories in 1848 there were 93,000 slaves in Guadeloupe and 74,000 in Martinique (M. J. Pellier). Emancipation brought a movement from the plantations, just as it did in the British colonies, and necessitated the introduction of indentured workers. It is estimated that 77,000 East Indians were introduced between 1852 and 1887, and 1,300 Chinese; the total number of immigrants was 78,000. It does not appear that these people participated to a large extent in the emigration to Latin America and the United States in which the peoples of the British Caribbean were so deeply involved. There have been some declines in mortality in recent years, and these have accelerated rates of growth, at least in Martinique. The suggested decline in Guadeloupe between 1954 and 1960 may merely indicate inadequacies in enumeration.

With approximately one person per square mile, French Guiana is the most sparsely settled country in the region. Like most of the other territories considered here, it resorted to immigration during the nineteenth century; some 10,000 Africans and East Indians were brought into the country (Pellier). Since this colony was developed as a penal settlement rather than for the production of plantation crops, population growth has been extremely small; only 28,500, according to the 1954 census.

The Dutch Islands

The Dutch islands of the Caribbean have also had a period of slavery, although the plantation systems there were never as fully developed as those in the British and French colonies, as the Caribbean Commission noted in 1957. When the islands came under Dutch rule in 1816 their populations were as follows: 12,000 in Curaçao; 1,700 in Aruba; 1,100 in Bonaire; 3,600 in St. Martin; 2,600 in St. Eustatius; and 1,100 in Saba. The total population of 22,000 probably changed little for a century. During this period there was some emigration, but not on a scale sufficient to have a marked influence on rates of growth. With the development of the petroleum industry in Curaçao and Aruba, population expanded very rapidly. In 1916, the population of the Dutch islands was 57,000 and by 1956 it had risen to 187,000; Curaçao alone experienced a four-fold expansion during this forty-year period. While immigration has been mainly responsible for this growth, there have been appreciable declines in mortality, and this has meant a rise in the rate of natural increase.

Dutch Guiana developed differently from the Dutch islands of the Caribbean. It was essentially a colony for the production of plantation crops, and as such depended largely on slaves during its early development. The Caribbean Commission estimated that between 300,000 and 350,000 slaves were imported into the country up to the time of the abolition of slavery in the Dutch territories in 1863. Nevertheless, in that year the entire population, including slaves and white settlers, numbered no more than 50,000. Additional labor was recruited by private individuals between 1853 and 1863, after which date the government granted premiums on laborers introduced. In 1872 indenture immigration under the complete control of the government was resorted to. Between 1853 and 1872, 5,400 immigrants entered Dutch Guiana. Of these, 500 came from Madeira, 2,500 from China, and 2,400 from the West Indies, the latter mostly from Barbados. Contract labor from India was introduced in 1872, the total of these immigrants amounting to 34,000. The Dutch possessions in Indonesia provided a more readily accessible source of labor. Between 1891 and 1939 about 33,000 Indonesians entered Dutch Guiana. Between 1919 and 1960 the population increased from 108,000 to 308,000, a threefold rise, which exceeds the comparable growth in British Guiana, that is, from 289,000 in 1921 to 560,000 in 1960.

SOME CHARACTERISTICS OF THE POPULATIONS

Ethnic Composition

There are marked differences in ethnic composition between the non-Spanish-speaking elements of the Caribbean and the populations of Spanish descent. These originate largely in two historical factors. First, the island populations were exploited by the early European settlers primarily for the production of plantation crops and not for the extraction of precious minerals, as was the case in the mainland countries. Gold and silver proved the great attraction to the Spanish conquerors on the mainland, and their effective exploitation did not call for the large-scale introduction of labor. Another contrast between the Caribbean territories and the Latin American countries, which contributed to ethnic differentiation, was the relatively large number of indigenous inhabitants in the latter. These could be impressed into work in the mines, which they were competent to undertake, whereas in the Caribbean islands they did not prove sufficiently robust to cope with the more arduous labor on the sugar plantations.

Indigenous elements in the islands were fewer than on the mainland and in general they suffered extinction or near-extinction soon after the arrival of the Europeans. In fact, the only territories in the non-Spanish-speaking groups where an appreciable number of indigenous people exist today are the three Guianas and British Honduras. It follows that the important *mestizo* element of Latin America has no counterpart in the English-, French-, and Dutch-speaking societies of the Caribbean.

Slavery has left its mark on the ethnic composition of the region, as is illustrated by the 1960 census data for the English-speaking peoples summarized in Table 3. The proportion classified as being of Negro descent is very high in those territories which received little indenture immigration. To be sure, the imbalance between the sexes of most of the immigrant populations has resulted in a degree of miscegenation, and a substantial proportion of some of the populations is returned as mixed. But it may be safely assumed that Negroes are generally strongly represented in the mixed categories, and therefore the two groups—Negro and mixed—may be taken as indicating the elements of predominantly Negro descent. As will be seen from Table 3, it is only in Trinidad and British Guiana, where relatively heavy indenture immigration took place, that the proportion of the population of Negro descent falls much below 90%.

East Indians account for 48% of the population of British Guiana, and 36% of Trinidad and Tobago. Their introduc-

TABLE 3.

Ethnic origin of the English-speaking populations of the Caribbean (1960).

	Negro	Mixed	East Indian	Chinese	White	Amer-indian	Other
Jamaica	76.8	16.9	1.7	0.6	0.8	—	3.2
Grenada	52.65	42.17	4.25	—	0.79	0.00	0.14
Dominica	66.05	32.72	0.00	—	0.42	0.66	0.13
St. Vincent	70.30	21.82	3.06	—	2.30	1.58	0.94
St. Lucia	68.82	26.89	3.48	—	0.54	0.17	0.10
Antigua	92.43	3.48	0.16		1.33	—	2.60
St. Kitts	89.44	8.78	0.21		0.94	—	0.63
Montserrat	95.60	2.36	0.00		0.42	—	1.60
Virgin Islands	93.40	4.71	0.00		0.59	—	1.26
Barbados	89.17	6.02	0.20	0.00	4.34	0.00	0.26
Trinidad & Tobago	43.31	16.27	36.47	1.01	1.90	—	1.04
British Guiana	32.83	11.99	47.79	0.73	0.54	4.54	1.54

Note: British Honduras has been omitted because of inconsistencies in the available ethnic data.

tion into other islands can be traced from the fact that small numbers are reported in Grenada (4%), St. Vincent and St. Lucia (3%), and Jamaica (2%). Chinese entered British Guiana and Trinidad under indenture and Jamaica as free immigrants, and small, but socially important, groups in these territories were classified as Chinese in 1960—1% in Trinidad and Tobago, 0.7% in British Guiana, and 0.6% in Jamaica.

Even in the early nineteenth century it appears that no dominant white group was present in large numbers in any of the colonies. Also of interest is the general decline in the proportion of the populations returned as European in the past century. This is well illustrated from the ethnic composition of Jamaica. At the first census of this island in 1841, 4.2% of its population was classified as white; this proportion fell steadily to 0.8% in 1960. At the 1960 census the largest concentration of Europeans, 4.3% of the total, was in Barbados, due to the indentured white labor imported during the early days of the island's history.

A substantial proportion of the population of British Honduras consists of indigenous Indians, but breakdowns of this population by race were not published for 1960 because of former inconsistencies in classification. Appreciable numbers of such ethnic groups are also found in British Guiana, where in 1960 they accounted for 5% of the total population. Small groups of persons of Carib descent are found in Dominica and St. Vincent.

It is therefore clear that a fairly wide range of racial intermixture characterizes these populations.

Education

The marked spread of education among the English-speaking populations is summarized in Table 4. The proportions of their adult populations who have not had any formal schooling are, by comparison with other developing countries, relatively low. Most favorably placed is Barbados, where the proportion without schooling is less than 2%, a level lower than that for most of the developing countries of the world. In five others—Virgin Islands, Antigua, St. Kitts-Nevis, Grenada, and St. Vincent—it ranges from 3% to 8%. In the mainland territory of British Guiana, 13% have received no formal schooling; for the largest unit of the group, Jamaica, the proportion is much higher (16%).

TABLE 4.

Education of the English-speaking population of the Caribbean, 1960.

	% with no schooling	% with primary schooling			% with secondary schooling		University education	Number of secondary school children per 100 primary school children
		Total	Less than 4 years	6–7 years	Without school certificate	With school certificate		
Jamaica	16.8	74.4	7.7	46.5	3.9	2.8	0.3	8.7
Trinidad & Tobago	11.3	72.9	12.8	37.1	9.9	3.7	0.7	13.5
Barbados	1.8	80.2	13.0	42.0	11.4	4.5	0.6	28.7
Grenada	6.7	84.7	19.1	29.6	5.4	2.3	0.5	6.6
St. Lucia	26.2	69.7	21.7	24.8	2.2	1.1	0.3	4.1
St. Vincent	7.9	85.4	28.1	21.2	4.2	1.6	0.3	4.7
Dominica	13.4	79.0	28.4	25.3	4.8	1.6	0.5	8.7
St. Kitts-Nevis	3.8	89.1	—	—	4.4	1.8	0.4	13.0
Antigua	3.3	83.1	—	—	9.4	1.9	0.4	4.5
Montserrat	11.1	81.1	—	—	2.3	2.0	0.4	6.6
British Virgin Isls.	3.2	88.0	—	—	4.0	2.2	0.5	5.7
British Guiana	12.9	75.5	12.3	38.6	7.1	3.3	0.4	8.1

Although a substantial proportion of adults in each of the territories has received primary education, these relatively high levels indicate that most students have had no more than three years of formal schooling, and must therefore be designated functionally illiterate. Apart from the Leeward Islands (where a somewhat different census classification of primary school students has been adopted), this proportion falls below one-fifth only in Jamaica (8%), Trinidad and Tobago (13%), and Barbados (13%), and it is highest (28%) in Dominica. Also of importance in considering primary schooling is the proportion who have completed six or seven years. Again, excluding the Leeward Islands, only Jamaica, Barbados, and Trinidad and Tobago show substantial numbers so qualified; here the proportions are 47%, 42%, and 37%, respectively.

In terms of secondary education, these populations appear in an even more unfavorable light in comparison to the more developed societies. The shortage of persons so qualified is a characteristic which the Caribbean shares with most of the developing areas of the world. Two levels of secondary school were recognized in the 1960 census, and in both it is clear that very few adults have had the benefit of secondary education. Of the population who have been to a secondary school but have failed to obtain a school certificate or its equivalent, the lowest levels, 2%, are recorded for St. Lucia and Montserrat. The highest proportion (11%) is that for Barbados. Even lower proportions have obtained the school certificate or its equivalent. Indeed, apart from Barbados (5%), Trinidad and Tobago (4%), Jamaica (4%), and British Guiana (3%), they are at a level of 2% or less. Even less satisfactory is the position of the region when measured in terms of the proportions of adults who have had any university training. In no case does this approach 1%, and for the majority of the populations it is under 0.5%. This marked shortage of persons with higher education is found throughout the Caribbean.

An examination of the composition of the school population in 1960 suggests that no significant improvement in the spread of higher education is impending, since the ratio between primary and secondary students is similar to that for adults. The school population also yields another statistic of significance, the number of secondary students per 100 primary students. This ratio is substantial only in Barbados, where it reaches 29%. Elsewhere it is much lower. In Trinidad and Tobago it is 14%; in St. Kitts-Nevis, 13%, while it is lowest in St. Lucia, 4%.

Strict comparisons between the French- and Dutch-speaking elements, and the English-speaking, cannot be closely drawn at this stage; but with one outstanding exception the former do not seem to differ much from the patterns outlined above. This exception is Haiti, where extremely low standards of schooling are apparent. According to the census of 1950, 89% of the adults have had no formal schooling, while only 2% had any secondary education, and the proportion with university training was at a level of only 0.1%.

Socio-economic Status

An attempt was made in the 1960 census of the Eastern Caribbean territories of the English-speaking group to utilize occupation as the basis for establishing a socio-economic classification of the working population. A few suggestive facts emerge from the simple preliminary summaries so far published from this census (Table 5).

From the percentage distribution the persistent dependence of these territories on agriculture is emphasized. This is clear in the Windward Islands, where the highest proportion of farmers and farm workers is in St. Lucia (57%) and the lowest is in St. Vincent (41%). Less marked is dependence on agriculture in the three larger units, where it ranges from about one-third to one-fifth.

Another significant aspect of these populations is the extent to which the male working force is involved in non-manual occupations. In the most economically advanced country of the English-speaking territories, Trinidad and Tobago, one-fifth are designated non-manual; in British Guiana it is 17%, in Grenada and Barbados about 14%, and much less in the others. The relative importance of profes-

TABLE 5.

Employment background of the English-speaking population of the Eastern Caribbean (1960). (Per cent of the total labor force).

	Agricultural		Non-Manual				Manual			
	Farmer	Agricultural worker	Professional worker	Manager and administrative worker	Other non-manual worker	Personal service worker	Skilled worker	Semi-skilled worker	Unskilled worker	Other
Male										
Trinidad & Tobago	7.53	13.76	5.37	3.58	11.65	4.72	35.58	2.41	13.37	2.04
British Guiana	15.58	20.53	4.59	4.09	8.49	3.37	29.01	2.12	11.11	1.10
Barbados	1.85	21.09	3.81	3.47	7.47	5.74	39.22	1.44	14.71	1.21
Grenada	14.99	28.03	3.94	3.41	6.63	4.12	25.48	1.35	8.74	3.30
St. Lucia	26.21	31.16	2.18	1.74	4.29	2.14	20.09	2.33	8.88	0.96
St. Vincent	16.60	24.80	4.17	3.04	5.19	3.47	25.24	3.32	12.19	1.99
Dominica	32.82	23.60	2.71	1.82	3.92	1.93	21.08	1.99	9.45	0.68
Female										
Trinidad & Tobago	3.45	12.96	10.02	3.53	18.73	30.25	6.76	0.98	5.84	7.47
British Guiana	5.88	19.41	11.22	3.17	11.96	27.67	4.90	0.97	6.96	7.86
Barbados	0.36	25.85	5.94	3.16	12.95	29.35	2.62	0.63	10.44	8.68
Grenada	6.22	26.55	6.33	4.09	8.53	20.56	3.20	0.34	11.03	13.14
St. Lucia	16.01	26.06	5.78	3.03	9.37	17.62	5.47	0.67	5.93	10.07
St. Vincent	5.51	32.17	7.28	2.98	7.41	17.30	2.37	3.40	12.37	9.21
Dominica	16.57	25.57	5.57	3.70	7.91	16.88	5.89	1.28	7.59	9.03

sional groups is about the same, the highest proportion being 5% in Trinidad and Tobago and British Guiana, and lowest (2%) in Dominica and St. Lucia. As is to be expected, most of the occupational classes in this non-manual category consist of clerks and lower-grade workers in commerce and industry; professional and managerial classes contribute only small proportions.

Because of the substantial numbers of skilled workers reported, a fairly large proportion of the working population appears in the manual category. The Windward Islands, which are more heavily dependent on agriculture, show smaller numbers classified as manual, largely because of the low proportion of skilled workers.

Classifications such as these have the merit of showing the heavy dependence on agriculture, but broader comparisons with advanced societies have to be made with caution. The skilled and semi-skilled elements present special difficulty. While to some extent these classes may be functionally equivalent to their counterparts in advanced societies, they do not necessarily adhere to standards of efficiency or craftsmanship comparable to those to be found in the technologically advanced societies.

Broadly, the patterns of distribution of the male working force are reflected among females, but the few contrasts noted are significant and help still further to underline the special features of the Caribbean. All population figures indicate that the proportion of females in the non-manual class exceeds that of males because of the comparatively high number of females returned as professionals. When more detailed tabulations from the census are available full analysis of this fact should be possible. It would be of particular interest to know which industries are responsible for this large proportion of females. More important is the number of females in personal service. Female participation in such occupations may well be a product of the social history of the region. In the slave period, females were heavily involved in occupations of this type, and although there has been, notably since the turn of this century, a steep decline

in female participation in agriculture, their equally traditional participation in personal service has persisted.

POPULATION GROWTH AND THE PROSPECTS
FOR FERTILITY CONTROL

Mortality Trends

The steep declines in mortality which commenced in the
1920's have continued and the death rates of the English-
speaking territories are now considerably lower than in the
early years of the century and compare favorably with most
developing countries of the world. Crude death rates have,
with the exception of four small territories, been reduced to
under 12 per 1,000, and in the larger units to less than 10.
Control has been most successful over those diseases which
exert their greatest force at younger ages, especially dysentery and diarrhea. This aspect of mortality is best illustrated
by infant mortality rates. In Barbados, the island which has
shown probably the greatest advances in the control of disease, infant mortality fell from a very high level of 275
deaths per 1,000 births in 1921, to 155 in 1946, to 129 in
1951, and to 63 in 1960; thus, the present rate is no more
than one-quarter of that which prevailed before. In 1921, infant mortality in the four larger units of the group—Jamaica, Trinidad and Tobago, Barbados, and British Guiana—
ranged from 275 in British Guiana to 144 in Trinidad and
Tobago. In 1960, the range was from 50 in Trinidad and
Tobago to 63 in Barbados.

Improvements in mortality rates are best summarized in
terms of the average length of life. In 1921, the average
length of life for females in the four largest territories
ranged from 31.9 for Barbados to 40.1 for Trinidad and Tobago. By 1960 the corresponding range was from 63.0 for
British Guiana to 67.4 for Barbados. Thus, there has been
not only a signal improvement but an equalization in the
death rates of the various countries of the area. As has already been observed, however, the gains registered in some
of the smaller islands are much less. Both St. Lucia and St.
Vincent have not shown any marked decline in mortality

rates in recent years, and death rates among children and infants remain high.

While the general death rate in the Caribbean remains somewhat higher than in the most advanced societies, much of this difference stems from the relatively high infant mortality with which the area still has to contend. In fact, if we compare the mean life expectancy after age one in the West Indies with corresponding levels for the advanced societies the differences are greatly reduced. Moreover, it is estimated that should the downward trend in the death rate continue, the over-all rate in the most favorably placed populations of the region within the next decade will approximate the death rate of those populations of the world with the highest standards of public health.

Fertility trends

The birth rate of the region is still that of a developing country. With the exception of some of the smaller units, birth rates in 1960 were generally above 40 per 1,000. In 1960, the highest rates were in St. Vincent (50.1) and St. Lucia (47.8). Other very high rates were those of Dutch Guiana (45.5), British Honduras (44.8), and British Guiana (43.7). The comparatively low rate to be found in Barbados (31.1) demands special attention. There is evidence that since the early years of this century birth rates in this very densely settled island have been somewhat lower than those for the neighboring territories. This suggests the operation of factors tending to curb fertility. These were probably associated with the severe imbalance between the sexes caused by the persistent and heavy male emigration beginning in the late 1880's. The preponderance of females remaining under these conditions might have resulted in a large number remaining unmarried, or not being involved in any of the less stable types of union characteristic of the region. At the same time, the possiblity remains that the pressure of population, which was evident since the mid-nineteenth century, could have led to the spread of some practices of fertility control long before they began to appear elsewhere in the region.

There is evidence of two trends in fertility in the British Caribbean which, on balance, may tend to cancel each other. On the one hand, there have been declines in the average size of the family, and on the other, declines in the proportion of childless females. The first trend can be illustrated by Jamaica, where crude birth rates declined from 37.7 in 1919-23 to 31.9 in 1944-48. When this trend is measured by refined rates (joint gross reproduction rates), a shift from 2.64 to 2.08 is equivalent to a substantial reduction of 21%. This reduction was to be found in all parishes of the island, especially the major urban districts. In fact, it seemed that the declines in fertility varied directly with the distance from Kingston-St. Andrew, the principal urban center. These declines, it should be noted, are inferred solely from annual rates. There are no data on the size of completed families prior to 1943, and we do not know how this may have varied.

Since 1943 the downward curve of the birth rate has turned upward. Taking Jamaica as an illustration, the birth rate, which up to 1949 was between 29 and 32 per 1,000, began to increase steadily after 1952 and by 1958 exceeded 40. The number of children per woman of completed fertility (over 45 years of age) in Jamaica fell from 4.87 in 1943 to 4.05 in 1960. Similar changes have been noted in other territories. Thus, in Trinidad the average number of children born to women aged 45-64, 4.10 in 1946, was down to 3.89 in 1960.

The second trend in fertility—the decline in the proportion of childless women—has appeared in most of these territories between 1946 and 1960. In Jamaica, for instance, more than half (52%) of the women aged 20-24 were childless in 1943. The corresponding figure in 1960 was 37%. In the Windward Islands—Grenada, St. Lucia, St. Vincent, and Dominica—there has also been a marked decline in childlessness between 1946 and 1960, the proportion of childless females falling from 42% to 33%.

Conclusion

In summary, despite the reductions in the level of completed fertility of the past few decades, the general position of the region has not changed materially, because of the larger proportion of women now having children. This decline in childlessness seems to have originated from improvements in public health such as campaigns to control venereal disease and yaws. These have tended to reduce the high incidence of sterility and sub-fertility, which has long been a feature of Negro populations in the Western Hemisphere.

The incipient declines in size of completed families which recent data indicate presage some ultimate reductions in fertility. But in view of the fact that further improvements in mortality levels are possible, it seems safe to assume that annual rates of natural increase in excess of 3% will continue for some time in most of the populations of the region. At the same time, the relatively low fertility in Barbados during the past two decades suggests that the program of family planning established there has had some success. Consequently, a closer examination of the prospects for fertility decline seem warranted.

Fertility Control

Continued social and economic development within the Caribbean may be expected to induce some reduction in levels of fertility. Urban expansion, the declining dependence on agriculture, and the growth of industry will contribute to the spread of the small family as an ideal. But, as with other countries similarly situated, pronounced declines may not appear in the near future unless definite steps are taken to institute policies aimed at stimulating such changes. It is therefore relevant to consider briefly the attempts to formulate such policies in Barbados over the past decade, and the more recent policy decisions in Jamaica to promote family planning.

Barbados, an island which as early as the mid-nineteenth century supported 740 persons per square mile, had long been trying to control the growth of its population. In some measure this could be done by promoting emigration, and this policy was pursued in the last century. But with the closing of most avenues of emigration in the early years of this century it became evident that other means of curbing population growth had to be explored. In 1954, the government appointed a committee to consider what could be done to slow down the rate of increase. It reported strongly in favor of stimulating family planning and its realistic recommendations were fully accepted by the government, which undertook to support action in this direction. The agency through which this policy was implemented was, in effect, a non-official body, the Barbados Family Planning Association; but it received full support, financial and otherwise, from the government. In its initial stages the Association launched a campaign for the spread of birth control information, and at the same time undertook to supply contraceptive material. Mobile film units, booklets, and other means were used in order to spread the ideal of the small family. This policy of positive promotion lapsed somewhat from 1959 to 1962 but under a revised program of large-scale promotion, utilizing media such as radio, television, and the press, it has been resumed.

As an integral part of its operations, the Barbados Family Planning Association runs several clinics where advice on the use of contraceptives and the necessary material can be obtained. Initially, reliance was placed on the diaphragm and on a specific brand of foam tablets. Of the patients attending the principal clinic in 1957, 51% were fitted with diaphragms and foam tablets were prescribed for 42%. Emphasis on the diaphragm declined, however, and by 1960 only about one-third of the clinic's cases were fitted with them, while less than one-fifth were in 1962. Another development was the greater use of spermicidal creams. After 1960 an aerosol foam product, *Emko,* came into prominence and was widely used in the clinics. In the last two years the clinics have introduced oral contraceptives and intra-uterine devices. Recent decisions to advocate the use of the latter on a large scale should considerably improve the type of service rendered by the clinics, and more firmly assure the spread of contraceptive practices.

Between 1957 and 1963 it is estimated that about 12,000

females came under the direct influence of the Association's clinics. As a result it seems certain that many more women were made aware of the possibilities of controlling their family size, and actually began doing so. In view of the fact that the number of women aged 15-39 in 1960 was 41,700, it can be safely concluded that an appreciable proportion of the island's female population of child-bearing age has been induced to adopt some form of contraception.

Jamaica, by no means as densely populated as Barbados and without the latter's dependence on a one-crop economy, has not been so strongly attracted to policies of population control. Throughout its history it has maintained a rate of growth much steadier than that of Barbados, which has meant a mounting pressure on the land. The full effects of rates of natural increase of between 2.5% and 3% per year, in evidence since the early 1950's, were largely offset by emigration to the United Kingdom, which assumed impressive dimensions after 1954. The passing of the Commonwealth Immigration Act of 1962, however, closed this outlet and brought home to the island the possibility of heavy unemployment and other aspects of increasing population pressure.

It had long been realized in Jamaica that some efforts at controlling fertility were desirable, and private Family Planning Clinics were in operation soon after the Second World War. But there was no public policy for the control of fertility. While field studies showed no widespread aversion to birth control, and some women were in fact eager to obtain knowledge about it, vocal opposition was raised, and the slogan "Birth control is a plan to kill the Negro" is widely known in Jamaica. But unquestionably the fall in fertility testified to the existence of a fairly widespread and efficient use of contraceptive measures, especially by urban elements of the population.

Important policy decisions were taken in 1963. In effect, the Government launched a campaign to spread the use of birth control throughout the island. Emphasis seems to be placed on the use of intra-uterine devices, largely because of their cheapness and efficiency. Plans have been completed for fitting these devices at a number of centers throughout the island.

What are the prospects for further plans for fertility control developing in other English-speaking territories? In both Barbados and Jamaica widespread awareness of existing pressure of population on limited resources has created a climate of opinion especially receptive to positive measures of birth control. In Barbados, a high level of schooling, dense settlement, a closely-knit urban center, and a negligible proportion of Catholics contributed to the crystallization of such policies. In Jamaica, the level of education was much lower than in Barbados and there was a sizeable proportion of Catholics—the 1960 census reported this as the religious denomination of 7% of the population. But a large and rapidly expanding urban center, and marked mobility of the people as exemplified in the large-scale emigration so prominent earlier in the century, provided the social basis for a program of fertility control.

Although many other territories of the region now have rates of natural increase greater than those of Jamaica, and a mounting awareness of the consequences of continued rates of growth in excess of 3% per year, it is doubtful if in the foreseeable future they will initiate policies similar to those of Barbados and Jamaica. One potent factor, however, is the possible future federation of the smaller islands of the Eastern Caribbean, which would have Barbados as its focus. A federation largely under the direction of Barbados might adopt a policy of fertility control, as the full implication of prevailing growth rates are realized by officials faced with the realities of economic planning.

4. Some Economic Aspects of Population Change in the Developing Countries

FRANK W. NOTESTEIN

Throughout the world there is great interest, even popular interest, in the problems of population growth. One hears them discussed everywhere by all manner of people, from the peasant and slum-dweller to the statesman and scholar. Curiously enough, in spite of this universal interest there is no universal understanding about either the nature of the problems or the paths along which the solutions must be sought. Indeed, it is difficult to find a proposition about population that has not been both made and contradicted by someone.

In a way, such confusion of opinion is surprising because the facts of the situation are basically clear. A great deal is known about the size and characteristics of the population and the processes of change through birth, death, marriage, and migration. These are definite events that can be counted and analyzed with mathematical accuracy. To be sure, they relate to aspects of human behavior that are individually imponderable, but when considered in the aggregate such events tend to run in orderly sequence.

Disagreement comes in substantial part because of the emotional content of the subject matter. Few events have deeper emotional significance than birth, marriage, movement of home, and death. When the age-old demographic balance of very high birth rates cancelled by very high death rates remained intact, there was little disagreement about the meaning of vital events. Confusion started when the age of modern science and technology began irresistibly changing the texture of life and the balance of birth and death. Under these new conditions the customary ways of attaining basic goals become inappropriate. The marriage customs, traditional teaching, and community rewards and sanctions essential to produce the abundant childbearing required for survival in the ages of uncontrolled disease become under modern conditions obstacles to the attainment of the goal of secure survival. Moreover, ancient means to basic goals become ends in themselves. Man is a social animal and, to survive, probably needs this nonrational loyalty of individual to individual, group to group, and the present to the past. Before accepting a need for change in his traditional ways, he typically argues that actually nothing has happened, that even if it has it probably will soon stop happening, and that in any case any reaction to the new situation involving a change of the ancient ways is immoral.

The confusion of opinion about population trends arises in spite of the clarity of the facts because the public is at a great variety of stages of awareness regarding the meaning of change in an age of science and technology. Fortunately man is also a rational animal and, as knowledge of the new developments becomes more widespread, the divergencies of its interpretation tend to narrow.

Before turning to the controversies of interpretation, we must, however, review the demographic situation of the world's major continents.

WORLD DEMOGRAPHY AND ECONOMICS

The density of the population of Europe is almost four times the world average, and that of Asia is almost three times the world average. Middle America, that is, Mexico and Central America, has only a few more persons per square hectare than the average for the world as a whole. On the low side, Africa, South America, the US.S.R., and North America have population densities ranging from only 40-43% of the world average. Oceania, with its vast deserts, has only one-tenth as many persons per square hectare as the world as a whole.

It is evident even from this brief review that there is no close relation between population density and economic prosperity. Both the most and the least densely settled continents are among the world's most properous. The second most densely settled continent, Asia, is about as low in the economic scale as Africa which, in turn, has about the same population density as South America, the U.S.S.R., and North America. Neither sparse nor dense populations guarantee either wealth or poverty. Actually, population density has an entirely different significance for the traditional self-sufficient agrarian economies than for the highly diversified and heavily capitalized economies that rely on inanimate energy and the sophisticated use of resources. In the former, high density spells poverty. In the latter, as the experience of Europe clearly shows, high population density, whatever its other disadvantages, is not a major obstacle to the achievement of high *per capita* income.

The relation of the birth rates of the world's continents to the nature of their economies is much simpler. There are only two groups of continents: those with very high birth rates, and those with low birth rates. The highest rates range from 41 to 46 births a year per thousand population and are found in the continents with the least technological development—South America, Middle America, Asia, and Africa. The remainder of the world's continents, that is, Europe, Oceania, the U.S.S.R., and North America, have birth rates ranging from 19 to 24, or roughly one-half those of the newly developing continents.

So far as death rates go, the situation is only a little more complex. Of the continents with very high birth rates, Asia and Africa have the highest annual death rates, about 20 and 23 deaths per thousand. Death rates for South and Middle America are about 13 and 14. It is these lower death rates that give these areas higher rates of growth than Asia and Africa. The remainder of the world's continents have death rates ranging from 7 to 10 per 1,000 population.

Classes of Population Growth

The rate of population growth, being virtually the difference between the birth and death rates, falls into four classes. The highest rates are those of Middle and South America which are between 2.5 and 3.0%. Next, with rates between 2.0 and 2.5%, come Asia, Africa, and Oceania. The last falls into this category partly because of heavy immigration. Next comes North America and the U.S.S.R., with rates between 1.5 and 2.0%. Lowest of all comes Europe with a rate of less than 1 per cent. If such rates of growth were to continue, Europe's population would require more than 75 years to double, the population of the U.S.S.R. and North America about 40 years, those of Africa, Asia, and Oceania only 27 to 35 years, and those of Middle and South America only between 23 and 27 years.

In a nutshell, then, the poorest continents have the highest birth rates, the highest death rates, and the highest rates of population growth. Conversely, the richest continents have the lowest birth rates, the lowest death rates, and the lowest rates of population growth. However, it must also be noted that even at their slow rates of growth, the continents of Europe, the U.S.S.R., and North America are generating a population increase that in terms of historical experience is very rapid. Except for North America, until the last few decades the developed regions of the world seldom grew by as much as 1% per year.

PROBLEMS AND OPINIONS

With this sketch of the world's demographic situation, let us examine some of the common opinions expressed about the question, first considering questions of population size and density.

A common view, especially in the rather sparsely settled agrarian societies, is that much larger populations are needed because, being poor, their only source of national, political, and military power lies in raw numbers. But from ancient times raw numbers have meant weakness, not power. Power has always been the product of advanced technology and organization, and never more so than in the age of nuclear technology. Political and military power are obtained through the development of technology, and not through the growth of population.

Another variant of this view is that large national populations are required to provide the market needed to reap the economies of large-scale production. In the first place, markets are built on total national income and are quite as responsive to prosperity as to population size. In the second place, the fast way to reap the very great economies of large-scale production is through consolidation of trading areas and reduction of tariff barriers rather than by the more gradual processes of population growth.

What, then, can be said about the most desirable population size? One hears a great deal about an optimum population size from an economic point of view. Much has been written about this concept and its wicked children, "over-population" and "under-population." Actually, I think these terms are almost useless. To use them in any precise way we have to think about the balance between the rewards of specialization and the penalties of diminishing returns, and the size of population at which their balance gives the largest possible *per capita* income. It is obviously impossible to think about the subject without specifying the state of the technology, the nature of the economic organization and, most important, the health, vitality, and education of the labor force. If we make the calculation in terms of today's conditions, it will be obsolete by the time the demographic goal can be reached. If we carry out the calculation for a future date, the whole operation is highly speculative. Moreover, the gains to be had from attaining the most desirable population size might well be more than nullified by the means taken to reach that goal. Indeed, it is my impression that the whole concept of an optimum population size has become more of a hindrance than a help to thought about the interrelations of demographic, social, and economic variables.

One thing is clear. As we have seen, the economic

significance of population size is entirely different in an extractive economy than in a diversified economy based on modern technology. In economies based on the production of agricultural and mineral raw materials, high population density must spell poverty. In the modern diversified and heavily capitalized economies, with their almost unlimited supplies of cheap energy, the economic limits to growth are virtually impossible to specify.

It is also clear that we need not trouble ourselves to calculate the world's carrying capacity by assuming, on the one hand, the maximum in technology and, on the other hand, the minimum standards of living. Societies that are able to maintain the maximum in technology will not accept the minimum in living conditions. Conversely, societies with living conditions that are under pressure cannot make the long-range investments in education and equipment that are required to achieve maximum production.

Irrelevance of Optimum Size

If we pursue this line of reasoning a bit further, we come to a rather startling conclusion. The relevant question is not the one posed by the discussion of the optimum population size. It is, instead, precisely the converse of that question. It makes little sense to ask what population size makes possible the largest *per capita* income. In the long run it makes a great deal of sense to ask what *per capita* income makes possible the largest population.

It makes sense because the major determinant of productivity is the nature of the technology and not the number of people. The traditional agrarian economy spells crushing poverty for Asia's present population, to say nothing of the doubled numbers that the next generation will bring unless death rates rise. The same thing is true in most of Africa and much of America below the Rio Grande, except that in these cases there remains much unoccupied land. Such available land is not likely to last long. Indeed, a century of growth at present rates would bring South America and Africa to twice the density of Asia's population today. Moreover, even when new land is available, peasant agriculture does not provide the economic basis for prosperity, vigorous health, and universal education. These goals can only be reached by rapid technological development in all sectors of the economy.

Modern technology has the capacity to support in plenty many times the population that subsistence agriculture maintains in poverty. The almost explosive increases in agricultural yields have come in the highly developed, and not in the agrarian economies.[1] It is precisely the advanced economies that today are having to come to the rescue of the agrarian economies by shipping cereal grain.

But modern technology cannot flourish when *per capita* income is low. It requires heavy investment of savings for equipment, health and advanced education. In short, it is only the very prosperous populations that, in the long run, have the capacity to maintain truly dense populations. It is a high, not a low, *per capita* income that permits the maximum population. The idea that a low average income makes possible a maximum population arises from looking at the pie of national income and noting that many people can have a slice if the slices are very small. A more realistic view notes that with much larger pies more people can have bigger pieces, and, if they get them, will also be better able to help make the bigger pies.

Thus far the analysis takes on something of the character of "pie in the sky" rather than on the earth. It is easy to say in the face of difficult economic situations that the remedy is high income. The obvious reply is, of course, that higher incomes are not only the means to modernizing but also the end—the object of the whole endeavor. Have we not, while objecting to the conventional analysis of optimum population size, only managed to say that questions of population are relatively unimportant, whereas those of technology are vital? Indeed, compared to the older neo-Malthusian arguments, I have gone some distance in this direction, agreeing with many Marxists that the way to a decent life lies in expanding production rather than in reducing population—if those ever were realistic alternatives. Neither view deals with the essential problem, which is the nature of the transition from the traditional self-sufficient economy to the technologically developed economy.

The real population problems are not those of present, or even ultimate, population size. The real problems lie instead in the extent to which rapid population growth itself becomes an obstacle to technological modernization. It was this problem that was never squarely faced either by the neo-Malthusians or the Marxists. The trouble was that they brought essentially static concepts to a dynamic problem.

THE PROBLEM OF GROWTH

The difficulty is not the size of population. The difficulty is the rate of population growth, and the way in which growth impedes the process of modernization. Given adequate economic organization and an abundance of workers, capital is the restraining factor in modernization. In agrarian economies undergoing development, it is often thought that the capital–output ratio may be as low as three. That is, an investment of three units will produce an annual addition of one unit to the income stream. If this is the situation, the investment of 9% of the national income would add 3% to the annual national income. Since a 3% rate of growth doubles the base in 23 years, an annual investment of 9% of the national income should double the national income in 23 years. Or, an annual saving and investment of 12% of the national income would double the national income in less than 18 years. Such development of the economy would represent solid achievement, but whether it would bring any improvement in living conditions, or additional ability to save and invest, would depend on the rate of population growth.

A 3% increase in the national income will bring no improvement in living conditions if the population grows at the same rate. A 4% growth in national income will bring only a 1% gain in *per capita* income if the population is growing by 3%. Indeed, national income increasing at the annual rate of 4% for a population growing at 3% requires about 70 years for a doubling of *per capita* income because, meanwhile, the population increases by more than eight-fold. Alternatively, the same rate of economic growth would yield a sixteen-fold increase in *per capita* income to a stable population.

This is precisely the situation that most of Asia, Africa, and Latin America faces. Generally their populations are growing faster than 2.0% and frequently they are growing at well over 3% per year. Even rather notable success in promoting economic development yields glacial rates of improvement in living conditions and the ability to lift the rate of savings and investment.

One may feel that to save only 9 or 12% of the national income is insufficient and, indeed, it is not enough to bring rapid improvement in living conditions when the population is also growing rapidly. Larger savings are not difficult to obtain in affluent societies. But they are difficult to the point of impossible without mass suffering in regions like Asia, where fully 80% of the family income goes for food alone and the people are malnourished.

Advantage of Reduced Birth Rates

The economic difficulties of the demographic situation relate less to long-run problems of population size than to the present problems of overriding growth.

Europe, too, in its nineteenth century of technological development, experienced what it thought to be rapid population growth. But its increase was seldom anywhere more than 1% per year. A reduction of the rate of growth in the newly developing countries from 2.5 and 3.5% to the 1% experienced by Europe during the nineteenth century would clearly make the problem of developing the technology much simpler.

In point of fact, a reduction of the rate of growth brought about by reducing birth rates has an additional advantage. High birth rates produce populations with very large loads of young dependents. Because of their history of very high birth rates, almost none of the newly developing countries has less than 40% of their total population under 15 years of age. A reduction of the birth rate can easily cut this figure below 30%. Slower growth means larger savings and investment and a population with more of its members in the working years of life. Beyond that, during the first 20 years of a falling birth rate the dependency load is being lightened without influencing the size of the labor force. Such child labor as is lost is probably more than replaced by the work of women freed from childbearing. The reduced load of dependency means more income for investment and a numerically unchanged labor force. There is every reason to think that a reduction of the rate of growth in this way would not only increase *per capita* income, but increase total income for smaller numbers. It was the development of this thesis that led Coale and Hoover in their study for Princeton University to conclude that a drastic decline in the birth rates of newly developing countries would yield in a generation *per capita* incomes 40% above those that could be expected if birth rates remained unchanged.[2]

So our argument comes full circle. Drastically reduced birth rates in the newly developing countries would permit much more rapid gains in *per capita* income, thus speeding the process of modernization, thus freeing the economy from long-range restraints on growth inherent in the traditional extractive economies. In short, the nation that chooses to be both prosperous and large in the long run can speed the day by reducing the birth rates drastically, and at once.

Our reversal of the usual question about optimum population size was warranted. The true problem is not the size of population that fosters maximum *per capita* income. The fact is that a high *per capita* income fosters the kind of technological revolution that can ultimately support a maximum population. Substantial assistance in the attainment of such income in the newly developing countries can come from cutting both the speed of growth and the burden of youth dependency through a drastic reduction in the birth rate. The vital problem is that of curtailing the rate of population growth in order to make rapid economic development possible.

Short- and Long-term Prospects

I have been speaking of action leading to the largest population as a possibility, not as something desirable in itself. I see no economic advantage and many esthetic disadvantages in maximizing population size. This, however, is a problem with which we need not be concerned. Any population that reduces its birth rate by enabling its people to regulate their family size as they see fit, and achieves a high stage of technological development, is surely in a position to make its own decision about the size of population it wants.

It should also be noted that those who warn against permitting married couples to regulate their fertility as they see fit because of the danger of race suicide are borrowing trouble that the record does not justify. The experience of Europe since the war shows a slow but healthy growth. The experience of the United States, Canada, Australia, and New Zealand shows that under conditions of great prosperity even populations that regulate their fertility grow at rates that will double their numbers in less than fifty years. The problem may continue to be too rapid growth, rather than too slowly growing numbers.

In the case of newly developing countries, anxiety that reduction of the birth rate will eliminate population growth is wholly unfounded. Most developing countries could cut their birth rate by half in two decades and still double their numbers within forty years. Growth may, indeed, stop, but if it does it will be because political and economic conditions deteriorate to such an extent that disease gets out of control. We are not faced with unending population growth in societies driven ever deeper into poverty. The world will not experience "standing room only." Long before the terrors of growth at compound interest become real, mortality will rise again because of political and economic disorganization. The question is not *whether* growth eventually ends, but *how*. If by the resurgence of disease, it will be because we have failed in our technological revolution. If by the reduction of human fertility, it will mean that through science and technology mankind has freed itself from the age-old bondage of poverty, ignorance and disease.

Demographic Fallacies

If the foregoing analysis is valid, then a number of rather common assumptions concerning the population question must be false.

One is particularly important to deal with because it is a potential obstacle to the reduction of fertility. It is a mixture of truth and error—truth in its premises and error in its conclusion. Briefly, the premise is that the motivation for the restriction of childbearing comes from the underlying social and economic situation. Experience has shown that birth rates of the traditional societies eventually fall under the impact of urban-industrial development, improvement of health, universal education, and the rising status of women. Interest in restricting childbearing comes when parents no longer aspire chiefly to perpetuate the family in an established social order. When the focus of parental interest shifts to opportunities that their children can achieve in the modern world, interest in a smaller family begins to emerge. From this sound generalization arises the baseless assumption that, in the absence of social and economic development, efforts to spread the practice of birth control are useless, and in the presence of social-economic development they are unnecessary. From this comes the exhortation that we should forget about birth control and get on with development.

In effect this is the sophisticated Marxist position, and one with which some Catholics are inclined to agree. It offers a rather painless resolution of intellectual difficulties for both groups. There are two basic weaknesses in the argument. The first is its failure to recognize that fundamental socioeconomic change has gone very far throughout the world today. The motivation to restrict childbearing is widely present in almost all societies. How else can we explain the widespread resort to criminal and dangerous abortion?

The second fallacy lies in the implicit assumption that,

given the motivation to restrict fertility, the process cannot be speeded by making appropriate information and supplies easily available. Note that urban-industrial development, education, etc., also reduce mortality. Literate people learn about the virtues of cleanliness and the dangers of contagion. The fact that social progress eventually reduces the death rate fortunately is never put forward as a reason for withholding efforts to control disease. There is ample evidence that special efforts to foster the practices of family planning are successful in speeding the reduction of fertility. Indeed, if they could not be successful we would have to call into question the entire role of education in fostering new behavior patterns. The demographic argument for forgetting about birth control and concentrating on economic development could be valid only if promoting the one involved sacrificing the other. But it does not. Indeed, the costs of a sound medical program are quickly returned in better public health—to say nothing of reduced rates of population growth.

Two other fallacies can be quickly disposed of for they are based on both ignorance and inhumanity. One is that public health and medical assistance should be withheld internationally until the newly developing countries reduce their birth rate. This proposition always relates to "other" people and never to one's own group. It sees medical achievement, not as the major triumph of our civilization but as the villain of the population problem. The major crime of its advocates is perhaps not their selfishness, but their stupidity. Improvement in health is not only an end in itself, but a means to the goal of economic development and social change, and incidentally to the motivation of parents to reduce their fertility. Since all peoples covet health, the reduction of the death rate involves only the question of obtaining efficient means. The control of fertility, however, requires changes of both ends and means. It seems probable that death rates will always decline before birth rates. The problem is to minimize the lag in order to simplify the difficulties of economic development.

It is also sometimes suggested that help in developing the

economy should be withheld pending a reduction in the birth rate. Perhaps enough has already been said about the factors governing the reduction of birth rates to make it clear that this proposition could only receive the support of persons wholly uninformed about the processes of social and economic change, and less than overburdened with the milk of human kindness.

We have sufficiently documented our thesis. Most of the confusion about the interrelation of demographic, social, and economic variables arises from the consideration of static systems within which we may intellectually manipulate a single element. It is such static thinking that leads to the conclusions:

—that large populations bring political and military power, and the economies of large-scale production;

—that it is somehow fruitful to think about the optimum size of population;

—that birth rates should be lowered before death rates, or before attempts are made to modernize the economy;

—that we should be concerned with the staggering populations that present rates of population growth will bring in a century, while neglecting the threat that such rates of growth now pose to the whole process of economic development.

REDUCED GROWTH SPEEDS MODERNIZATION

A more reasonable view considers the processes of an entire changing social system—a system in which the variables are neither firmly locked nor wholly independent. It is clear from the consideration of such dynamic systems that their large populations will not live in indefinite poverty. Long before that, death rates will rise. In the long run, growth, far from inevitable, is impossible. In this view, in the short run, immediate curtailment of the rate of population growth will greatly facilitate the kind of technological development that can provide long-run support for populations both large and prosperous. The major difficulties are not ultimate but immediate, not hypothetical but real and urgent. They are

those of at once reducing the rate of growth in order to foster economic development. If growth soon can be reduced,
the risks of temporary and tragic failure in modernization
will be greatly lessened. Once the major transformation has
been made, mankind will have an excellent chance for the
first time in history to attain health, education, and reasonable prosperity for all.

FOOTNOTES

1. Lester R. Brown, *Increasing World Food Output, Problems and Prospects,* Foreign Agricultural Economic Report No. 25, United States Department of Agriculture, Washington, 1965.
2. Ansley J. Coale and Edgar M. Hoover, *Population Growth and Economic Development in Low-Income Countries,* Princeton University Press, Princeton, New Jersey, 1958.

5. Housing, Population Growth, and Economic Development

*OCTAVIO CABELLO**

HOUSING AND ECONOMIC DEVELOPMENT

The problem of housing in Latin America is one aspect of the area's general underdevelopment; not a symptom or an effect, but an integral part. Not only is there a general lack of building funds, but in some countries poor use is made of what funds are available. In general, there is a correlation between *per capita* income and the amount of money spent on housing. Thus a higher level of income will enable more money to be spent on housing also. National investment in housing (including maintenance and repair of existing housing) appears to fluctuate between 2 and 6%.

In general, the greater the national income, the greater the percentage of money that is invested in housing; but as richer countries have more housing to maintain, one must assume that the proportion of the national income invested in new housing will remain approximately constant. One may assume also that funds available for housing will increase as the gross national product (GNP) increases. Therefore, it should interest housing planners to analyze the relationship between population growth and the GNP as it affects the availability of housing funds.

POPULATION GROWTH AND DEVELOPMENT

According to José A. Mayobre, Executive Secretary of CEPAL (the Economic Commission for Latin America), dis-

* Although the author is a staff member of the United Nations, the views expressed in this paper are his own and may not coincide with the official position of the U.N.

TABLE 1.

Latin America.

National investment in housing.

	Year	Housing investment (a) as a percentage of		Percent of the budget spent on public housing (b)	Per capita income 1961 (c) (current $)
		GNP	Total nat'l investment		
Argentina	1962–3	3.5	14.4	2.8	779.0
Bolivia	—	—	—	—	122.3
Brazil	—	—	—	—	374.6
Colombia	1962	—	—	4.2	373.4
"	1953	2.7	—	—	
Costa Rica	1960–2	2.4 (d)	15.0 (d)	4.6	361.7
Cuba	1957–8	3.5	20.2	—	516.0
Chile	1961–	—	18.1 (e)	—	452.9
"	1960–61	—	—	6.1	
"	1954	3.3	—	—	
Ecuador	1961–2	—	—	1.6	222.7
"	1960–2	2.0	13.3	—	
El Salvador	1962	—	—	3.7	267.5
Guatemala	1961–4	—	—	1.6	257.7
Haiti	1962	—	—	1.5	149.1
Honduras	1960–1	3.6	30.1	—	251.7
"	1962	—	—	0.1	
Mexico	1960	—	—	4.3	415.4
"	1955	2.4	—	—	
Nicaragua	1961–2	—	—	0.3	288.4
Panama	—	—	—	—	371.0
Paraguay	—	—	—	—	193.2
Peru	1961	—	—	7.7	268.5
Dominican Republic	—	—	—	—	313.2
Uruguay	1960–1	6.2	44.6	1.6	560.9
Venezuela	1960–1	1.6	9.9	—	644.5
"	1962	—	—	1.5	

(a) United Nations: ST/ECLA/CONF. 9/L. 11 and *Statistical Bulletin of Latin America*, Vol. 1, No. 1.

(b) Interamerican Development Bank, *Fondo Fiduciario de Progreso Social*, second (1962) and third (1963) annual report.

(c) CEPAL, *The Postwar Economic Development of Latin America.* Vol. II, E/CN. 12/659/Add. April 17, 1963.

(d) Instituto Nacional de Vivienda y Urbanismo, *Diagnóstico preliminar del sector vivienda*, San José, Costa Rica, April 1964.

(e) Central Savings and Loan Bank, *El sistema de ahorro y préstamo en Chile*, 1963, Santiago, Chile.

cussion of the relation of population growth to economic development has been made difficult by conflict between two schools of thought: (1) those who maintain that since increases in the GNP are entirely absorbed by the rapid population growth, birth control constitutes a pre-condition for any realistic economic development; and (2) those who affirm that the population growth figures (although high) should not worry us because of the extent of our resources, our low population density, and the possibility of attaining a much higher economic development than Latin America now enjoys. Mayobre indicates that the problem is much more complex than these two extreme positions suggest.[1] Most of the governments that replied to a UNESCO survey of Latin American urbanization in 1962 also recognized the complexity of the relationship between population growth and economic development.

The U.S. Government, commenting on the effect of population growth on the growth of U.S. *per capita* income during the last fifty years, points out that:

> It has not been clearly established whether the growth of population increased or retarded the growth of *per capita* income. . . In any case, the rate of economic growth in the U.S. is more influenced by factors other than the size of the population—such as the increase of capital, the improvement of the quality of human resources, and technical progress. . . The exact role that population growth plays in the stimulation of demand, and thus in the full use of resources, is not clear. For one thing, population growth increases consumption needs, thereby producing pressure on production capacity. For another, the rise in consumer spending tends to reduce the relationship between savings and income; thus limiting the funds available for expansion of productive capacity. In view of these limitations, population growth cannot be considered a principal cause of bettering the standard of living. . .

As for the relationship between population growth and economic development in underdeveloped countries, the U.S. Government says this.

Certain relationships are more important in one particular stage of a country's development than in another. For example, a high growth rate can cancel out economic growth in its early stages, when a rapidly growing population consumes the profits of a less rapidly expanding economy. On the other hand, the rapid growth of population can stimulate development, if it can count on a wide range of natural resources, and ample capital...[2]

Let us consider some essential aspects of the problem in Latin America. In the first place, for economic development to occur production must exceed consumption and the surplus must be invested in capital goods. The rate of GNP growth consequently will depend primarily on the rate of capital investment.[3]

Of the basic factors essential to national economic development—labor, natural resources, and capital—capital is the most important since it is scarcest. We can state this simply below:

$$(1) \qquad X = \left(\frac{1}{R}\right)^{c}$$

where X = rate of increase of the GNP
  C = rate of capital investment
  R = ratio between product and the capital needed to produce it

This formula shows that a given rate of capital investment (C) will yield a predetermined rate of increase in the GNP. But in order that the GNP grow on a *per capita* basis, the GNP itself must increase at a more rapid rate than the population. The need for this can be represented as follows:

$$(2) \qquad Y = (X - P)$$

where Y = *per capita* growth rate of the GNP
  P = annual population growth rate

The necessary rate of capital investment (C) can then be determined by

$$(3) \qquad C = R(Y + P)$$

Formula (3) shows that in order to produce a given increase in the *per capita* GNP, capital investment is needed in proportion to the rate of population growth. For example, if it is supposed that in Latin America the product/capital ratio is 0.40-0.45, and if it is desired that the *per capita* GNP should increase 2.5% annually (the goal fixed by the Alliance for Progress), an annual capital investment of 11% of the GNP is needed, if we figure the population growth rate to be 2%; or 13%, if we figure the population growth rate to be 2.9% (as it is estimated it will be during 1965-75).[4] (C = 2.35(.02 + .025) = 10.6%; or C = 2.35(.029 + .025) = 12.7%)

These calculations are quite crude and serve only to illustrate how population growth influences the investment necessary to produce a given rate of development. It is worth noting that, in reality, the rate of investment is never independent of the rate of population growth, and that the two rates influence each other. In South America it is possible that an important immediate increase in the GNP might be produced by better utilization of productive capacities as a result of more effective planning, apart from any increase in investment.

According to Joseph J. Spengler, Professor of Economics at Duke University, there are three categories of investment that contribute directly to increasing a country's productivity: (1) the physical industrial equipment; (2) the economic superstructure—transportation networks, communications, electricity, etc.; and (3) the social superstructure—sanitation services, education, housing, etc. Of these three, the first contributes most directly to increasing the GNP. When the population grows rapidly, however, there are great demands for investment in the second and third categories, thus reducing the possibilities for investment in the physical industrial plant and slowing up the rate of growth of production of goods and services.

Spengler also indicates[5] that it would be correct to interpret the GNP as a function of the labor force, of the available capital, and of the productivity of labor and capital, as follows:

$$GNP = AK^aL^bv$$

A = a constant
K = capital
L = labor force (which can be considered a constant propor-
    portion of the total population (P)
a = elasticity of the product with respect to capital (K)
b = elasticity of the product with respect to the work force
    (L)
v = residual variable

The above formula indicates that an increase in the GNP depends directly, although in a limited way, on an increase in the labor force (L) which, in turn, depends in part on population growth and in part on other factors that condition the demand for work. So we see that an increase in the population ought, if other conditions are maintained, to increase the product. It should also be noted that variations in occupational structure can cause "a" to vary significantly, and thus the GNP, and the variations in the GNP, in turn cause variations in the growth rate of the population.

Because the relationship between population growth and economic development is so complex, it cannot be satisfactorily interpreted by the simple formulas we have given. Urquidi points out that demographers

. . . persist in clinging to a notion of a relationship of population to natural resources, which does not seem to have anything to do with the structure of a modern economy. But it is evident that Latin America's future standard of living depends less on this relationship (if it has any significance at all) than on the capacity of Latin American countries to integrate their industrial structures, either among themselves or with non-Latin nations, so that they may increase their exports of raw materials and manufactured goods to the rest of the world; and on whether the process of substitution of imports can be accelerated, that is, that it include capital goods and—through regional integration—take advantage of the economy implicit in mass production. Besides, taking Latin America as a whole, there exist great reserves of agricultural resources and of potential productivity which, through regional economic integration, can be used for the benefit of this region; and, in so far as it gives more impulse to industrialization and the development of exports, the demand for food can be filled in part with supplies from the temperate zone of the northern hemisphere, where the productivity and agricultural conditions, faced with a flexible demand, tend to create permanent surpluses.[4]

Estimates of population and of gross national product for countries of South America indicate that for short periods— five to ten years—the rate of population growth and the rate of growth of the GNP have been directly correlated. That is to say, countries that have had a high rate of population growth have generally also been those with the highest rates of growth of both the GNP as well as *per capita* income. This statement is based on the figures of Table 2, below.

TABLE 2.

Latin America.

Percentage growth of the population and the gross national product (1955–1964).

| | Population growth (a) | | Gross national product | | | |
| | | | Overall Growth (b) | | Growth per capita | |
	1955–59	1960–64	1955–59	1960–64	1955–59	1960–64
Latin America (except Cuba)	2.9	2.9	4.7	4.0	1.8	1.1
Uruguay	1.2	1.2	0.3	0.1	−0.9	−1.2
Argentina	1.9	1.8	2.7	1.2	0.8	−0.6
Bolivia	2.2	2.3	−0.2	5.0	−2.4	2.7
Chile	2.4	2.4	3.8	4.0	1.4	1.6
Paraguay	2.5	2.5	2.4	3.6	−0.1	1.1
Peru	2.6	2.7	4.7	6.4	2.1	3.7
Colombia	2.8	2.8	5.3	5.3	2.5	2.5
Panama	2.7	2.8	5.3	5.3	2.5	2.5
Guatemala	2.9	2.9	5.1	5.4	2.2	2.5
Brazil	3.1	3.0	5.8	3.9	2.7	0.8
Ecuador	3.2	3.1	4.5	3.7	1.3	0.5
El Salvador	3.0	3.2	3.0	8.3	0.0	5.1
Mexico	3.3	3.4	6.2	6.2	2.9	2.8
Honduras	3.3	3.5	4.8	4.3	1.5	0.8
Venezuela	3.9	3.5	6.5	5.3	2.5	1.7
Nicaragua	3.5	3.5	1.7	7.3	−1.8	3.8
Costa Rica	4.2	4.0	4.9	3.3	0.8	−0.7

(a) Based on estimates published by the *Bulletin of Statistics* of CEPAL, Vol. I., No. 1.

(b) CEPAL. *Economic Study* 1964. Table 1–2.

This Table indicates that:

1) In general, countries with the highest rates of population growth (for example, over 3%) were also those that showed the highest rates of GNP growth in both five-year periods.[6]

2) Those countries with the lowest rates of population growth (Argentina and Uruguay) had the lowest rates of GNP increase.

3) In all but one of the countries, a higher rate of population growth corresponds to a higher rate of GNP growth. Reductions in the rate of population growth were followed by reductions in the rates of growth of the GNP and *per capita* GNP. This is the contrary of what might be predicted by adherents of the first school of thought described by Dr. Mayobre, above.

4) Great variations in the rates of GNP increase were related to very small variations in the population growth rate. The latter were much more stable than the former, which indicates—after taking into account possible errors in calculation—that, for short periods, variations in the rate of GNP growth depend more on other factors than population growth.

5) A positive correlation between variations of the GNP and the *per capita* GNP can be observed. This is a consequence of the previous point, above.

To summarize, a cause and effect relationship cannot be established between changes in the rate of population growth, fluctuations in the GNP, and increases in *per capita* income. However, statistics suggest that during the last decade in Latin America there has been a direct though limited connection between the rate of population growth and the rate of increase of the GNP.

Thus, it would be risky to affirm that the reduction of the population growth rate can by itself stimulate economic development. It is illogical to hope that a program of birth control alone can contribute significantly to stimulating economic development in this region. On this point, Dr. Mayobre draws the following conclusion in his work presented to the World Conference on Population (1965):

> It seems justified to conclude that a reduction in the rate of population growth would not of itself stimulate economic development, and that policies that seek such a reduction cannot be considered *the key* to the solution of the problem of development in Latin America. At the same time, a profound examination of the specific characteristics of population growth in this region suggests that some reduction in the rate could *facilitate* development and reduce the magnitude of some of the alarming sub-products of unbalanced and uncontrolled processes of economic development and of the current social changes that are taking place.

THE PROBLEM OF HOUSING IN LATIN AMERICA

In Latin America a high proportion of the population occupies housing which does not meet minimum standards established by the United Nations. The large proportion of families living in slums has increased in the decade 1950-60. There is a very high proportion of houses with neither running water nor toilets, and a high proportion of buildings that, for lack of adequate maintenance or because of the deficient quality of building materials, are neither comfortable nor healthy.

Changes in the situation in the period 1950-64 can be partially assessed by studying the following statistical information: comparison of the 1950 and 1960 censuses,[7] estimates of the growth of marginal neighborhoods based on special studies in affected countries, tendencies in the volume of residential construction, and estimates of the accumulated housing deficits.

Available census data for this period indicate that the total number of dwelling units of all types increased in proportion to the growth of the population. Nevertheless, in order to appreciate the changes in the nature of housing it is essential to classify housing according to type of structure.[8]

Although lack of adequate census data impedes our knowledge of changes in the entire region, the following figures may reflect similar situations in specific countries. In Chile, the number of houses and apartments rose from 764,000 in 1952 to 973,000 in 1960. The new dwellings sheltered 86% of the population increase in the period between censuses. The remaining 14% swelled the number of occupants of "collective" dwellings, "improvised" dwellings, and others. Thus the tenements and shacks (including *callampas*) increased from 130,000 units in 1952 to 196,000 in 1960; the number of occupants went from 645,000 to 1,044,000; and the percentage of the population that occupied this type of housing increased from 10.9 in 1952 to 14.2 in 1960.

In Venezuela, although the percentage of the population that lived in shacks declined from 45.8 in 1950 to 34.6 in 1961, the number of shacks increased from 409,000 to 478,000, and the number of their occupants rose from 2,143,000 to 2,488,000.

The increase in the number of "homes of a permanent type" has not been commensurate with the growth of the population in either Venezuela or Chile. The number of marginal dwellings increased considerably, thus worsening the housing shortage and increasing the accumulated housing deficit.

In Honduras the total number of dwellings of all types increased from 213,000 in 1949 to 325,000 in 1961. Dwellings "with walls of cane or poles" also increased from 39,000 to 56,000, showing that the construction of houses and apartment buildings was insufficient to absorb the population increase.

In respect to the provision of running water and to the quality of building materials in existing housing, progress can be reported. Dwellings with running water increased in Chile from 48% in 1952 to 56% in 1960; in El Salvador, from 40% in 1950 to 77% in 1961; in Honduras, from 10% in 1949 to 25% in 1961; in Mexico, from 17% in 1950 to 24% in 1960; in Panama from 44% in 1950 to 46% in 1960; and in Venezuela, from 30% in 1950 to 48% in 1961.[9]

In sum, in countries from which we have been able to compare the results of the last decade's housing censuses, we find an insufficient increase in "permanent living quarters" in relation to the population growth and, as a result, an increase in the number of improvised dwellings. Nevertheless, the six countries studied have registered appreciable progress in the provision of running water to existing dwellings.

A most important aspect of the housing problem has been the appearance and growth of vast slum areas in major cities. For example, it is estimated that the population of the *favelas* (slums) in Rio de Janeiro grew from 400,000 inhabitants in 1947 to 650,000 in 1957, and to 900,000 in 1961, when their inhabitants constituted approximately 38% of the city's population.[10] According to the figures from another source, between 1950 and 1960 the percentage of *favela* dwellers in the population rose from 7.1 to 10.2. In this same period, nearly 50% of the population of Recife was made up of inhabitants of *favelas*.[11]

In Colombia, the four cities most affected by the expansion of slums are Barranquilla, Buenaventura, Cali, and Cartagena. It is estimated that 80% of the population of Buenaventura live in slums.[12] In Chile, the number of people who occupy tenements, shacks, and housing of this nature has increased from 10% of the population in 1952 to 14% in 1960. In Peru, the slum population of Lima rose from 10% in 1940 to 21% in 1961. In other Peruvian cities the proportion is even higher, reaching a maximum of 70% in Chimbote and 40% in Arequipa.[13] In Mexico City, 14% of the population lived in workers' colonies in 1952. In Uruguay, a national sampling showed that there were 30,000 urban dwellings of the tenement or shack type, housing about 100,000 people, at the beginning of 1963. Finally, 17.4% of the homes in Caracas were classified as shacks or improvised dwellings, according to the 1950 census.

If the housing situation is not to deteriorate in the face of continuous population growth, it is necessary (once minimum standards are achieved) for residential construction to grow at the same rate as the number of families, a rate which differs in urban and rural areas. Available statistics indicate that residential construction has not increased at a rate commensurate with urban population growth, and that in some countries it has been constantly decreasing. The rate of residential construction remained stationary or decreased in the ten-year period after the early Fifties, except in Colombia, Costa Rica, and Chile. Statistics for the cities in Argentina and the city of Montevideo also show a considerable drop in the rate of construction. If these statistics are accurate, they indicate a considerable worsening in the housing situation, since population growth and the formation of new families has been more rapid than the rate of construction. However, we must take into account that these statistics are quite unreliable, as they generally reflect only the capital cities and in many cases give information only up to 1960.

The expression "housing shortage" has been used in many ways by various regional and national organizations concerned with the housing problem in Latin America. Calculation of housing needs has generally been limited to determining the need for replacing those houses which are unacceptable because of faulty construction or inferior building materials. Uniform criteria have not been used to arrive at these estimates, which generally reflect only the number of dwellings which ought to be replaced at the time of the census. Thus the housing deficit according to the 1951 census conducted by the Pan American Union was estimated to include 19 million units, the construction of which "was not compatible with human dignity, and which should be demolished." In 1962 the International Development Bank estimated that the deficit of urban dwellings in this region was approximately 14 million units.[14] In spite of reservations as to the validity of census data, the estimates suggest that the housing shortage is extensive, has increased in the last decade, and that remedying it in a short time is beyond the economic capabilities of all of the countries mentioned. Above all, therefore, housing policy should aim at avoiding any increase in the existing housing deficit by means of annual construction of a minimum number of houses and apartments rather than at the impractical end of totally eliminating the deficit in a few years.

It is well known that the housing problem is much more

acute in rural areas than in cities. Moreover, if we take into account that about 50% of the population of Latin America lives in population centers of less than 2,000 inhabitants, it becomes evident that the major part of the housing deficit is concentrated in rural areas. Nevertheless, the housing shortage is not as dramatic in rural areas, due to the cultural differences between rural and urban populations and because of the rapid growth of the latter.

A great part of the housing problem is caused by the displacement of the population from the countryside to the city. While the urban population of Latin America grew 4.0% annually between 1950 and 1960, the rural population grew only 1.4%. This can only be explained as an effect of internal migration, motivated as much by the attraction of the cities as by the lack of housing and other incentives for living in rural areas. Thus the development of incentives to live in rural areas, such as the construction of housing in areas which have been depleted of people through migration, could be one good solution. We must attack on both fronts, keeping in mind that while construction of urban dwellings resolves a more urgent problem, developing rural areas will prevent the urban problem from becoming more acute. The first is an immediate solution, the latter a long-range one.

Even if it be granted that rural dwellings make an unfavorable impression because they are constructed of rustic materials—mud, straw, cane, stones, etc.,—it cannot be denied that a great proportion of Latin American rural dwellings are sub-standard. In 1950, for example, 70% or more of the rural dwellings of Honduras, Panama, Paraguay, and Venezuela had earth floors. On the whole, rural houses are smaller than urban ones and, in consequence, the density of persons per room is even higher than in urban areas. Moreover, the proportion of homes with running water is very low. In 1960, it was higher than 10% only in Cuba, Uruguay, and Venezuela, and hygienic facilities are also scarce.[15]

The situation in Peru is of interest. According to the 1961 census, 39% of the rural dwellings consisted of one room, and 29% of two rooms. Of the total dwellings, 44% are occupied by three or more persons per room. Lack of windows and light is usual in a large part of the country. About 70% of the Peruvian population live in huts of cane or mud.[16] The same deficiencies exist to greater or lesser extent in all other countries. Even today, the majority of Latin Americans in rural areas live in conditions that approach the most primitive. Wide dispersion of the houses makes it difficult to provide adequate sanitary facilities at reasonable cost, and services such as schools, clinics, etc., seem justified only where there is a concentration of homes.

In general, the problem of rural housing is tied to agricultural development. There is no attempt, as in urban housing, to finance rural housing by long-term loans, since rural housing is indispensable for the private economic exploitation of agricultural property.

There are several common factors involved in the housing problem in all rural zones. Construction methods are bound by tradition and difficult to improve because of the dispersion of the population, their low incomes, the scarcity of adequate building materials and qualified construction workers, and the slight importance that the inhabitants themselves, for cultural reasons, assign to the necessity of bettering their homes. Also it is clear that inhabitants of dwellings in agricultural areas are not inclined to make an effort to improve houses which they do not own. The cultural backwardness of the rural population vitiates efforts to better conditions in rural housing for the immediate future.

More effective rural cooperation, an increase in the proportion of rural landowners, an elevation of cultural levels, and the general development of agriculture constitute essential prerequisites for the betterment of rural housing. Despite the importance and severity of the problem, efficient means for facing up to it on a large scale have not yet been found.

POPULATION GROWTH AND THE NEED FOR HOUSING

Estimates of housing needs must be considered in a larger perspective, in which housing policy forms a part of over-all economic development. It is a case of simultaneously resolving the following problems:

1. Funds destined for housing ought to permit, as a *minimum*, the maintenance of existing dwellings, taking into account the increase in the number of urban and rural homes, as well as the necessity of maintaining a certain number of vacant houses to permit the real estate market to function;

2. Funds that are destined for housing ought to be of a magnitude, origin, and type that do not compromise economic stability or the maintenance of sustained economic growth. That is, they ought to be compatible with the resources that are available, and not create inflationary pressure, nor divert investment funds from the more productive sectors of the economy to such an extent that economic growth is hindered;

3. The existing housing gap should be filled as soon as possible. The growth of urban slums, which constitute not only a social problem, but also a social sickness whose propagation can seriously jeopardize economic development, should be controlled.

Points (1) and (3) above are to a certain extent in conflict with point (2). The problem of fixing goals consists basically in the establishment of a better equilibrium between the various positions. Point (1) permits us to fix a minimum social goal, and point (3) a more desirable one. Between these two extremes, a practical goal must be determined by the economic considerations in point (2).

The determination of housing goals can only be worked out in conjunction with other demands on the resources of a country; between the need for new housing, and the available funds; between prices of new homes, and the ability of families to pay; between the volume of construction needed, and the capacities of construction firms; between the future availability of construction materials, and the need for such; between the availability of skilled workers, and the quota of such workers needed. In addition, it is necessary to examine closely the structure, capacity, and functioning of fund-raising and use of funds for housing. Only after making these and other comparisons will it be possible to establish achievable goals which satisfy the above criteria.

The first problem in the aforementioned chain of operations is an estimate of the annual need for new dwellings. This may be approached from the following angles:

1. Determination of the number of dwellings which must be constructed to satisfy the actual aspirations of the population;
2. Determination of the actual demand, in number of houses, using marketing concepts; and
3. Estimates of the number of dwellings needed to reach a given level of housing conditions, using politico-social criteria.

Each of these points requires some comment:

1. Estimates based on aspirations present practical difficulties. For example, it is common to find a large proportion of the population living in unacceptable sanitary conditions, yet satisfied with their lot. Furthermore, it is practically impossible to determine how their desires will change in the next five to ten years. Although a study of the aspirations of the public might be needed to determine the importance which the public assigned to its housing, it would be of little use in calculating housing needs for a particular segment of the population.
2. Calculating the actual demand for houses is an imprecise process, because of the difficulty of defining parts of the market, the disparity between supply and demand, and other factors that influence the housing market. It does not seem possible in Latin America to estimate the actual national demand for housing.
3. This seems to be the only practical way to estimate housing needs on a national scale.

Consequently, if maintenance of present levels and conditions of housing is taken to be the objective of housing policy (other objectives might be set, such as the achievement of certain indices, 20%, 30%, for the absorption of the deficit in approximately 10, 20, etc., years), it is possible to calculate how many dwellings must be constructed annually in order to achieve our goal, taking into account the population growth rate, the rate of formation of new families, migrations of the population, the changes in social structure, the need for maintaining the number of existing houses, etc.

Accepting the fact that the family is the unit which demands housing, we must study the formation of new homes, which in turn is dependent on demographic, economic, and cultural factors. The following demographic factors directly influence the formation of new homes: the growth rate of the population between 20 and 59 years of age, and the marriage, death, and divorce rates.

Factors that influence growth of the total population and those that influence growth of the number of families are distinct. Population growth during a given period will be determined by the balance between national increase (the difference between deaths and births) and migratory movements. In contrast, the number of new families formed will be determined by the adult population that will become "heads of families." The following factors may lead an individual to become head of a family: he reaches a certain age, he marries, he gets an increase in his income, he adopts new forms of living, etc.

An important determing factor in the variation of the number of homes is the number of people between the ages of 20 and 30, because this is the most common age at which people marry. At this age also the greatest number of people move from rural to urban areas. Therefore, a great part of the population forming new homes in 1965-74 will come from those people born 20 to 30 years previously (1935-45). In addition, children born in 1965-74 are going to increase the demand for space in existing dwellings during this same period, although they will not need new housing until approximately 1985-94. Therefore, reductions in the birth rate during the next decade could relieve the living pressure on existing dwellings, but could have no influence on the demand for new houses during this period.

An estimate of housing needs should begin with the number of families that will be formed in the next 5-10 years. There is no practical value in making long-range plans. For purposes of this study we have estimated on an even simpler basis. The index of the annual need for new housing per thousand inhabitants has been calculated on the basis of the percentage of the population expected to inhabit permanent houses or apartments, the rate of annual replacement of existing houses, and the annual growth rate of the population.

Taking these variables into account, housing needs for Latin America for the years 1960-75 can be estimated. If 80% of urban families and 60% of rural families are to inhabit their own houses or apartments, it will be necessary to construct 11.6 dwellings annually per 1,000 urban inhabitants, and 4.6 dwellings per 1,000 rural inhabitants. On an average, Latin America's minimum annual need will be for about 8 dwellings per 1,000 inhabitants. This figure is less than that recommended by a committee of experts of the United Nations (10 dwellings per 1,000 inhabitants) because it does not foresee absorbing the accumulated housing deficit of more than 20 million housing units.

Applying the above figures to the total population of the 20 countries involved, calculated for 1965 at 231 million, we find that Latin America will have to construct annually, in the decade 1960-70, a minimum of approximately 1,850,000 houses per year. To achieve a more rapid and wide-reaching improvement in housing, existing dwellings would, of course, also have to be improved. In the short run, the housing needs would depend directly on population growth rates, and inversely on the average size of the dwellings. On the basis of direct studies of the number of families, derived

TABLE 3.

Latin America.

Minimum annual need for housing units (1960 and 1975).

(in 1,000s)

	1960 (a)			1975 (b)		
	Total	Urban	Rural	Total	Urban	Rural
All Latin America	1,141	785	356	2,627	1,889	738
Argentina	162	129	34	222	185	38
Bolivia	15	7	7	49	32	17
Brazil	289	169	120	634	336	297
Chile	45	40	6	110	99	11
Colombia	91	67	24	225	212	43
Costa Rica	12	7	5	19	11	8
Cuba	55	42	13	80	63	17
Dominican Republic	14	7	7	52	34	18
Ecuador	24	12	12	63	38	25
El Salvador	11	9	2	36	25	11
Guatemala	16	12	4	63	40	23
Haiti	15	6	9	50	33	17
Honduras	12	6	6	26	13	13
Mexico	228	159	69	587	465	123
Nicaragua	7	4	3	24	15	8
Panama	6	4	2	16	11	5
Paraguay	5	3	2	21	16	4
Peru	61	34	27	171	125	46
Uruguay	19	17	2	21	19	2
Venezuela	55	51	4	127	116	11

(a) Units needed annually to maintain the 1950 percentage of families living in houses or apartments.

(b) Based on the premises: a) that in 1975, 95% of families will have houses or apartments; and b) that the average size of families will be reduced to 4 people in urban, and 5 people in rural areas.

from the composition of the population as to sex, civil status, and age, the annual minimum need for housing for urban and rural areas in each of the Latin American countries has been calculated. Table 3 shows the results.

To sum up, it is necessary to estimate present and future needs for new housing on the basis of standard criteria in order to use such calculations to formulate housing programs. In effect, an estimate of the minimum annual need determines the minimum goal for housing construction, the achievement of which implies building new housing units to take care of population growth, and replacing existing dwellings as they are lost through demolition, fire, change of use, or other causes.

CONCLUSIONS

1. The most obvious signs of the housing crisis in Latin America are the rapid growth of slums in most of the major cities, and the enormous number of shacks in rural zones.

2. The housing deficit in Latin America is enormous and has grown larger in the last decade. It is estimated that it will be necessary to replace about 20 million units which are considered absolutely inadequate. As this is impossible to achieve in a short period, we have suggested that efforts should be concentrated on avoiding an even greater increase in the housing deficit. This will require an increasing rate of construction until annual construction is in balance with the "minimum annual need for housing." In the last few years, the number of dwellings constructed annually has been far below the minimum necessary to prevent the housing gap becoming greater.

3. In view of the fact that from 1955 to 1964 the growth of the GNP in Latin American countries underwent variations independent of the variations in the population growth rate, it is surmised that variations in the birth rate in the next decade will not produce appreciable change in the growth of the GNP nor in demand for new housing.

4. On the basis of very crude hypotheses—which are necessary because of lack of adequate statistics—we arrive at the conclusion that Latin America will have to construct at least 1,850,000 dwellings annually during the period 1960-70 in order to prevent the housing situation from continually deteriorating.

FOOTNOTES

1. J. A. Mayobre, *Economic Development and Population Growth in Latin America,* United Nations World Population Conference, August 30-September 10, 1965, Belgrade, Yugoslavia.

2. E/3895/ Add. 1.

3. J. Tinbergen, *La planeación del desarrollo,* México, Fondo de Cultura Económica, 1959.

4. *El crecimiento demográfico y el desarrollo económico latinoaméricano,* Víctor L. Urquidi, World Population Conference, 1965, (A.9/I/ S/118).

5. *Points of contact between the growth of population and the growth of national product,* Joseph J. Spengler. World Population Conference, 1965, (A.10/I/E/140).

6. For the two periods there exists a positive correlation by ranks (if the coefficients of Spearman or Kendall are calculated), significantly different from zero. However, the coefficients' value is small and its variance is large.

7. In recent years dwelling censuses have been made in the following countries: *Argentina:* 1947 & 1960; *Brazil:* 1950 & 1960; *Costa Rica:* 1949 & 1963; *Chile:* 1952 & 1960; *El Salvador:* 1950 & 1961; *Honduras:* 1940 and 1961; *Mexico:* 1950 and 1960; *Panama:* 1950 and 1960; *Peru:* 1940 and 1961; *Dominican Republic:* 1950, 1955, & 1960; and *Venezuela:* 1950 and 1961. However, it has been impossible to explain the changes which occurred in several of these countries during the inter-census period. In some instances it may be because the outcome of the last census is not available; in others, because different basic assumptions were employed; and in other cases, because tabulations showing these changes were not obtained.

8. Except for a few countries, classifications of this type are not available. It would be especially interesting to know the number of "ordinary private dwellings (permanent)," that is, the number of houses and apartments whose structural characteristics could be considered adequate, and which are designed and constructed to serve as private homes. It would also be interesting to know the number of "impoverished" dwellings, for these represent a specific aspect of the housing problem. Unfortunately, census information dealing with this type of housing is available for very few countries. See definition, for example, recommended by the United Nations for this type of dwelling in *General Principles for Census on Dwellings,* United Nations, Number of sale: 58/XVII.8, paragraph 304.

9. Figures for different countries are not comparable, as there are variations on the basic ideas submitted. Further information on the nature and limitations of these statistics appears in *Summary of Social Statistics,* United Nations, 63.XVII.3, pp. 270 and 278-80.

10. United Nations Educational, Scientific and Cultural Organization (UNESCO), *Urbanization in Latin America, 1962;* and Inter-American Development Bank, *Fiduciary Funds for Social Progress, First Annual Report, 1961.*

11. Brazilian Institute of Geography and Statistics, National Service

of Re-Census (State of Guanabara), *Preliminary Synopsis of Demographic Census, 1960.*

12. Institute of Territorial Credit, *Plan for the eradication of huts,* Bogotá, April, 1963.

13. National Board of Dwellings: *Report on dwellings, construction and urban development situation,* Lima, 1963. (Preliminary version)

14. Inter-American Development Bank, *Fiduciary Funds on Social Progress,* Second Annual Report, 1962, p. 148.

15. Detailed statistical information appears in CEPAL, *Statistical evaluation on living conditions (dwellings), existing deficit and future need for homes in the Latin American countries,* ST/ECIA/CONF. 9/L.10.

16. Pan American Union, *Dwelling conditions in Peru,* Washington, D.C., 1963, p. 291.

6. *Population Growth and Education*

*JORGE V. ARÉVALO**

Population growth can be analyzed in terms of its components: birth, death, and migration. The proportions of the components determine not only the speed of growth but the age structure which, in turn, gives rise to the problem of the size of the population of school-age children and the proportion of the potentially active population which must eventually support them.

The speed at which the school-age population grows, together with other factors, exerts pressure on the available resources. On the other hand, these resources are affected by the proportion of the total population which is economically active and that proportion, without considering migration, is affected by birth and death rates, especially the former. Latin American countries which have high proportions of people under the age of 15 also have high birth rates. Sixteen countries have birth rates over 40 per 1000, resulting in a proportion of people under the age of 15 that fluctuates between 38% and 48%. While age structure is little affected by mortality, in those cases in which the birth rates are equal, the proportion of people under 15 years of age is nearly always greater when the death rate is lower. This is due to the tendency for mortality to decrease with greater speed in the ages between 1 and 14, resulting in more survivors within the groups born in the most recent five-year period.

* The views expressed in this paper are the writer's, and do not necessarily reflect those of the Latin American Demographic Center, of which he is a member.

THE SCHOOL-AGE POPULATION

The rapid growth of the population of Latin America gives rise to serious educational problems. Practically half of the population over 15 years of age is illiterate, and a great number of people have only had two or three years of elementary instruction. Country by country, the situation is even more discouraging. The countries which are less developed in terms of education require a greater proportional investment in this regard in order to reach the levels of the more developed countries. On the other hand, the more the countries grow, the greater the portion of the national product which must be allocated to satisfy basic needs such as education, with the result that the resources to be invested in economic development are scantier. Growth is slower in those countries which are more developed economically and educationally, such as Uruguay and Argentina, and to a lesser degree Chile and Cuba. Moreover, as a consequence of their low or moderate birth rates, such nations have more satisfactory age structures, in the sense of the relationship between the economically active and the dependent population.

The rate of growth of the total population is not necessarily equal to the growth of the school-age population. Before presenting projections to illustrate this point, some definitions will be discussed.

"School-age population" refers to the range of ages within which school attendance is legally compulsory. In general, elementary school attendance is obligatory, but this is not the case with respect to secondary school. Enrollment in elementary school occurs at 6 or 7 year of age. (In five countries the age of 6 has been established as the lowest limit, and in 15 countries, the age of 7.) The age at which school attendance is no longer compulsory is 12 years in two countries, and 14 years in 13 countries. The maximum, in Peru, is 16 years. In this report the age range 7-14 years is used. As there are no legal limitations on the age to which attendance is compulsory for secondary school, we shall utilize the age range 15-19 years.

Projections of the population 7-14 years of age, 15-19 years of age, and of the total population are given in Table 1, below:

TABLE 1.

Latin America.

Projections of age groups 7–14, 15–19, and total population 1960–80.

(*in thousands*)

	Age Groups	1960	1965	1970	1975	1980	Growth rate 1960–80 (per cent)
Argentina	7–14	3 244.0	3 525.0	3 626.0	3 611.0	3 726.0	6.9
	15–19	1 749.0	1 984.0	2 183.0	2 301.0	2 262.0	12.8
	T P	20 669.0	22 360.0	24 064.0	25 769.0	27 515.0	14.2
Bolivia	7–14	722.9	816.4	926.7	1 057.4	1 193.8	24.6
	15–19	383.9	418.9	474.1	538.4	613.5	23.0
	T P	3 696.0	4 136.0	4 658.0	5 277.0	6 000.0	23.8
Brazil	7–14	14 222.6	16 592.2	19 202.5	21 914.9	24 775.4	27.1
	15–19	7 000.3	8 273.8	9 741.5	11 292.9	12 965.0	29.9
	T P	70 308.9	81 300.1	93 751.9	107 862.8	123 566.3	27.5
Chile	7–14	1 458.1	1 705.6	1 940.3	2 132.1	2 453.2	25.4
	15–19	737.0	860.0	1 005.0	1 183.0	1 272.0	26.6
	T P	7 791.0	8 786.0	9 969.0	11 349.0	12 912.0	24.7
Colombia	7–14	3 095.0	3 550.0	4 000.0	4 560.0	5 170.0	25.1
	15–19	1 490.0	1 790.0	2 100.0	2 380.0	2 660.0	28.2
	T P	15 468.0	17 787.0	20 514.0	23 774.0	27 691.0	28.3
Costa Rica	7–14	211.8	248.5	275.6	303.5	334.7	22.5
	15–19	109.2	122.6	148.0	165.2	182.5	25.1
	T P	1 171.0	1 424.0	1 718.0	2 049.0	2 419.0	34.8
Cuba	7–14	1 215.0	1 340.0	1 450.0	1 565.0	1 685.0	16.2
	15–19	670.0	730.0	805.0	885.0	975.0	18.5
	T P	6 797.0	7 523.0	8 307.0	9 146.0	10 034.0	19.2
Dominican Republic	7–14	587.9	683.2	797.1	922.3	1 055.0	28.3
	15–19	305.4	343.7	399.1	467.2	543.9	28.1
	T P	3 030.0	3 588.0	4 277.0	5 124.0	6 174.0	34.3
Ecuador	7–14	834.3	956.7	1 095.7	1 273.5	1 489.3	28.2
	15–19	427.9	485.2	560.6	639.7	743.7	27.0
	T P	4 355.0	5 013.0	5 819.0	6 809.0	7 981.0	29.4
El Salvador	7–14	511.5	618.4	733.8	885.0	1 029.6	33.6
	15–19	234.8	292.4	362.0	423.1	512.2	37.1
	T P	2 486.6	2 917.8	3 426.1	4 007.4	4 686.7	30.7
Guatemala	7–14	802.6	940.3	1 068.1	1 214.2	1 388.9	26.8
	15–19	405.2	462.9	551.4	628.9	715.3	27.7
	T P	3 765.0	4 343.0	5 033.0	5 867.0	6 878.0	29.3
Haiti	7–14	804.7	939.4	1 083.1	1 266.4	1 497.2	30.1
	15–19	422.4	464.0	549.4	633.9	740.8	27.4
	T P	4 140.0	4 645.0	5 255.0	6 001.0	6 912.0	25.1
Honduras	7–14	393.6	505.1	583.5	648.7	780.7	33.0
	15–19	176.9	221.2	287.5	354.8	587.7	37.3
	T P	1 845.6	2 154.0	2 538.2	3 036.6	3 668.5	33.1
Mexico	7–14	7 430.8	9 038.8	10 904.4	12 909.4	15 406.6	34.9
	15–19	3 590.0	4 256.0	5 255.0	6 417.0	7 638.0	36.1
	T P	36 018.0	42 681.0	50 733.0	60 554.0	72 659.0	33.7
Nicaragua	7–14	263	323.2	353.2	383.6	415.8	22.5
	15–19	146.4	146.5	191.1	210.1	229.9	22.2
	T P	1 403.0	1 666.0	1 979.0	2 350.0	2 791.0	33.1

TABLE 1.—*(Continued)*

	Age Groups	1960	1965	1970	1975	1980	Growth rate 1960–80 (per cent)
Panama	7–14	207.1	240.0	285.9	338.5	398.7	31.7
	15–19	102.3	121.9	139.8	167.2	198.8	32.0
	T P	1 021.5	1 191.5	1 395.5	1 638.7	1 928.1	30.8
Paraguay	7–14	325.0	355.0	400.0	455.0	519.0	23.1
	15–19	165.0	180.0	200.0	225.0	255.0	21.6
	T P	1 720.0	1 952.0	2 233.0	2 573.0	2 981.0	26.7
Peru	7–14	2 048.5	2 424.0	2 916.1	2 364.3	3 863.2	30.8
	15–19	1 010.4	1 203.4	1 399.2	1 720.9	1 997.5	32.9
	T P	10 076.0	11 709.3	13 655.9	15 950.1	18 622.0	29.8
Uruguay	7–14	361.1	363.5	356.9	344.0	333.2	−4.2
	15–19	208.6	223.4	226.8	224.9	216.8	2.0
	T P	2 491.0	2 647.0	2 802.0	2 960.0	3 126.0	11.1
Venezuela	7–14	1 529.1	1 852.1	2 194.8	2 695.0	3 195.9	35.3
	15–19	708.8	879.3	1 099.8	1 268.7	1 586.0	38.3
	T P	7 442.6	8 827.5	10 509.8	12 518.7	14 909.6	33.3
Total	7–14	40 268.6	47 017.4	54 193.7	61 844.1	70 711.2	27.5
	15–19	20 043.5	23 459.6	27 678.3	32 126.9	36 695.6	29.3
	T P	205 695.2	236 651.2	272 638.4	314 616.3	363 454.2	27.8

The children alive in 1965 will constitute the population aged 15-19 in 1980, 10-19 in 1975, and 5-19 in 1970. This shows that part of the future population already exists, and that its numbers can only be affected by mortality. These generations are the product of the fertility levels of the recent past. Future levels will only affect those under age 15 by 1980. The future levels of mortality will, of course, affect all ages throughout the entire period of the projection.

In general, population projections which imply moderate decreases of fertility have been chosen, except in a few cases where such declines seem unlikely.

The assumptions about the death rate project a decrease in all cases, greater in those countries which in 1960 had higher rates. As mortality decreases at a faster rate in the 1-14 year age group, it can bring about an effect very similar to an increase in the birth rate, since a greater proportion of survivors occurs in the age of childhood. However, for this to have a significant effect, the decrease in the death rate must be very sharp. In the projections to be examined this is scarcely observable.

In Table 1 projections up to 1980 are given. The first noteworthy aspect is the unequal size of the 20 Latin American countries. Brazil, in 1940, had 34% of the total population. With Mexico it included 52%, and with Argentina and Colombia 69% of the total population. By 1980, according to the projections, the first two countries will have 54% of the total and, if the other two countries are added, 69% of the total population will be included.

Of the four countries mentioned, three have high proportions of illiterates. In 1950, 51% of Brazil's population over the age of 15 was illiterate, Mexico 35% in 1960, Colombia 30% in 1951. Argentina had 9% illiterate in 1960. Of the remaining population of Latin America, Uruguay has as low an illiteracy rate as Argentina, while Costa Rica and Chile registered 16%, and all others exceeded 20%. Guatemala and Haiti, where the rates were 71% and 89% in 1950, are extreme cases.

Between now and 1980, the populations of eight countries will grow at very high rates, over 3.0%. Seven countries will grow at a rate between 2.5% and 2.9%, and only three at a rate of 2% or less. Three-fourths of the countries, with 84% of the population in 1980, will continue growing rapidly.

But the rhythm of growth of the total population is not necessarily the same as that for the groups between 7 and 14 years of age and between 15 and 19 years of age, nor does it have the same meaning. In ten countries the total population will grow more rapidly than any of the two age groups we are considering. They are Argentina, Colombia, Costa Rica, Cuba, Ecuador, Guatemala, Nicaragua, Paraguay, the Dominican Republic, and Uruguay. In seven others, Chile, El Salvador, Haiti, Mexico, Panama, Peru, and Venezuela, the total populations will grow at a slower rate than the specified age groups. In Bolivia, Brazil, and Honduras, the population will grow at a speed between the two age groups. The differences bear little relation to the rhythm of growth. Whether it is slow, moderate, or rapid, discrepancies occur.

TABLE 2.

Latin America.
Projection of 7–14, 15–19 age groups as per cent of total
population, by country, 1960–80.

	Age	1960	1965	1970	1975	1980
Argentina	7–14	15.7	15.8	15.1	14.0	13.5
	15–19	8.4	8.8	9.0	8.9	8.2
Bolivia	7–14	19.6	19.7	19.9	20.0	19.9
	15–19	10.3	10.1	10.1	10.2	10.2
Brazil	7–14	20.2	20.4	20.5	20.3	20.1
	15–19	9.9	10.1	10.3	10.4	10.4
Chile	7–14	18.7	19.4	19.5	18.8	19.0
	15–19	9.4	9.7	10.0	10.4	9.8
Colombia	7–14	20.0	20.0	19.5	19.2	18.7
	15–19	9.6	10.0	10.2	10.0	9.6
Costa Rica	7–14	18.1	17.5	16.0	14.8	13.8
	15–19	9.3	8.6	8.6	8.0	7.5
Cuba	7–14	17.9	17.8	17.5	17.1	16.8
	15–19	9.8	9.7	9.6	9.6	9.7
Dominican Republic	7–14	19.4	19.0	18.6	18.0	17.1
	15–19	10.0	9.5	9.3	9.1	8.8
Ecuador	7–14	19.2	19.1	18.8	18.7	18.7
	15–19	9.8	9.6	9.6	9.3	9.3
El Salvador	7–14	20.6	21.2	21.4	22.1	22.0
	15–19	9.4	10.0	10.5	10.5	10.9
Guatemala	7–14	21.3	21.7	21.2	20.7	20.2
	15–19	10.7	10.6	10.9	10.7	10.3
Haiti	7–14	19.4	20.2	20.6	21.1	21.7
	15–19	10.2	9.9	10.4	10.5	10.7
Honduras	7–14	21.3	23.4	23.0	21.4	21.3
	15–19	9.5	10.2	11.3	11.6	10.5
Mexico	7–14	20.6	21.2	21.5	21.3	21.2
	15–19	9.9	9.9	10.3	10.5	10.5
Nicaragua	7–14	18.8	19.4	17.8	16.3	14.9
	15–19	10.4	8.7	9.6	8.9	8.2

TABLE 2.—(*Continued*)

	Age	1960	1965	1970	1975	1980
Panama	7–14	20.3	20.1	20.5	20.7	20.7
	15–19	10.0	10.2	10.0	10.2	10.3
Paraguay	7–14	18.9	18.2	17.9	17.7	17.4
	15–19	9.5	9.2	8.9	8.7	8.5
Peru	7–14	20.3	20.7	21.4	21.1	20.7
	15–19	10.0	10.2	10.2	10.7	10.7
Uruguay	7–14	14.5	13.7	12.8	11.6	10.7
	15–19	8.3	8.4	8.0	7.5	6.9
Venezuela	7–14	20.5	21.0	20.9	21.5	21.4
	15–19	9.5	9.9	10.4	10.1	10.6
Total	7–14	19.6	19.9	19.9	19.7	19.5
	15–19	9.7	9.9	10.2	10.2	10.1

Source: Table 1.

The situation will not change markedly between 1960 and 1980 if the projections are accurate. The proportion of school-age children will vary in only a few countries. In Table 2 we see that for all of Latin America the proportion of people between 7 and 19 years of age was about 29% in 1960 and is expected to be the same in 1980 because of the very moderate decreases expected in fertility in most of the countries.

The situation can be summarized as follows:

Per cent of population between 7 and 19 years of age	Number of countries	1960	Number of countries	1980
less than 25.0	2	Argentina, Uruguay	4	Argentina, Costa Rica, Nicaragua, Uruguay
25.0 to 27.4	2	Costa Rica, Cuba	3	Cuba, Paraguay, Dominican Republic
27.5 to 29.9	8	Bolivia, Colombia, Chile, Ecuador, Haiti, Nicaragua, Paraguay, Dominican Republic	3	Colombia, Chile, Ecuador

30.0 and over	8	Brazil, El Salvador, Guatemala, Honduras, Mexico, Panama, Peru, Venezuela	10	Bolivia, Brazil, El Salvador, Guatemala, Haiti, Honduras, Mexico, Panama, Peru, Venezuela

At least three countries, however, will have undergone striking changes in their age structure by 1980. In Costa Rica and Nicaragua the proportion of the school-age population will decrease, and in Haiti it will increase. The case of Costa Rica is explained by the fact that very pronounced decreases in the birth rate have been forecast, which cannot be offset by decreases in the death rate. In Haiti, since the predicted decrease in the death rate is sudden and is associated with a very slight decrease in the birth rate, its effects are noticeable in the increase of the school-age population. In the other countries the variations are slight and can be accounted for in the same way.

School Enrollment

Not all school-age children attend school. The reasons are various. Poverty, the need to work at an early age, ignorance and negligence of parents, the distance from school, insufficient number of schools, and shortage of teachers are among the causes for failure to attend primary school. At the secondary school level non-compulsory attendance is an additional cause of leaving school. The attendance ratio, defined as the proportion of people between 7 and 14 years of age who attend elementary schools, and the proportion of people between 15 and 19 years of age who attend secondary schools, respectively, shows considerable variation by country.

The Elementary School Population, 7-14 Years of Age

Table 3 below shows that attendance at elementary schools varies between 112.6% in Cuba and 29.6% in Haiti. The first figure is a result of the massive incorporation of those who have exceeded the age at which attendance is obligatory and who did not attend when they were supposed to, or of

TABLE 3.

Latin America.

Projection of elementary school-age population by country, 1960–80.

(*in thousands*)

	Attendance in 1960 (per cent)	1960	1965	1970	1975	1980 (a)	(b)	(c)
Argentina	89.5	2 902.0	3 154.9	3 245.3	3 231.8	3 334.8	3 651.5	126
Bolivia	58.7	424.0	479.2	544.0	620.7	700.8	1 169.9	276
Brazil	56.4	8 014.0	9 357.4	10 830.2	12 360.0	13 973.3	24 279.9	303
Chile	76.0	1 108.0	1 296.3	1 474.6	1 620.4	1 864.4	2 404.1	217
Colombia	54.1	1 674.0	1 920.6	2 164.0	2 467.0	2 797.0	5 066.6	303
Costa Rica	93.5	198.0	232.5	257.7	283.8	312.9	328.0	166
Cuba	112.6	1 368.0	1 508.8	1 632.7	1 762.2	1 897.3	1 651.3	121
Dominican Republic	84.9	499.0	580.0	676.7	783.0	895.7	1 033.9	207
Ecuador	71.3	595.0	682.1	781.2	908.0	1 061.9	1 459.5	245
El Salvador	56.7	290.0	350.6	416.1	501.8	583.8	1 009.0	348
Guatemala	37.0	297.0	347.9	395.2	449.3	513.9	1 361.1	458
Haiti	29.6	238.0	278.1	320.6	374.9	443.2	1 467.3	617
Honduras	52.1	205.0	263.2	304.0	338.0	406.7	765.1	373
Mexico	64.7	4 807.0	5 848.1	7 055.1	8 352.4	9 968.1	15 098.5	314
Nicaragua	58.2	153.0	188.1	205.6	223.3	242.0	407.5	266
Panama	78.2	162.0	187.7	223.6	264.7	311.8	390.7	241
Paraguay	93.9	305.0	333.3	375.6	427.2	487.3	508.6	167
Peru	70.0	1 433.0	1 696.8	2 041.3	2 355.0	2 704.2	3 785.9	264
Uruguay	89.2	322.0	324.2	318.4	306.8	297.2	326.5	101
Venezuela	71.6	1 095.0	1 326.1	1 571.5	1 929.8	2 288.3	3 132.0	286

Source: Table 4, and "UNESCO estadísticas relativas a aspectos de la educación," UNESCO/IAC-LAMP/IV/8. Table A.2.
(a) The proportion of school attendance is assumed to be constant between 1960 and 1980. This proportion is the percentage of the 7–14 year old population attending school.
(b) Assuming that school attendance will increase linearly to 98% by 1980.
(c) Relative growth by 1980, 1960 = 100. Assumes attendance increase to 98%.

those who did not complete elementary schooling within the legal age limit.

The size of the future school population will depend not only on demographic variables, but also on the attendance goal. It is undoubtedly the goal of all Latin American countries to place all school-age children in school, with the exception of the one or two per cent not intellectually capable of obtaining an education. Therefore, 98% is considered a reasonable maximum of elementary school attendance, and this figure is used in the last two columns of Table 3. This percentage may vary, because the elementary curriculum usually has a shorter duration than the period of ages here considered. Some students complete their studies before reaching the age of 14. On the other hand, there may be repeaters who keep on attending school after having reached this age.

Except in Cuba, where the attendance exceeded 100% of the age group, the projected school population is obviously

greater than that calculated, assuming no change in attendance proportions. The pattern of growth is better observed
through the relative figures seen in the last column of Table
3. If they are compared with the growth attained in 1980 by
the school population, projected according to the constant
rate of attendance of 1960, large discrepancies are apparent
in some cases.

We have seen that the rates of school attendance in 1960
are not strictly related to the population increase, as is also
evident from the following summary.

Projected percentage growth of the elementary school-age population		*Projected percentage increase in elementary school attendance in 1980 at maximum rate of 98%*					
	Number of Countries	*Less than 50%*	*50– 99%*	*100– 149%*	*150– 199%*	*200– 249%*	*250 and more*
Less than 50	3	3	—	—	—	—	—
50–66	4	2	—	2	—	—	—
67–85	6	2	1	2	—	—	1
86–106	5	1	1	1	1	—	1
107– and over	2	—	1	1	—	—	—
Total	20	8	3	6	1	—	2

In eight countries, with a wide range of growth caused by
demographic factors, there is an additional growth resulting
from an increased school-attendance rate of less than 50%.
This occurs because the rates of attendance in those countries were already relatively high in 1960. Thus, while it is
possible that accelerated population growth is a barrier to
increasing school attendance, there are also economic, social,
and political factors which may exert an even more decisive
influence.

The Secondary School Population, 15-19 Years of Age

The lack of compulsory secondary school enrollment is
another factor affecting attendance. Table 4 below shows the
rates in 1960 to be considerably lower than those in the elementary cycle, ranging from 42% in Uruguay to 4% in

TABLE 4.

Latin America.

Projection of the secondary school-age population, by country, 1960–80 (a).

	Attendance in 1960 (per cent)	Number of students (in thousands)				
		1960	1965	1970	1975	1980
Argentina	34.6	606.0	686.5	755.3	796.1	782.7
Bolivia	14.0	53.6	58.6	66.4	75.4	85.9
Brazil	17.7	1 238.1	1 464.5	1 724.2	1 998.8	2 294.8
Chile	31.3	230.5	269.2	314.6	370.3	398.1
Colombia	19.2	286.0	343.7	403.2	457.0	510.7
Costa Rica	32.1	35.1	39.4	47.5	53.0	58.6
Cuba	18.2	121.9	132.9	146.5	161.1	177.5
Dominican Republic	7.1	21.6	24.4	28.3	33.2	38.6
Ecuador	15.7	67.3	76.2	88.0	100.4	116.8
El Salvador	14.3	33.6	41.8	51.8	60.5	73.2
Guatemala	6.8	27.4	31.5	37.5	42.8	48.6
Haiti	4.4	18.6	20.4	24.2	27.9	32.6
Honduras	8.4	14.8	18.6	24.2	29.8	32.6
Mexico	13.6	486.7	578.8	714.7	872.7	1 038.8
Nicaragua	7.0	10.3	10.3	13.4	14.7	16.1
Panama	38.0	38.9	46.3	53.1	63.5	75.5
Paraguay	16.8	27.7	30.2	33.6	37.8	42.8
Peru	20.0	202.2	240.8	279.8	344.2	399.5
Uruguay	41.9	87.5	93.6	95.0	94.2	90.8
Venezuela	20.8	147.5	182.9	228.8	263.9	329.9

Source: Table I and UNESCO, *op. cit.*, Table S.2.
(a) The proportion between the total number of students attending school and the entire 15–19 age group has been assumed as constant during 1960–1980.

Haiti, the Table also gives projections for the secondary school population, assuming that the 1960 attendance rates remain constant until 1980. This projection, which varies only according to the behavior of demographic variables, is probably a minimum estimate of the future school population.

It is reasonable, however, to expect that the proportion of people attending secondary school will increase, as it has in fact in recent years. Consequently we have made a second estimate, assuming various increases for different countries.

TABLE 5.

Latin America.

Projection of the secondary school-age population by country, 1960–80 (a).

Country	Attendance (per 100)		1960	1965	1970	1975	1980	Incre. 1960– 1980 (1960 =100)
	1960	1980						
Argentina	34.6	60.0	606.0	813.4	1 032.6	1 235.6	1 357.2	224
Bolivia	14.0	45.0	53.6	91.3	139.9	200.8	276.1	515
Brazil	17.7	45.0	1 238.1	2 027.1	3 058.8	4 313.9	5 834.3	471
Chile	31.3	60.0	230.5	331.1	459.3	624.6	763.2	331
Colombia	19.2	45.0	286.0	460.0	674.1	918.7	1 197.0	419
Costa Rica	32.1	60.0	35.1	47.9	68.2	87.6	109.5	312
Cuba	18.2	45.0	121.9	181.8	254.4	339.0	438.8	360
Dominican Republic	7.1	30.0	21.6	44.0	74.2	113.5	163.2	756
Ecuador	15.7	45.0	67.3	111.6	170.4	241.2	334.7	497
El Salvador	14.3	45.0	33.6	64.3	107.5	157.8	290.5	686
Guatemala	6.8	30.0	27.4	58.3	101.5	152.2	214.6	783
Haiti	4.4	30.0	18.6	50.1	94.5	149.6	222.2	1 195
Honduras	8.4	30.0	14.8	30.5	55.2	87.3	116.3	786
Mexico	13.6	45.0	486.7	915.0	1 539.7	2 387.1	3 437.1	706
Nicaragua	7.0	30.0	10.3	18.8	35.4	51.1	69.0	670
Panama	38.0	60.0	38.9	53.0	68.5	91.1	119.3	307
Paraguay	16.8	45.0	27.7	43.0	61.8	85.5	114.8	414
Peru	20.0	45.0	202.2	316.6	454.7	667.7	898.9	445
Uruguay	41.9	60.0	87.5	103.7	115.7	124.8	130.1	149
Venezuela	20.8	45.0	147.5	236.5	361.8	494.8	713.7	484

(a) Under three assumptions: 1) countries that had over 25% school attendance in 1960 would reach 60% in 1980; 2) those that had 10–24% in 1960 would reach 45% in 1980; 3) countries with less than 10% in 1960 would reach 30% in 1980.
Source: Table 1 and UNESCO, *op. cit.*, Table S.2.

There are extreme cases, such as Haiti, where to enroll 30% of the 15-19 year olds in secondary school by 1980 would require enrollment of *twelve times* the number of pupils attending in 1960. As was the case at the elementary level, there seems to be no relation between the speed of population growth and projected increases resulting from higher proportions attending school.

	Projected percentage growth of the secondary school-age population	*Projected percentage increase in secondary school attendance in 1980 at maximum rate of 98%*					
	Number of Countries	*Less than 100%*	*100– 199%*	*200– 299%*	*300– 399%*	*400– 499%*	*Over 500%*
Less than 50	3	2	—	1	—	—	—
50–66	3	—	—	1	1	—	1
67–85	8	—	2	2	1	—	3
86–106	2	—	1	1	—	—	—
107– and more	4	—	—	1	—	2	1
Total	20	2	3	6	2	2	5

Four estimates regarding elementary school teachers will be made, utilizing different assumptions about the school population and the teacher-student ratio. One set of projections for the former assumes that the rate of school attendance will remain constant, while another assumes that it will reach 98% in 1980. Another set assumes that the teacher-student ratio in 1960 will remain constant, while the other assumes a ratio of 25 students per teacher in 1980.

The optimum number of students per teacher will vary according to time and place. It will depend, for example, on the ultimate attendance goal, the intellectual level and qualifications of teachers and pupils, the curricula, the quantity, quality, and variety of the teaching material, and on the teaching methods. If the ratio of 25 pupils per teacher is a realistic figure, the situation in Latin America is not favorable. Of the 20 countries, 10 have 35 or more pupils per teacher, while 17 have 30 or more:

No. of Pupils Per Teacher	No. of Countries	Countries
less than 25	1	Argentina
25–29	2	Bolivia, Paraguay
30–34	7	Peru, Uruguay, El Salvador, Guatemala, Honduras, Nicaragua, Panama
35–39	3	Brazil, Venezuela, Cuba
40–44	6	Colombia, Chile, Ecuador, Costa Rica, Haiti, Mexico
45 and over	1	Dominican Republic

Of the four estimates, the one assuming the same rate of school attendance and teacher-student ratio observed in 1960 varies for demographic reasons. The estimates which assume that the teacher-student ratio will remain constant, but that attendance will reach 98% in 1980, will vary according to demographic attendance factors. Both estimates will be affected by the evolution of the elementary school population, the rhythm and consequences of which were analyzed above.

The introduction of an ideal goal for the proportion of pupils per teacher adds a new factor of variation which lessens the importance of figures on the growth of the population of school age.

It is obvious that the greater the increase in population, the greater the problem of providing school children with enough teachers. But growth is not the only obstacle to edu-

TABLE 6.

Latin America.

Projection of elementary school teachers needed in 1980, by country.

	Students per teacher in 1960	Number of teachers in 1960 (in thousands)	Number of teachers in 1980 according to four hypotheses			
			(a)	(b)	(c)	(d)
Argentina	22.4	129.7	148.9	163.0	133.4	146.1
Bolivia	25.1	16.9	27.9	46.6	28.0	46.8
Brazil	36.7	218.4	379.8	661.6	558.9	971.2
Chile	41.7	26.6	44.7	57.7	74.6	96.2
Colombia	40.0	41.8	69.9	126.7	111.9	202.7
Costa Rica	39.6	5.0	7.9	8.3	12.5	13.1
Cuba	35.6	38.4	53.3	46.4	75.9	66.1
Dominican Republic	57.4	8.7	15.6	18.0	35.8	41.4
Ecuador	41.3	14.4	25.7	35.3	42.5	58.4
El Salvador	33.3	8.7	17.5	30.3	23.4	40.4
Guatemala	30.6	9.7	16.8	44.5	20.6	54.5
Haiti	44.1	5.4	10.0	33.3	17.7	58.7
Honduras	31.5	6.5	12.9	24.3	16.3	30.6
Mexico	43.3	111.1	230.2	348.7	398.7	603.9
Nicaragua	34.0	4.5	7.1	12.0	9.7	16.3
Panama	30.6	5.3	10.2	12.8	12.5	15.6
Paraguay	28.5	10.7	17.1	17.8	19.5	20.3
Peru	34.2	41.9	79.1	110.7	108.2	151.4
Uruguay	32.5	9.9	9.1	10.0	11.9	13.1
Venezuela	35.4	30.9	64.6	88.5	91.5	125.3

(a) School attendance in 1980 equal to that in 1960. Student-teacher ratio in 1980 equal to that in 1960.

(b) School attendance in 1980 equal to 98%. Student-teacher ratio in 1980 equal to that in 1960.

(c) School attendance in 1980 equal to that in 1960. Student-teacher ratio of 25.

(d) School attendance in 1980 equal to 98%. Student-teacher ratio 25.

Source: Table 3, and UNESCO, *op. cit.*, Table M.1.

TABLE 7.

Latin America.
Elementary school teachers needed in 1980, by country
(Based on four assumptions)
Base year: 1960 = 100.

	1980 (a)	1980 (b)	1980 (c)	1980 (d)
Argentina	115	126	103	113
Bolivia	165	276	166	277
Brazil	174	303	256	445
Chile	168	217	280	362
Colombia	167	303	268	485
Costa Rica	158	166	250	262
Cuba	139	121	198	172
Dominican Republic	179	207	411	476
Ecuador	179	245	295	406
El Salvador	201	348	269	464
Guatemala	173	458	212	561
Haiti	186	617	328	1 087
Honduras	198	373	251	471
Mexico	207	314	359	544
Nicaragua	158	266	216	362
Panama	193	241	236	294
Paraguay	160	167	182	190
Peru	189	264	258	361
Uruguay	92	101	120	132
Venezuela	205	286	296	406

(a) School attendance in 1980 equal to that in 1960. Student-teacher ratio in 1980 equal to that in 1960.
(b) School attendance in 1980 equal to 98%. Student-teacher ratio in 1980 equal to that in 1960.
(c) School attendance in 1980 equal to that in 1960. Student-teacher ratio of 25.
(d) School attendance in 1980 equal to 98%. Student-teacher ratio of 25.
Source: Table 6.

cational progress. Other factors of an economic and social nature necessarily exert an important influence. The slight or non-existent relationship between the rate of population growth and the proportion of pupils per teacher around 1960 seems to support this point of view.

Tables 6 and 7 below contain estimates of future teacher needs according to the four combinations of assumptions. In the *a* and *b* estimates, where it is assumed that the rates observed in 1960 will remain constant, growth is equal to the growth in the school-age population previously analyzed. In the *c* and *d* estimates, on the other hand, the variability between countries increases, since population growth, pupil attendance, and the various ratios of pupils per teacher affect the estimate. The estimates *b* and *d* are higher than *a* and *c* as they assume that school attendance will reach 98%. With the exception of Argentina, the estimates are lower than *c* and *d* since all school attendance is below 98% and, with the exception mentioned, the number of pupils per teacher is over 25. The situation varies by country depending on whether the growth of the school-age population, attendance, or the proportion of pupils per teacher is considered.

According to estimate *a* Guatemala must increase the number of teachers by 73%, and Mexico by 107% if one considers only the growth of the population of school age. But if attendance is also considered, Guatemala will need 358% more teachers, whereas Mexico will need a 214% increase. While El Salvador must increase its teachers by 101%, according to the *a* estimate, the Dominican Republic teachers will increase by 79%, if only growth of the population of school-age children is taken into account. But if we consider the pupil-teacher ratio of 25, the situation is reversed. El Salvador will only need a 169% increase in teachers, while the Dominican Republic will require a 311% increase. Thus it would appear that, so far as the need for teachers is concerned, other factors appear to be more important than the mere growth of the school-age population, whether it be slow, moderate, or rapid.

Financial Resources

In the last section of this paper the problems of financing and the growth of the school-age population will be briefly examined. While there is information available for only half of the countries, all levels of growth are represented. We shall focus on expenditures per pupil and educational budgets.

Expenditures Per Pupil

This figure usually comprises all the investments and expenditures made per pupil, and thus measures the educa-

TABLE 8.

Latin America.

Elementary and secondary school budgets 1960–1980.

| | National Budget (Millions of national currency) | | | | Expenses per students (Units of national currency) | | | | | | |
| | Elementary | | Secondary | | 1960 | | 1980 | | | | |
	1960	1980*	1960	1980*	Elementary	Secondary	(a)	(b)	(c)	(d)
Argentina	6 676.9	8 888.4	4 531.8	6 032.8	2 301	7 478	2 665	2 434	7 708	4 445
Chile	58.9	97.6	32.1	53.2	53	139	52	41	134	70
Colombia	100.6	180.1	27.2	48.7	60	95	64	36	95	41
Costa Rica	70.4	145.4	16.0	33.1	356	456	465	443	565	302
Cuba	67.1	99.1	14.3	21.1	49	117	52	60	119	48
Ecuador	110.8	203.1	55.4	101.5	186	823	191	139	869	303
El Salvador	18.2	34.3	2.6	4.9	63	77	59	34	67	21
Mexico	1 303.7	2 629.9	495.5	999.6	271	1 018	264	174	962	291
Nicaragua	24.0	47.7	7.7	15.3	157	748	197	117	950	222
Venezuela	176.7	354.0	83.7	167.7	161	567	155	113	508	235

* Assuming growth at same rate as projected population.

School attendance assumptions:

(a) Elementary school attendance remains constant between 1960–1980.
(b) Elementary school attendance will reach 98%.
(c) Secondary school attendance remains constant between 1960–1980.
(d) Secondary school attendance will reach 60% in 1980 in Argentina, Costa Rica, Cuba, Ecuador, El Salvador, Mexico, and Venezuela; 30% in Nicaragua.

Sources: "Nota sobre financiamiento y costos de la educación en algunos países de América Latina," UNESCO/ED/CEDES/ 18; ST/ECLA/CONF.10/L.18; PAU/SEC/18; N.U. February 26, 1962; pp. 4, 13, and Tables 1–5 of present paper.

tional effort and the expected achievement. In the present instance it is used only to measure the financial impact of the growth of the school-age population. No attempt will be made to judge the adequacy of the investment per pupil.

It is assumed that the budget for elementary and secondary education will grow in proportion to the total population. If the 1960 rate of school attendance remains constant, the expenditure per pupil will increase in those countries in which the population of school age grows more slowly than the total population, and conversely. Table 8 above presents the different figures obtained by utilizing the two assumptions of attendance for elementary and secondary school. Since local currencies are used in these calculations, direct comparison between countries is not possible.

However, in Table 9 below we compare the necessary percentage increase in expenditure between 1960 and 1980 for each country according to our four different assumptions.

In the *a* and *c* estimates the level of school attendance remains at the 1960 level and the variations are due exclusively to the difference between the speed of growth of the total

TABLE 9.

Latin America.

Elementary and secondary school expenses per student in 1980.

(*Based on the four assumptions of Table 8*)

Base Year: 1960=100

	Expenses per student in 1980			
	a	b	c	d
Argentina	116	106	103	59
Chile	98	77	96	50
Colombia	107	60	100	43
Costa Rica	131	124	124	67
Cuba	106	122	102	41
Ecuador	103	75	106	37
El Salvador	94	54	87	27
Mexico	97	64	94	29
Nicaragua	125	75	127	30
Venezuela	96	70	90	41

Source: Table 8 of present paper.

TABLE 10.

Latin America.

Projected elementary and secondary school budgets in 1980.[1]

	Elementary schools		Secondary schools	
	1980 (a)	1980 (b)	1980 (a)	1980 (c)
	(in thousands of national currency)		(in thousands of national currency)	
Argentina	7 673.4	8 402.1	5 853.0	10 149.1
Chile	98.8	127.4	55.3	106.1
Colombia	167.8	304.0	48.5	113.7
Costa Rica	111.4	116.8	26.7	49.9
Cuba	93.0	80.9	20.8	51.3
Ecuador	197.5	271.5	96.1	275.5
El Salvador	36.8	63.6	5.6	17.7
Mexico	2 701.4	4 091.7	1 057.5	3 499.0
Nicaragua	38.0	64.0	12.0	51.6
Venezuela	368.4	504.3	187.7	406.1

[1] School-attendance assumptions:

(a) Attendance remains constant, 1960–80.

(b) Elementary school attendance will reach 98% in 1980.

(c) Secondary school attendance will reach 60% in 1980 in *Argentina, Costa Rica,* and *Chile;* 45% in *Colombia, Cuba, Ecuador, El Salvador, Mexico,* and *Venezuela;* and 30% in *Nicaragua.*

Note: Budget in 1980 = expense per student in 1960 times projected students in 1980.

Source: Table 3, 4, 5 and 8 of present paper.

population and of the population of school age. Only in Argentina, Colombia, Costa Rica, Cuba, Ecuador, and Nicaragua does the expenditure per pupil increase, since the school-age population will grow more slowly than the total population. Estimates *b* and *d,* which assume increased school attendance, are lower than those previous, except for Cuba, which had an elementary school attendance over 100% in 1960. By 1980, Argentina and Costa Rica also will increase their expenditure per pupil according to the *b* estimate, whereas remaining countries will be below their 1960 level. This shows that in some cases an increase of school attendance rate will more than counterbalance a decreased rate of growth of the school-age population, while in others it will greatly enhance the difficulties attendant on a rapid growth of the numbers of these young people.

Educational Budgets

Another way of analyzing financial aspects of the question is through different assumptions about the growth of the educational budget, which are connected with the rhythm of growth of the total population, school attendance, and the expenses per pupil. For purposes of this analysis the level of expense per pupil in 1960 is assumed to remain constant. The results are given in Table 10.

SUMMARY

The population of Latin America is growing at a rate faster than has been observed anywhere at any time. This acceleration has taken place since the Second World War as a result of marked decreases in the death rate without modification in the high level of fertility. This situation affects education, since great increases in all types of educational investment are required. Growth of the total population, however, is not as important as growth of the school-age groups. In some cases the population of school age grows more rapidly than the total population, and in other cases the opposite happens; phenomena apparently independent of the speed of growth of the total population. Speed of population growth also has little effect on the proportion of the population attending school and the ratio of teachers to pupils, a fact which indicates that these things are probably a function of other factors of an economic and social nature. Expenditure per pupil and the educational budgets themselves are a function of the growth of population of school-age children and of attendance at school, among other variables. Both growth and attendance may operate in the same direction, enhancing their favorable or unfavorable influence, or they may tend partially to balance each other; but the predominance of the influence of school attendance over growth is always apparent.

Appendix

ARGENTINA Arévalo, Jorge V., "República Argentina. Proyección de la población hasta el año 2000." CELADE, Santiago, Chile, 1965 (unpublished).

BOLIVIA Somoza, Jorge L., "Bolivia. Proyecciones Demográficas." CELADE D.B. 61/4.2/3.1. Santiago, Chile, Table 9.

BRAZIL Arretx, Carmen, "Proyección de la población del Brasil, por sexo y grupos de edad. Período 1940 a 1980." Serie C E/CN.CE-LADE/C. 34 B.63.3/3.1, 1965. Santiago, Chile, Table 2.

CHILE Alvarez, Leonel, "Proyecciones de la población de Chile por sexo y groupos de edad, 1960-2000." Santiago, Chile, 1965 (unpublished).

COLOMBIA CEPAL—Social Affairs Division, "Proyección de la población urbana, población rural y fuerza trabajadora de Colombia." CEPAL 1960. Table I.

COSTA RICA Ducoff, Louis J., "Los recursos humanos de Centroamérica. Panamá y México en 1950-1980 y sus relaciones con algunos aspectos del desarrollo económico." N.U. CEPAL 1960, p. 107, Table I.

CUBA CEPAL—Social Affairs Division. "Proyección de la población urbana y rural de Cuba. (con estimaciones de la fuerza de trabajo de la población en edad escolar y del grado de alfabetismo)." CEPAL 1960, Tables I and II.

DOMINICAN REPUBLIC Mellon, Roger, "Estimación de los principales índices demográficos de la República Dominicana en el año 1950 y proyección de la población total por sexo y grupos quinquenales de edad (1950-1980)." CELADE SERIE C. E/CN. CELADE/C.16B. 62. 2/7.1. Santiago, Chile, 1963, p. 27, projection II.

ECUADOR Nieto Terán Bolívar, "Proyección de la población de Ecuador 1950-1980." CELADE B. 60.2/5.4, 1961. Santiago, Chile, p. 41, Annex 13.

EL SALVADOR Alens Z., Alex A., "República de El Salvador. Proyección de la población por sexo y groups de edad 1961-1981." CELADE Serie C E/CN. CELADE/C.25. B.64.2/2.1, Santiago, Chile, 1964, p. 26, Table 2.

GUATEMALA Barrios, Berta and Ruiz, Carlos Haroldo, "Análisis de la situación demográfica de Guatemala en 1950 y proyección de la población entre 1950 y 1980." CELADE B. 60.1/3-9, Santiago, Chile, 1960, Table IIIa.

HAITI Saint-Surin, Jacques, "Estimation de quelques indices démographiques et perspective de la population d'Haiti de 1950 à 1980." CELADE B.61.1/14. Santiago, Chile, 1961, Table 10.

HONDURAS Cambar, Manuel C., "Proyecciones de población para Honduras de 1961 a 1981." CELADE B.62.1/4. Santiago, Chile, 1962. Table 3.

MEXICO Recchini, Zulma L. and Chavira O., Miguel, "Proyección de la población de México por sexo y grupos de edad, 1960-1980." Serie C E/CN.CELADE/C.33 B.63.2/3.2.Rev.I, Santiago, Chile, 1964, p. 32, Table 13.

NICARAGUA Ducoff, Louis J., "Los recursos humanos de Centroamérica, Panamá y México en 1950-1980 y sus relaciones con algunos aspectos del desarrollo económico." N.U. CEPAL, 1960, p. 119. Table V.

PANAMA   Médica, Vilma N., "Análisis de la situación demográfica de la República de Panamá en el período 1950-1960 y proyección de la población total 1960-1980." Santiago, Chile, 1965 (unpublished).

PARAGUAY   ST/SOA/SER.A/28, model CDEF of Appendix B, with an initial life expectancy in 1950 of 45 years, and supposing a net emigration of 15,000 persons as calculated in ST/SOA/SER.A/30, Table III, the population of rural areas—composed of localities with less than 2,000 inhabitants, according to the definition set forth in the *Economic Bulletin for Latin America*—will increase at an annual rate of 0.5%.

PERU   Dirección Nacional de Estadística y Censos—"Proyecciones de la población total por sexo y grupos quinquenales de edad, 1960-1980." Documento de trabajo, República del Perú, Instituto Nacional de Planificación, August 1964, p. 12, Table 2.

URUGUAY   Cataldi, Alberto, "Uruguay. Determinación de algunos índices demográficos y proyección de la población total por sexo y edad. 1950-1980." CELADE B.61.2/2.2, Santiago, Chile, 1961. Appendix, p. 19, Table 18.

VENEZUELA   Silvero M. and Arnaldo A., "Proyecciones de la población urbana y rural de Venezuela, en los períodos 1950-1960 y 1960-1980 con especial referencia a la migración interior." CELADE B.63.1/11, Santiago, Chile, 1963, p. 24, Table 10.

7. Health, Population, and Development

ABRAHAM HORWITZ AND MARY H. BURKE

The relationship between health and population is being analyzed today in terms of economic trends. This does not imply that health is not recognized as wealth for each human being, but acknowledges that as a social service it requires an investment of funds from the national income. Following this line of thinking, prevention of diseases, treatment of the ill, and extension of life are interpreted by the effects they have on the investments of current and future funds of each country. These actions are therefore components of development, understanding this as the end result of an increase in the economy and of the structural changes intended to improve the living conditions of the population. To reduce development exclusively to growth in the economy is to forget that it is of at least equal importance to give to each human being the opportunity for self-development, that is, to progress as far as possible in accordance with his biological and cultural heritage. Thus, as income increases, it should be distributed in proper balance between directly productive investments and those which meet the most urgent needs of the population, among them education and health. Even as an efficient economic infrastructure contributes to improving the welfare of communities, a social infrastructure assures the success of the directly productive investments.

Today no economic system is conceived which does not have goals of humanitarianism and social progress. However, the great imbalance between needs and resources in Latin America forces the assignment of priorities to the distribution of funds which, in the absence of programs, do not always correspond to the most prevalent problems or benefit the greatest number of people, either immediately or on a long-term basis. The governments of the region agreed in the Act of Bogotá[1] and the Charter of Punta del Este[2] to plan economic and social development as a harmonic entity, and established general objectives to be achieved in the decade beginning in 1962. Health was included among these goals.

For these reasons we believe that health and development are two variables with the same purpose, the welfare of the population which as it evolves in size and structure requires a realignment in the methods to achieve such a purpose. In other words, we consider societies as differential entities in which it is possible to identify various interacting activities intended to improve the life of its components. It is not possible to attribute exclusively to one of the activities specific effects on the social structure because these usually result from factors operating simultaneously or successively, but never separately. This viewpoint conforms to the ecologic concept which considers health as a reflection of the subtle and continuing process of adaptation of the individual to his environment, which is undergoing constant modification from stimuli of various types. This capacity differentiates man from other living species and allows him to conquer and dominate his environment so as to satisfy his biological and cultural requirements. Health and disease are considered variations in the phenomena of his adaptation to agents of various types which produce specific reactions in different persons. Therefore, there can be no single cause for each disease, but multiple causes from which one is singled out and can usually be identified.

". . . we regard aetiology as the disclosure of a *causal nexus* in contradistinction to the identification of a singular cause. . . . disease, dysfunction, and malformations, no less than what we call characters of the healthy organism, are, like all attributes of a living being, end-products of an immensely intricate interplay between the class of antecedents subsumed by the terms "nature" or "inheritance" as already defined and the class of variables subsumed by the expressions nurture or environment."[3]

Analysis of the consequences which the protection, promotion, and restoration of health have on the size and structure of populations must take into account their close dependency on other factors which contribute to the creation and evolution of life in society. It is in this context that we wish to analyze the problems of health in Latin America, the resources and the instruments which are used to solve them, the progress achieved in the course of this century, and the trends for the future. First, we will present background demographic information which has a direct bearing on this approach.

POPULATION: CHARACTERISTICS AND ESTIMATES OF GROWTH FOR THE AMERICAS

Latin America has at present the highest rate of population growth of the large regions of the world. In Figure 1 is shown the population of the three areas of the Americas from 1920 to 1960 and projections to the year 2000. To make these estimates the United Nations assumed that in Latin America levels of natality, although reduced, would remain high and that there would be a regular decline in mortality. In 1920, the population of Latin America was only 44% of the total for the Americas; in 1960, in contrast, it was slightly over 50%, and if there are no changes from the assumptions on birth-death relationships, it may reach 64% by the year 2000.

By decades since 1920—as is shown in Table 1—the annual growth rate rose from 1.8% between 1920 and 1930 to 2.7% between 1950 and 1960. A maximum growth rate of 2.9% is projected between 1960 and 1970 followed by a gradual decrease to 2.5% in the last decade of the century. Between 1920 and 1960 the population increased from 91,000,000 to 212,000,000; it is predicted that by the year 2000 it will triple, reaching 624,000,000. In contrast, in the same period (1920-2000) in North America the growth rate

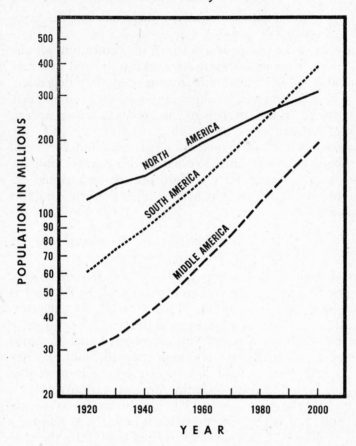

Source: United Nations, Statistical Yearbook, 1958
United Nations, ST/SOA/Series A/28

Figure 1. Growth of population in three regions of the Americas, 1920-1950, and estimated growth, 1950-2000.

fluctuates considerably. From the 117,000,000 in 1920 the population may increase to 354,000,000 at the end of the century.

The growing disparity between birth and death rates, which has been reflected in the accelerated growth of the population, is shown in Figure 2. In Middle America, an-

TABLE 1.

Estimated population of North and Latin America at ten-year intervals, 1920–2000.

Year	Population in millions			Annual percentage increase	
	Total	North America	Latin America	North America	Latin America
1920	208	117	91		
1930	244	135	109	1.44	1.82
1940	277	146	131	0.80	1.85
1950	330	167	163	1.29	2.21
1960	411	199	212	1.77	2.66
1970	509	227	282	1.33	2.89
1980	636	262	374	1.44	2.86
1990	794	306	488	1.56	2.70
2000	978	354	624	1.46	2.49

Source: For 1920–1960, UN *Demographic Yearbooks*.
For 1960–2000, UN, ECOSOC, E/CN.9/186.

nual registered mortality has decreased from 25 per 1,000 in the period 1926-30 to 12 per 1,000 between 1957 and 1961 or, that is, by one-half. In the same years, in South America the existing data show a decrease of one-third in death rates, that is, from 16 to 10.5 per 1,000 population. It is quite probable that registration was at least as deficient in the earlier as in the later period and thus has not accentuated the decrease in rates. Present estimates of mortality rates adjusted for under-registration and lack of data in some countries are 14 per 1,000 population in Middle America and 13 in South America.

On the other hand, birth rates remained at the same high level or increased between 1920 and 1960 in most of the countries of Latin America. Recent data indicate a rate of 43 per 1,000 in Middle America and 34 in South America, excluding Brazil. In Costa Rica, Guatemala, and El Salvador rates are around 50 per 1,000, while in Argentina and Uruguay they are only 22 per 1,000, close to that of the United States.

The natural increase of the population, derived from the difference between births and deaths, has been continuous,

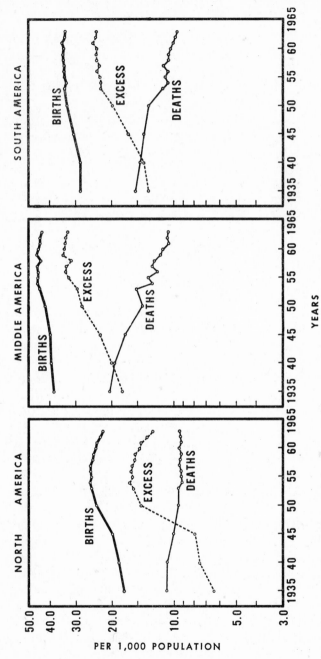

Figure 2. Births, deaths, and excess of births over deaths per 1,000 population in three regions of the Americas, 1935-1963.

reaching 3.4% in 1963 in Middle America and 2.4% in South America, excluding Brazil. In North America it was 1.3% in this same year.

The rate of increase of the population accelerated in the two decades between 1940 and 1960, in varying amounts in the different countries and within the countries. In no country was annual growth greater than 3% in the earlier decade, while in ten it was higher than this in the second, and reached 4% in two.

With regard to age structure, the population of Latin America is young, with its high natality and infant and child mortality, quite different from that in North America. If projections are made of this structure, as in Table 2, significant changes do not appear up to 1980, but between 1980 and 2000 a decrease is expected in the percentage of the population under fifteen years of age. In effect, the numbers of persons in the reproductive ages in 1980 will come from those already born. The size of the group at old ages will be related to present numbers of adults.

TABLE 2.

Percentage distribution of the population by age in North and Latin America, 1960–2000.

	North America			Latin America		
	1960	1980	2000	1960	1980	2000
Under 15 years	31.3	29.9	29.8	41.7	41.6	37.8
15–64 years	59.7	60.7	61.3	55.0	54.4	57.8
65 years and over	9.0	9.4	8.9	3.3	4.0	4.4

Source: UN, ECOSOC, E/CN.9/186.

The urban-rural distribution of the population is a highly variable factor in the Americas. In a few countries a high proportion lives in large cities and in other urban areas, but the opposite is more frequently the case. From addition of data for countries shown in Figure 3, 55% of the population of Latin America is rural and lives in communities of less than 2,000 inhabitants. Projections for 1980 show only 40% living in rural areas.

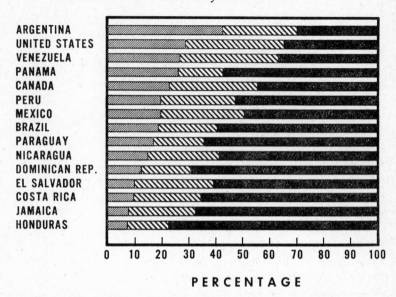

Figure 3. Percentage of population living in cities with 100,000 or more inhabitants, in other urban areas, and in rural areas, according to censuses taken around 1960.

The rapid urbanization in Latin America and, in particular, the migration to the very large cities is one of the most remarkable demographic features in this century. The largest proportion of migrants to the large cities is between 15 and 29 years of age and frequently includes more women than men. During the decade from 1950 to 1960 population in urban localities of 20,000 or more inhabitants increased at an annual rate of 5%. Closely related to urban migration is the steady decrease in the agricultural labor force. However, large numbers are still required to maintain production levels, due to the underdevelopment of agricultural methods in Latin America.

HEALTH PROBLEMS

Health reflects the capacity of each individual to adapt to his continually changing environment. The environment in turn is modified and improved with development, that is, with the application of modern techniques to promote well-being. As a result, all improvements of the environment will react favorably on health and will be the result of man's creativity and work. In the Americas, as in other regions of the world, the health problems in each country reflect the level of development. From an analysis of demographic indices, such as those of morbidity and mortality, the growth rate and age structure of the population, its urban-rural distribution, and the characteristics of the labor force, it is possible to infer the nature of the principal health problems. If these data are related to others of an economic nature—such as national income, industrial and agricultural production, real *per capita* income—and to those which describe the environment—with special reference to sanitation, to nutrition, and to housing—these health problems can be differentiated with even greater clarity. Moreover, they appear as the total of factors which condition diseases and their distribution in each society. These factors are of a biological, economic, historical, and cultural nature.

Available data show that Latin America is beset by infectious diseases, undernourishment, poor sanitation, unhealthful housing and working conditions, illiteracy, lack of proper clothing, and a low *per capita* real income. Together they produce a high general mortality, a high infant and child mortality, (over 40% of all deaths), as well as accidents of pregnancy and motherhood which limit life expectancy at birth. They are also responsible for the poor scholastic performance of school children; for low productivity of the labor force, not to mention a pessimistic outlook on life. The distribution of these health problems among the countries varies as it does among parts of the same country and between cities and rural areas.

It is evident that in the areas and countries of the Americas with a higher socio-economic level, with urbanization and with full industrialization, chronic diseases, both degenerative and mental, as well as accidents, are leading causes of illness. The rest of the region, which includes the greatest part of Latin America, has a predominance of the acute diseases, in particular the infectious diseases.[4] The methods of health protection and promotion, combined with prompt treatment of the ill, can produce effects comparable to those already achieved in the technically advanced countries. The scientific knowledge exists; its application is limited by socio-economic conditions.

There is probably no other group for which this situation is displayed with greater intensity in Latin America than for children under five years of age. As we have seen, they account for more than 40% of total deaths from all causes. The aggressions of the environment on children with a weak reactive capacity to build up immunity are the bases of the

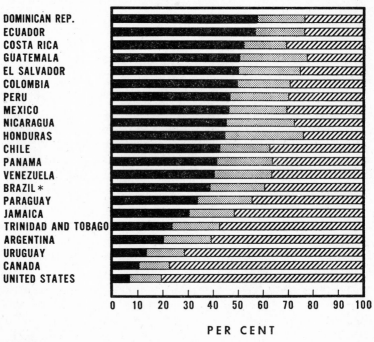

* (STATE OF SÃO PAULO)

Figure 4. Percentage of deaths in three age groups in countries of the Americas, around 1961.

most frequent infectious diseases, in particular the diar-
rhoeas. And the effects are more intense the more deficient
the sanitation and the greater the ignorance. The build-up of
immunity is slower when undernutrition is severe. Also related to this situation are the real income of each family, its
capacity to obtain or to reach the indispensable services, the
weight of customs, of superstitions, and of traditions. This
means that health is an asset in itself for each person, an essential factor for his progress, so that "he may become
better, knowing more." But at the same time in society
health is a component of development from which it benefits
and to which it contributes.

In North America, only 7% of deaths occur among children less than five years of age while in Latin America this
percentage is 42, varying between 58% and 13% in the various countries (Figure 4). The progress to reduce these indices
has been slow in the region, thus giving rise to the objective
in the Charter of Punta del Este to lower mortality of children under five years of age to one-half of the present rates.
In Figures 5 and 6 are shown the trends between the years
1954 and 1963, together with the projected rates in 1970
which would meet this goal. In the countries for which data
are shown, infant mortality in the early years of the present
decade has not been reduced enough to reach the stated objective. In the 30 preceding years, although a greater degree
of under-registration in the earlier periods may in part
conceal the total decrease, the over-all reduction has averaged less than 50% in the same seven countries for which
data are shown in Figures 5 and 6, ranging from 11% in one
country to 62% in another. However, the decline in mortality among children 1 to 4 years of age in the present decade
seems closer to fulfilling the objectives of the Alliance for
Progress.

Mortality early in life looms much greater when fetal
deaths are included. Abortions have reached the level of a
major health problem in many areas. Data from hospitals
show a steady increase in admissions of complicated cases,
and abortions cause a large proportion of maternal deaths.

In all the countries of Latin America the leading causes of

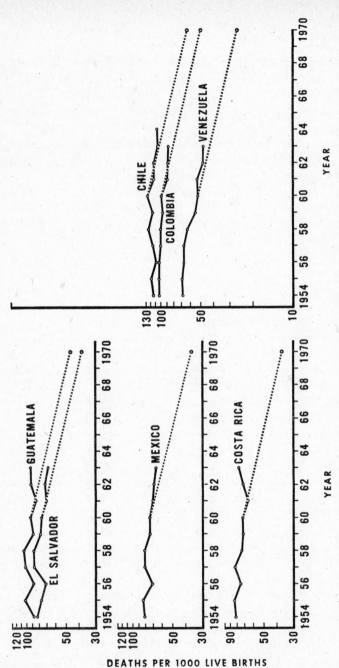

Figure 5. Deaths of children under 1 year of age per 1000 live births, 1954-1963, and projected goal for 1970, in seven Latin American countries.

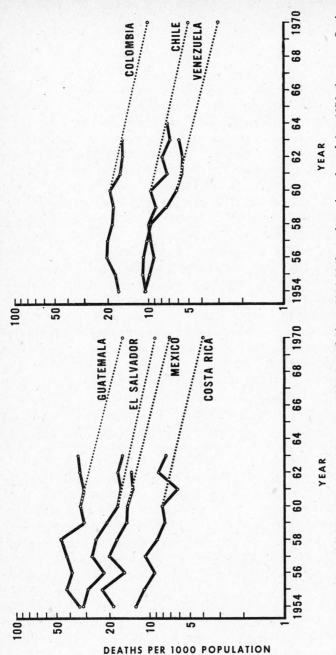

Figure 6. Deaths of children 1-4 years of age per 1000 population, 1954-1963, and projected goal for 1970, in seven Latin American countries.

mortality in infancy and early childhood include gastritis, enteritis, influenza, and pneumonia. In addition, in some countries other infectious diseases—tetanus, measles, malaria, tuberculosis, dysentery, and whooping cough—are also among the principal causes. The distribution by age is shown in Table 3, where avitaminosis and other nutritional deficiency diseases and anemias also appear. The frequent association of nutritional deficiency with other diseases to which death may be ascribed leads to understatements of the impact of nutritional problems in Latin America.

Probably the group 1 to 4 years of age is the one requiring the most concerted action by national health and development programs to reduce, through methods of prevention and early treatment, the excessive illness and deaths. Medical techniques produce lasting results when combined with improvement of nutrition, sanitation, and housing, and the elimination of illiteracy and ignorance. But this process is also true for other population groups. For this reason, social progress is stimulated in proper balance when the funds and resources are concentrated on priority problems. Once the order of importance is established, each problem has its own characteristics and its own methods of solution. It is on this basis that we wish to analyze some of those health problems which are most frequent today in the Americas.

The Great Epidemics and Endemics

With respect to the frequency of the quarantinable diseases which decimated populations in the past, Latin America today is a region in transition where the epidemic is an exception, endemic disease appears with a decreasing incidence, and the chronic diseases already occupy a place among the principal causes of death. Smallpox is an example of this transition. In 1921, around 125,000 cases were reported from six countries; 100,000 were in the United States and the rest in Latin America, where it is likely reporting was very incomplete. In 1947, fourteen countries of the hemisphere reported cases of smallpox, while in 1963 this figure was reduced to five, with a total of 7,126 cases.

TABLE 3.

Ranking of principal causes of death for children under one year old, and age 1–4 years, in 18 Latin American countries, 1962.

Under one year of age

Cause of death	Total*	1st	2nd	3rd	4th	5th
Certain diseases of early infancy	18	16	2	—	—	—
Gastritis, enteritis, etc.	18	2	11	3	—	2
Influenza and pneumonia	18	—	3	10	2	3
Bronchitis	11	—	—	3	6	2
Congenital malformations	10	—	2	—	3	5
Tetanus	8	—	—	2	2	4
Accidents	3	—	—	—	2	1
Malaria	2	—	—	—	1	1
Whooping cough	1	—	—	—	1	—
Measles	1	—	—	—	1	—

1–4 years of age

Cause of death	Total*	1st	2nd	3rd	4th	5th
Gastritis, enteritis, etc.	18	11	3	2	—	2
Influenza and pneumonia	18	4	11	3	—	—
Bronchitis	12	—	1	4	3	4
Measles	11	—	2	3	4	2
Accidents	10	2	1	2	2	3
Whooping cough	5	—	—	1	2	2
Avitaminoses and other metabolic diseases	4	1	—	—	2	1
Congenital malformations	3	—	—	2	—	1
Malignant neoplasms, etc.	3	—	—	—	3	—
Malaria	2	—	—	1	1	—
Diphtheria	1	—	—	—	—	1
Dysentery, all forms	1	—	—	—	1	—
Tuberculosis, all forms	1	—	—	—	—	1
Anemias	1	—	—	—	—	1

* Of countries in which this disease ranked as one of the five principal causes of child death.

In the past year the Pan American Sanitary Bureau received reports of 3,046 cases, of which 80% were in a single country. In this period of 40 years the human race has advanced physically and intellectually due to its own ingenuity, as displayed in scientific and technical progress. Thus, the smallpox virus has been displaced, even though everyone has not been immunized against the disease. Many years ago, exactly 169, Jenner discovered with great intuition a simple and inexpensive method of preventing smallpox. In the Americas many countries have succeeded in eradicating the disease, but an adequate level of immunity is not maintained in all of them sufficient to stop the spread of the virus if eventually it re-enters from outside. In others where the disease is endemic, a systematic program of vaccination has not been organized. The knowledge exists and techniques for application of the vaccine, which is produced in sufficient quantities, have been widely disseminated. The concerted action of the people, of experts, and of governments is essential to end the constant threat of smallpox.

Of similar significance is the problem of yellow fever. At the end of the nineteenth century epidemics were frequent in many countries of the Americas, especially in ports. Today only a limited number of cases are reported. In fact, in the last ten years the highest number reported in a single year was 141 cases, all of jungle origin, while no case of urban yellow fever has occurred since 1954. This has resulted from the continent-wide program for the eradication of *Aedes aegypti* begun in 1947 with a Resolution of the Pan American Health Organization, whose success is a credit to the governments. The vector has been eliminated from all of South America except Venezuela, Surinam, French Guiana, and Cúcuta in Colombia. It has been eradicated also in Mexico and Central America (though re-introduced into El Salvador and Mexico in the summer of 1965) and persists only in the countries and territories of the Caribbean region as well as in the southern United States. Unfortunately, in some areas the mosquito has acquired resistance to the insecticides in use. However, investigations underway give hope for new preparations happily to conclude this continental undertaking.

In 1954 the governments of Latin America gave their support to the eradication of malaria and in 1956 initiated a systematic program in the countries where the disease was

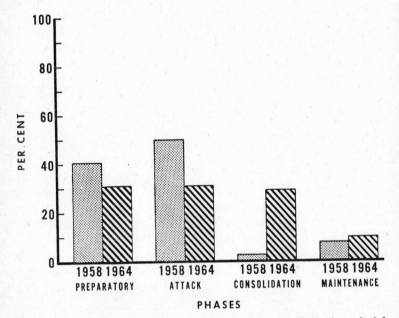

Figure 7. Latin America: Percentage of the population living in malarial areas, 1958 and 1964, by phase of malaria eradication campaign.

prevalent. In Figure 7 is shown the progress achieved. In 1956, the population of malarial areas was 87,951,000 persons. At the end of 1964 the inhabitants in the same areas had increased in number to 112,131,000.

In the short period of seven years, malaria has been almost completely eradicated from an area in which more than 43 million people live and work so that it remains only a potential danger, in view of its existence in other regions of the Americas from which it can be reintroduced by migration, internal or external. This requires rigorous and constant vigi-

lance by health services. Not only have the people been successful in improving their living conditions and their future
but the countries have increased their natural resources in
previously unpopulated areas with a rich potential for agriculture and economic development. The 69 million others
still in malarial areas expect to obtain similar benefits. This
will be possible if the governments and the international organizations maintain their dedicated support, if technicians
apply proven knowledge in an efficient manner, and if research discovers new methods to accelerate the process.
These conditions have become most urgent for solving the
so-called "problem areas" which, by definition, are those
where the transmission of malaria has not been interrupted
despite a well planned program. These areas exist in 13
countries and two territories with an estimated population of
7 million. Through research, characteristics of the epidemic
have been identified which justify the application of additional measures. Of value are the trials of mass preventive
treatment of the population; the use of larvicides; trials of
new insecticides with residual action; methods of overcoming
the repellent capacity induced by DDT. These studies
should be intensified in the laboratory and in the field. At
the same time it will be necessary to understand the nature
of the relations between parasite and man, and the essence of
immunity to malaria; for on this basis it should be possible to
find a method of protection which would surely respond
better to the characteristics of the disease.

In two recent seminars[5] in which health authorities of all
the countries of the region participated, the role of the general health services in various phases of the malaria eradication program was analyzed. There was agreement that a
greater coordination between the general health services and
the malaria service was needed. The measures which should
be adapted for this were specified. Evidence was presented of
the inadequate coverage of extensive rural areas of the Americas with minimal health services, especially of areas in the
consolidation phase. Therefore it did not appear possible to
maintain the spectacular results from a control or eradication

program for a communicable disease without some form of health services which have a fundamental role to play throughout development of the program. As organized activities to eradicate malaria continue, their coordination with normal activities of the various units of the health ministries should proceed.

Schistosomiasis, produced by *Schistosoma mansoni,* is endemic in the Dominican Republic, Puerto Rico, Antigua, Guadeloupe, Martinique, and Santa Lucia. It also occurs in Venezuela and Surinam, and is widespread in Brazil. It is estimated that there are now 5.5 million infected persons in the region, of which 5 million are in Brazil, principally in coastal states. Schistosomiasis is a chronic debilitating disease which lowers productivity and affects the economy by increasing the cost of public health and medical care. The control of the disease is based on the interruption of the cycle of the parasite by means of sanitation, and measures directed against the snail, which acts as an intermediate host. Wherever there are extensive irrigation programs, steps should be taken to avoid outbreaks, because irrigation tends to spread the sources of infection.

Chagas' disease is endemic in large areas of South America, especially in Argentina, Brazil, Chile, Paraguay, Uruguay, Colombia, and Venezuela. The disease extends north through Central America to Mexico where the incidence is believed to be very low. In certain states of Brazil the frequency is very high and produces a high mortality in adolescents and adults from myocardial complications and "megasyndromes" of the digestive system and other organs. Chagas' disease is not only a problem of health but one of wellbeing, closely related to the quality of housing. Effective methods are known for the control of the vectors, which should be systematically applied. However, the basic need is for improvement in housing in the extensive endemic areas of Latin America. In addition, longitudinal epidemiological studies are essential to establish the pattern of the disease and its consequences in the areas in which it is prevalent in the region.

Only two cases of cholera—both laboratory-acquired infections in June and July, 1965—have been reported in the Americas since 1911.

The incidence of exanthematic typhus, epidemic and murine, has decreased markedly. Epidemic outbreaks are an exception and the number of reported cases is relatively low. In 1964, the Pan American Sanitary Bureau was informed of 281 cases of epidemic typhus. The extensive use of insecticides with residual action to which the vectors of typhus are sensitive has had an influence on the reduction but it is not easy to determine the extent.

Foci of bubonic plague persist in border areas of Peru and Ecuador, in Venezuela, Bolivia, northeast Brazil, and in the western United States. Forest reservoirs are the source of the increase in incidence and of some epidemic outbreaks in recent years, especially in Ecuador where they have been a grave danger to the economy and commercial exports. 423 and 653 cases were reported in 1963 and 1964, respectively. A control program in areas known to have a high incidence is urgent, particularly in the ports, while studies proceed to determine the epidemic cycle of the disease in the forest.

The progress in the reduction of tuberculosis in the last 15 to 20 years is impressive (Figure 8). Registered mortality rates have been reduced to one-third of those in 1946. To this have contributed, in varying degree, chemotherapy and antibiotics, vaccination with BCG (Bacillus Calmette-Guérin), early diagnosis and treatment, and, of no less value, the relative improvement in socio-economic and environmental conditions. To all these factors should be added the education that has been disseminated in urban communities on the possibilities of recovery with modern methods, alleviating the terror of the inevitable which used to influence attitudes toward the disease. However, much needs to be done to achieve the mortality rates of technically advanced countries. The attack against tuberculosis should be planned and evaluated as a permanent process which includes measures

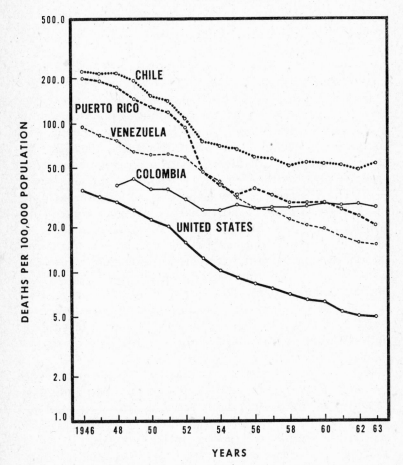

Figure 8. Deaths from tuberculosis per 100,000 population in five areas of the Americas, 1946-1963.

for prevention and treatment as a part of the activities of existing health services, whatever their level of development. In this way a more rational use will be made of available resources, obtaining better results at a smaller cost within the general health program. An indispensable complement to this plan is the proper combination of medical techniques with those of development and welfare. Another essential element of equal or greater importance to be included in the process of coordination is nutrition.

Nutrition

High death rates in infancy and early childhood are one of the most severe consequences of malnutrition. As has been pointed out, a health goal of the Charter of Punta del Este is to cut these death rates in half in the period 1962-72. This should contribute greatly to increasing average life expectancy at birth by five years as is proposed in the same document. However, this will not be possible through the exclusive action of techniques of individual and community medicine, which, although essential, require the simultaneous action of all techniques which promote development and improve nutrition. Among the last are the production, conservation, distribution, and consumption of fundamental foods—animal and vegetable proteins. To the lack of these, in any analysis of the problem of undernutrition, must be added the low purchasing power of families, and the influence of customs and tradition on the appreciation of the value of certain foods.

Figure 9 shows the relation between population growth and total and *per capita* production of food in North and Latin America. In the former both variables have increased annually, resulting in a relatively constant and sufficient average quantity of food per person. In Latin America, between 1953 and 1958, production of food increased rapidly, at the same or faster rate than the population. Since 1958 the upward trend has continued but at a slower pace, resulting in 1963 in a lower *per capita* amount of food than in 1953. To this problem must be added the present tendency to produce food for export, thus diminishing that available for the population. In Figure 10 are shown the hours of work required in seven countries to buy three basic foods. The comparisons are made on the basis of average income of skilled workers in selected cities. While in the United States they earn enough in twenty minutes to buy one kilo of meat, in five countries

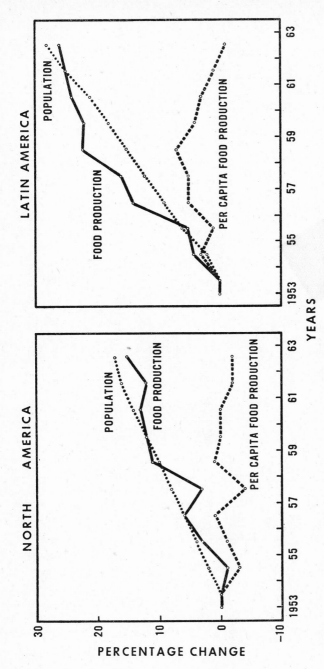

Figure 9. Percentage change in total and per capita food production and in population in North and Latin America from 1953-54 to 1962-3.

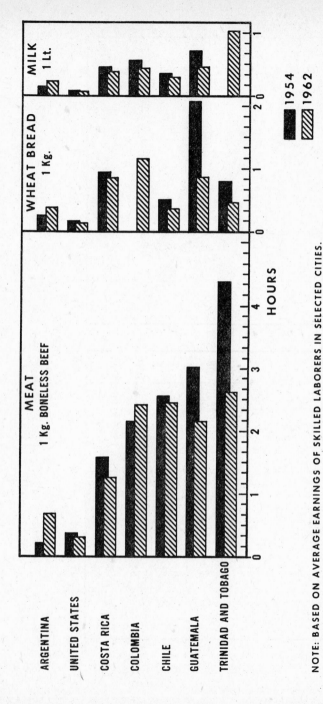

NOTE: BASED ON AVERAGE EARNINGS OF SKILLED LABORERS IN SELECTED CITIES.

Figure 10. Work-time required to purchase three basic foods in selected countries of the Americas, 1954 and 1962.

they must work over one hour and a half to accomplish this. A similar situation is observed for other basic foods.

"With regard to basic nutritional requirements, quite apart from the well known and persistent deficiency in proteins and protective foodstuffs, in 1964 the available daily food supply was still below the minimum of 2,500 calories per person in 14 countries and under 2,000 calories in three countries. As a remedy the governments resort to the import of essential food, which reached $900 million in 1962-63 and an even higher figure in the following year."[6] This emphasizes the need to accelerate modernization of the techniques of land cultivation, reform in its use and tenancy, and the study of the indispensable crops in relation to environmental conditions and the social and cultural characteristics of the countries of Latin America. At the same time, a redefinition of agricultural policy is essential to balance the food requirements of the population against the need for foreign exchange derived from exports. We believe that not all countries will be able to produce everything their populations need—here is the advantage of the common market; however, it does not seem right to promote the cultivation of crops which promise good income but which have no nutritive value. In such a redefinition must be included the modernization of methods of conservation, distribution, and consumption of food, even if the expense appears to be enormous (and it would be of interest to measure it), and in each of these areas there are reasonably proven methods.

The nutritional responsibilities of the ministries of health and agriculture in the communities are not clearly delineated. As a result, it is left to the decision of the families, according to their income, their customs, and the available food, without the benefit of educational work to guide them in improving their diet with what is available. By maintaining continuing relations with the communities, the ministries of health should incorporate a nutrition program into their normal activities. This should include not only the prevention and treatment of the most prevalent diseases such as protein-calorie malnutrition, anemia and goiter—which have a higher frequency—but also improvement of the average diet by more consumption of basic foods. Education is basic, but must begin with school children by teaching new diet habits.

The research developed by the Institute of Nutrition of Central America and Panama on mixtures of vegetable proteins of a nutritional value comparable to milk deserves special mention. Utilization of cotton seed in a preparation called "Incaparina" has had excellent results and at a cost within reach of rural families. This substance is now being produced in Guatemala and Colombia, and it is hoped that this will also take place in other Latin American countries. Meanwhile, studies continue to identify other indigenous foods which contain vegetable protein of nutritional value.

> Hunger is still a disease of millions. And this should not be, for man has managed to overcome the caprices of nature in order to provide the essential food in quantity and quality for life and reproduction of the species. He has acquired through the centuries the knowledge and means to control the process of providing food to the extent that now it is the environmental factor most susceptible to his orders. However there is much evidence of the failure in the world today to exercise an intelligent and constant control on this phase of the environment. Therefore hunger is still a disease of millions and affects more severely children under 5 years of age, pregnant women, nursing mothers and the laborers whose work demands a large expenditure of energy.[7]

Environmental Health

Environmental health exerts a significant influence on the socio-economic progress of Latin America. There exist great deficiencies in housing, in water supplies, in sewerage systems, and in control of contamination of air and water. However, great progress is occurring.

The normal existence and growth of a community depends on a sufficient quantity of potable water. Its lack creates serious health problems, degrades living conditions, hampers business and industrial development, and is a major obstacle to economic and social welfare. This was recognized

in the Charter of Punta del Este which established the goal
". . . to supply potable water and sewage disposal for at least 70
per cent of the urban population and 50 per cent of the rural
population during the present decade as a minimum."[8] On
analyzing this objective the Task Force on Health at the
Ministerial Level recommended that these programs should
be intensified to the maximum in urban areas, basing them
on self-financing methods through reasonable interest rates
and an organization with sound administrative principles.[9]

For 1961, estimates were made of the population needing
water in urban and rural areas and of the costs of construction to reach the goals of the Charter in 1971. Table 4 shows
these estimates by country and the totals for the region. The
magnitude of the financial and administrative task is evident. To these resources must be added as essential elements
the determination of the government, the motivation of the
communities to contribute reasonably toward the installation and maintenance of the systems, and the support of international sources of capital.

During the last five years dramatic advances in the provision of potable water have been made by many countries of
Latin America. Activity has been concentrated on the extension and improvement of existing systems in capitals and
large cities. The trend today is to include more communities
of moderate size in the program. In rural areas most projects
involve new installations. Table 5 summarizes the international loans from 1960 to 1964 for water and sewerage systems, by country and source, with accumulated totals which
have reached $309,897,829, and the contribution from na-
tional funds, totalling $527,572,987, an investment which
benefits around 40,000,000 persons. The Inter-American Development Bank has been the largest contributor of foreign
capital. In the short period of four years it has become the
principal agency financing economic and social progress in
Latin America. In addition, the Bank has displayed leadership in initiating economic integration and related policy to
accomplish it. The Agency for International Development of
the United States has also contributed substantial amounts to

TABLE 4.

Ten-year plan for water supply in urban and rural areas in Latin America, 1961-71.

Country	Estimated urban population (in thousands)				Average number to be supplied yearly (in thousands)	Annual cost of construction at $50 per capita (in $1000 U.S.)	Estimated rural population (in thousands)				Average number to be supplied yearly (in thousands)	Annual cost of construction (in $1000 U.S.)	
	Total		Without water				Total		Without water			at $10 per capita	at $15 per capita
	1961	1971	1961	1971			1961	1971	1961	1971			
Total	101,661	147,630	41,297	87,266	4,441.9	233,248	107,000	128,009	—	—	5,825.6	58,256	87,385
Argentina	15,531	18,743	5,385	8,597	297.4	14,870	5,570	6,744	5,495	6,669	329.7	3,297	4,946
Bolivia	1,448	2,120	640	1,312	67.6	3,380	2,367	2,755	—	—	137.8	1,378	2,067
Brazil	32,963	49,807	14,932	31,776	1,683.4	84,170	40,125	48,300	—	—	2,415.0	24,150	36,225
Chile	4,874	6,830	1,285	3,241	143.8	7,190	2,486	2,610	2,086	2,190	90.5	905	1,358
Colombia	6,289	9,437	1,334	4,482	248.1	12,405	8,663	10,587	5,171	7,095	180.2	1,802	2,703
Costa Rica	421	676	—	264	25.0	1,250	766	969	487	690	20.6	206	309
Cuba	3,855	5,100	1,673	2,918	138.8	10,410[a]	3,121	3,452	—	—	172.6	1,726	2,589
Dominican Republic	867	1,580	375	1,088	61.4	3,070	2,095	2,556	1,719	2,180	90.2	902	1,353
Ecuador	1,248	2,337	522	1,611	91.0	4,550	3,183	3,533	—	—	177.0	1,770	2,655
El Salvador	799	1,403	322	936	51.5	2,575	1,675	1,854	875	1,602	92.7	927	1,390
Guatemala	961	1,206	590	439	47.3	2,365	2,900	3,628	—	—	80.1	801	1,202
Haiti	402	541	300	667	27.7	1,385	3,700	4,740	3,700	4,740	237.0	2,370	3,555
Honduras	618	879	406	—	40.3	2,015	1,373	1,703	1,270	1,600	75.0	750	1,125
Mexico	18,398	28,152	8,316	18,070	962.4	48,120	17,490	20,359	—	—	1,018.0	10,180	15,270
Nicaragua	568	890	353	675	40.8	2,040	950	1,164	947	1,161	57.9	579	868
Panama	514	741	81	308	19.1	955	574	703	—	—	35.2	352	528
Paraguay	624	980	452	808	51.4	2,570	1,146	1,220	1,146	1,220	61.0	610	915
Peru	4,878	7,288	1,517	3,927	174.1	8,705	5,487	7,620	—	—	381.0	3,810	5,715
Uruguay	1,750	1,950	460	660	14.7	735	620	680	605	665	32.5	325	488
Venezuela	4,653	6,970	2,335	4,652	256.1	20,488[a]	2,709	2,832	—	—	141.6	1,416	2,124

[a] At $75 per capita for Cuba, and $80 for Venezuela.

NOTE: "Urban" refers to cities of 2,000 or more inhabitants, except for Colombia (5,000) and Cuba (1,000).

TABLE 5.

Funds allotted for the construction of water and sewerage systems in Latin America (1960–64) (U. S. Dollars).

Country	Inter-American Development Bank		International Bank for Reconstruction and Development	Agency for International Development	Export-Import Bank	Estimated contributions from Governments	Estimated population benefited
	Water	Sewerage	Water	Water and sewerage[a]	Water		
Argentina	5,500,000	—	—	—	—	8,800,000	1,970,000
Brazil	55,110,000	14,650,000	—	12,300,000	—	62,230,000	13,400,000
Chile	11,145,000	—	—	2,840,000	—	10,604,000	1,580,000
Colombia	26,165,930	7,833,000	—	8,000,000	—	36,334,158	6,030,000
Costa Rica	100,000[b]	140,000	—	5,400,000	4,500,000	2,450,000	550,000
Dominican Republic	1,340,000	—	—	—	9,000,000	1,260,000	190,000
Ecuador	5,200,000	3,568,000	—	—	—	2,933,000	1,300,000
El Salvador	7,680,000	1,520,000	—	—	—	4,540,000	1,950,000
Guatemala	5,730,000	1,200,000	—	—	—	4,285,000	440,000
Haiti	2,360,000	—	—	3,050,000	—	160,000	280,000
Honduras	2,550,000	—	—	3,700,000	—	650,000	400,000
Jamaica	—	—	—	—	—	—	200,000
Mexico	8,650,000	500,000	3,000,000	—	—	6,080,000	1,730,000
Nicaragua	—	185,000[b]	—	600,000	—	3,000,000	240,000
Panama	2,762,000	—	—	9,815,000	8,250,000	2,553,000	720,000
Paraguay	—	—	—	1,000,000	6,500,000	—	540,000
Peru	4,389,539	1,171,360	—	8,800,000	1,900,000	7,939,000	1,410,000
Uruguay	5,743,000	2,500,000	—	—	7,500,000	18,257,000	3,120,000
Venezuela	36,000,000	—	—	—	—	45,600,000	2,370,000
Total[c]	180,425,469	33,317,360	3,000,000	55,505,000	37,650,000	217,675,158	38,420,000

— None.

[a] The amount allotted for potable water projects cannot be separated from that for sewerage projects but the proportion for sewerage is known to be low.

[b] Loans solely for studies.

[c] International loans, $309,897,829; contributions of governments for the same projects, $217,675,158.

the sanitation program. The Export-Import Bank and the International Bank for Reconstruction and Development have also supplied smaller amounts. While it is obvious that the rate of investment and construction must be accelerated, nevertheless the advances which have been made are significant for health and the economy, and the goals set appear reasonable. Venezuela is an excellent example of a country which has achieved its objective. Under the goals of the Charter of Punta del Este, 230,000 new persons in urban areas in Venezuela were to be provided with water service each year between 1961 and 1971. By December 1964, 3,200,000 persons should have had water service in their homes. Actually the number reached 3,856,000, and funds budgeted for the coming years exceed the amounts needed to meet the goal. The rural situation in Venezuela is developing similarly.

However, the rural problems of the region are especially serious, both in size and difficulty of solution, due to the primitive methods of land cultivation, the lack of industrial decentralization and the very low average income of the population, the tendency to migrate to cities, and the erroneous interpretation of the attitude of individuals and communities in rural areas as reflected in ancestral customs. To meet the objectives of the Charter it will be necessary to provide basic sanitation services to 58 million persons who live in communities of less than 2,000 inhabitants.

The Task Force of Ministers of Health recommended that the Pan American Sanitary Bureau study the establishment of a Special Fund for Rural Welfare, based on contributions from the governments, from foreign capital, and from organized communities whose inhabitants would contribute in addition by working on the installation of services. The proposal was presented at the XIVth Meeting of the Directing Council of the Pan American Health Organization, and the XVth Meeting of the Regional Committee of the World Health Organization for the Americas in 1963.[10] This idea has not yet crystallized. However, the foundation has been laid and has been proved practical in the experience of the last two years.

It is even more evident today that it will not be possible to resolve the problem of rural sanitation—and the entire rural question—without motivating the communities to coordinate their efforts for the common good. We believe rural inhabitants of Latin America have been waiting for this stimulus, to which they will react positively when they observe that the objective is their own welfare. In their response they reveal their sense of responsibility in organizing to carry out works for community improvement to which they contribute their labor, money, and other resources. Moreover, they have

TABLE 6.

Latin America: Estimates of housing deficit, annual requirements, and annual construction. *
(Thousands of units).

	Estimated Deficit[1]			Housing Units Required Annually to meet Population Growth and Replacement Needs[2]			Annual Construction Total
	Urban	Rural	Total	Urban	Rural	Total	
Argentina	800	400	1,200	121.6	30.9	152.5	55.0
Bolivia	100	280	380	8.0	10.8	18.8	5.0
Brazil	3,000	4,000	7,000	277.0	179.0	456.0	150.0
Chile	270	130	400	45.0	7.4	52.4	33.0
Colombia	300	500	800	72.0	28.8	100.8	40.0
Costa Rica	30	70	100	6.8	4.5	11.3	3.0
Dominican Republic	60	140	200	12.3	11.8	24.1	4.0
Ecuador	180	320	500	15.1	13.6	28.7	4.0
El Salvador	60	140	200	8.5	6.4	14.9	2.0
Guatemala	110	390	500	12.6	11.4	24.0	2.0
Honduras	30	100	130	6.3	7.0	13.3	3.0
Mexico	1,000	600	1,600	194.0	85.3	279.3	57.0
Nicaragua	50	100	150	5.9	3.8	9.7	1.2
Panama	30	70	100	5.2	3.0	8.2	2.5
Paraguay	30	120	150	5.1	2.1	7.2	1.0
Peru	370	450	820	46.3	22.5	68.8	10.0
Uruguay	40	60	100	14.6	2.9	17.5	11.0
Venezuela	500	100	600	54.3	8.6	62.9	40.0
	6,960	7,970	14,930	910.6	439.8	1,350.4	423.7

[1] *Source:* United Nations, Economic Commission for Latin America.
[2] Obtained from various sources.
* *Source:* Inter-American Development Bank, Social Progress Trust Fund, Fourth Annual Report, 1964, page 117.

learned their own value in a cooperative endeavor. The success of the program in three countries, and the formulation of similar projects in eight, has resulted from this initiative in 1964. To its materialization the Inter-American Development Bank has contributed.

The problems of urban and rural sewage disposal are very great in Latin America. In Middle and South America only 17% and 47%, respectively, of the urban population live in houses connected to sewerage systems. Considerable progress has been made, but at a slower rate than for water services. Similar problems exist with respect to housing. Table 6 shows the estimated deficit of houses, the requirements and the annual construction in eighteen countries of the region. Among the factors to which this situation is attributed are the lack of a defined policy in the responsible agencies; domestic financing problems which delay or hinder the utilization of foreign loans; the lack of technicians at the intermediate level; and a weakness in the system of administrative regulations and procedures. An additional problem is the high cost of construction attributed in large part to inefficient and traditional building methods.[11] The influence of housing on health is evident.

HEALTH RESOURCES

Of all resources the most essential are people, that is, the university-trained professionals and their auxiliaries, to carry out functions of prevention and treatment of disease and of health promotion. To determine their number and quality, a comprehensive study is underway in Colombia sponsored by the Ministry of Health, the Association of Medical Schools, the Milbank Memorial Fund and the Pan American Health Organization. Through a stratified survey of the population a profile of the health conditions is being obtained based on indices of morbidity and mortality and on the results of various special studies, including an estimate of the effective demand and need for such services. From the findings, data will be assembled on the number of health technicians now needed, together with projections for the coming years. At the same time, information is being obtained as the basis for improving and expanding medical education and other disciplines in Colombia. It is hoped that the methods and procedures used will be applicable in other countries, taking into consideration that the estimates currently being used represent experience in societies where health conditions are very different, as are their requirements for professional personnel and institutions.

Although such studies have considerable value for rational programming, the lack of technicians and of health units to cover the entire territory of each country and to serve the increasing population in the next decade is, nevertheless, evident. Even on the basis of very incomplete information, it is clear that there are extensive rural areas in Latin America which have no health services. This is due in large part to the lack of trained staffs and to the inadequate living conditions offered to such staffs in these areas of extreme underdevelopment. Education and training of various types of professionals, technicians, and health auxiliaries in growing numbers, will be essential to meet present and future demand. At the same time, new or expanded educational institutions will have to be provided. For various professions requiring extensive years of education careful programming will be needed. However, many activities can be carried out, particularly in rural areas, by well-trained auxiliaries under adequate supervision.

The plans to prepare specialists and technicians in each country for future years must take into consideration factors such as the growth of the population, the needs and demands of health in relation to socio-economic development for both urban and rural areas, activities for prevention and cure of disease, the changing patterns of health services, the progress of science, and the nature of the health problems.

In Table 7 the number of physicians, the ratios per 10,000 population, the number of medical schools, and the annual number of graduates are shown for the countries and territories of the Americas around 1962. In South and Middle America there are less than half as many physicians as in North America. However, there are now comparable numbers of both medical schools and graduates in Latin and

TABLE 7.

Number of physicians, schools of medicine, and medical graduates, with ratios of physicians per 10,000 population in the Americas, recent years.

Area	Year	Physicians Number	Physicians Ratio	Medical Schools Number	Medical Schools Graduates (annual)[a]	Area	Year	Physicians Number	Physicians Ratio	Medical Schools Number	Medical Schools Graduates (annual)[a]
North America	1962	281,441	13.8	98	7,940	Antigua	1962	17	2.9	—	—
Middle America	1963	34,207	4.9	33	1,696[b]	Bahama Islands	1962	65	5.9	—	—
South America	1960	88,936	6.0	70	4,659[b]	Barbados	1962	82	3.5	—	—
Argentina	1962	31,831	14.9	9	1,770	Bermuda	1960	37	8.4	—	—
Bolivia	1963	1,032	2.9	3	55	British Guiana	1960	145	2.6	—	—
Brazil	1960	26,392	3.7	31	1,342	British Honduras	1962	20	2.1	—	—
Canada	1962	21,000	11.3	12	817	Canal Zone	1962	103	22.9	—	—
Chile	1961	4,729	6.0	4	220	Cayman Islands	1962	3	3.8	—	—
Colombia	1962	7,453	5.0	7	442	Dominica	1960	8	1.3	—	—
Costa Rica	1962	575	4.5	1	—	Falkland Islands	1962	4	20.0	—	—
Cuba	1962	5,841	8.3	2	335	French Guiana	1962	23	6.8	—	—
Dominican Republic	1960	442[c]	1.5	1	85	Grenada	1962	20	2.2	—	—
Ecuador	1962	1,620	3.5	3	—	Guadeloupe	1962	122	4.2	—	—
El Salvador	1961	526	2.1	1	29	Martinique	1962	122	4.1	—	—
Guatemala	1962	954	2.4	1	35	Montserrat	1962	3	2.3	—	—
Haiti	1961	400	0.9	1	41	Netherlands Antilles	1960	137	7.2	—	—
Honduras	1957	365	2.2	1	34	Puerto Rico	1962	1,721	7.0	1	45
Jamaica	1961	655	4.0	1	25	St. Kitts, Nevis and Anguilla	1962	12	2.0	—	—
Mexico	1960	20,590	5.7	21	1,011	St. Lucia	1962	10	1.1	—	—
Nicaragua	1960	524	3.5	1	22	St. Pierre and Miquelon	1962	4	8.0	—	—
Panama	1962	502	4.4	1	14	St. Vincent	1960	10	1.2	—	—
Paraguay	1962	1,082	5.8	1	97	Surinam	1960	149	5.5	1	6
Peru	1962	6,010	5.7	4	378	Turks and Caicos Islands	1962	2	3.3	—	—
Trinidad and Tobago	1962	350	3.9	—	—	Virgin Islands (U.K.)	1962	2	2.5	—	—
United States	1962	260,400	14.0	86	7,123	Virgin Islands (U.S.)	1960	24	7.3	—	—
Uruguay	1962	2,700	9.3	1	91						
Venezuela	1962	5,766	7.3	6	258						

[a] Data usually for 1960 for WHO World Directory of Medical Schools, Third Edition, 1964. Other sources include the following: Supplement to the Second Report on the World Health Situation (Cuba, Guatemala, Peru); Anuario Estadístico do Brasil, 1963, Brazil; Servicio Nacional de Salud, Desarrollo Socioeconómico y Planificación, 1963, Chile; Medical Education in the United States, 1961–1962, JAMA, Vol. 182 (Canada, United States and Puerto Rico); Demografía; 1961, Dirección de Estadística y Censo, Panama.
[b] Incomplete.
[c] Ministry of Health only.

North America. In the last twenty years the number of medical schools in Latin America has been doubled, reaching 108 in 1964.

From the available data on physicians in Latin America in 1962 estimates have been made of the number required for 1980, if the same ratios of physicians to population are to be maintained. For the present population of 244 million there are now an estimated 134,000 physicians, or 5.5 per 10,000 population. To have the same services available in 1980 for a projected population of 374 million, 206,000 physicians will be needed, an increase of 72,000. During the next 15 years some physicians will withdraw from practice through death, disability, or retirement. Assuming this loss is 1% per year, and it may be greater, over 15 years it will amount to roughly 15%, or 25,000 physicians who must be replaced to maintain the original ratio. Thus, approximately 97,000 physicians should be trained in the next 15 years. The present 108 medical schools now graduate approximately 6,500 physicians per year, which in the next 15 years would total close to 100,000 physicians. From this it appears that by continuing as at present, it should be possible to maintain the present availability of physicians in Latin America.

These estimates, based on incomplete data, do not imply that the situation is the same or satisfactory in all countries. The ratio of physicians ranges from 14.9 in Argentina to 0.9 per 10,000 population in Haiti; moreover, it is below 3 per 10,000 in six countries. However, every country except Trinidad and Tobago has at least one medical school, and much can be done to strengthen existing schools by improving the quality of the instruction, by providing internships, and by increasing the number of students where teaching resources and materials permit. When the needs of the country clearly indicate that new schools are essential, it will be necessary to establish them, for the problem will not be solved—possibly it would be aggravated—by over-saturating the present schools at the risk of educating physicians incapable as professionals of advancing their own preparation.

Considering that for many of the principal health problems in Latin America preventive measures are available to reduce their incidence, the proportion of 5.5 physicians per 10,000 population is not excessively low. With their services and experience it should be possible to accelerate the decrease in morbidity and mortality provided the geographical distribution of physicians were better in relation to needs. Table 8 presents this problem in the countries of Latin America. For each are shown the number of physicians who work in capitals and in large cities of 500,000 or more inhabitants, and the number in the rest of the country. 21% of the population of Latin America lives in the first group of cities served by 54% of the physicians. By country, the ratios of physicians in these cities vary between 7 and 29 per 10,000 inhabitants. In the second group, which includes the smaller cities and the rural areas, the inhabitants form 79% of the country total, the physicians 46%, and by country the ratios

TABLE 8.

Latin America: Number of physicians, and ratios per 10,000 population in capitals and large cities, and in remainder of these countries, in 13 countries, around 1962.

Country	Year	Capital and large cities [a]		Remainder of country	
		Physicians	Ratio	Physicians	Ratio
Total		56,653	15.1	48,159	3.4
Argentina	1962	20,353	28.8	11,478	8.0
Bolivia	1963	456	9.7	576	1.8
Brazil	1960	11,684	12.8	14,708	2.4
Chile	1960	2,929	11.4	1,692	3.3
Colombia	1962	3,784	7.4	3,669	3.8
Costa Rica	1962	408	9.3	167	2.0
El Salvador	1960	329	7.3	176	0.9
Guatemala	1958	571	10.1	159	0.5
Mexico	1960	10,047	11.9	11,094	4.2
Nicaragua	1960	246	9.0	278	2.3
Panama	1960	245	9.1	156	2.0
Peru	1957	2,843	19.2	998	1.3
Venezuela	1962	2,758	21.0	3,008	4.6

[a] Includes federal districts, capital cities or departments with capital city, and other cities of at least 500,000 population, or departments with a city of 500,000 population or more.

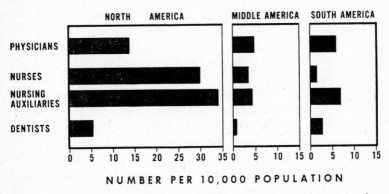

Figure 11. Number of physicians, nurses, nursing auxiliaries and dentists per 10,000 population in the three regions of the Americas, 1962.

of physicians vary from 0.5 to 8 per 10,000 population. The variation in development within each country of Latin America is reflected in the distribution of those with university training. Regionalization of services has been proposed as one solution, together with the improved use of services of technicians and auxiliaries, while intensifying the efforts to graduate more physicians.

The lack of nursing resources, probably the most serious deficiency with respect to health personnel in Latin America, is seen in Figure 11. The inverse relation of the ratio of physicians to nurses in Middle and South America as compared to North America stands out. As has been said, we cannot hope to solve in this generation the rural health problems exclusively with university graduates. Auxiliaries must be trained to assume greater responsibilities, and the time of the university graduates must be directed to the more difficult functions and to supervision. This is the orientation of the present policy of the governments and of the international organizations which stresses obtaining from the resources a production adapted to the needs.

The number of dentists in Latin America is also insufficient. As seen in Figure 11, the ratio per 10,000 population is one-seventh in Middle America and one-half in South America of that of North America. In 1965, there were in Latin America an estimated 51,000 dentists, a number which should be increased to 79,000 in 1980 to maintain the 1965 ratio. Approximately 3,000 are graduated annually, or an estimated 45,000 in a 15-year period. Clearly, the universities are equipped to educate enough dentists to maintain the present level of services, providing for the increase in the population and for replacements for those who retire. However, the present ratio of dentists to population is inadequate by all standards. Part of the problem will be solved through preventive measures, such as the fluoridation of water. In any case, it is essential to improve the present teaching and to prepare the additional dentists each country requires. With the exception of Jamaica and Trinidad and Tobago, all countries have dental schools, graduating each year an average of 20 dentists per school in Middle America and 40 in South America. The possibilities for improvement and expansion are evident.

In view of the priority placed on environmental health programs, particularly water supply, it is urgent to expand the education of sanitary engineers. With the exception of Argentina and Brazil there are approximately 300 engineers working in health services in Latin America and another 1,700 in ministries of public works, in *municipios,* and in other agencies concerned with construction of water supplies and sewerage systems. 4,000 engineers are needed immediately, and possibly 8,000 additional. Schools in Latin America have been graduating around 100 each year, and schools in other countries prepare another 20 annually for Latin America. With contributions from the Special Fund of the United Nations, teaching programs have been initiated in four universities of Venezuela and in Rio de Janeiro for this purpose. Organization of similar courses in other countries is planned. Also, for the past two years special short courses for engineers have been given on selected problems of environmental health.

Sanitary inspectors, too, have an important function to carry out in the installation of basic sanitation services. Presently around 7,500 are working in health services in Latin

America, but twice as many are required to meet the most urgent needs.

A comparable situation exists for other professional groups, technicians, and auxiliaries who are indispensable for the complex tasks of promoting health and preventing and curing diseases of man and animal diseases transmitted to man. In the society of today, health, as a social function, is one of those which requires the greatest diversity of specialists. Their preparation and training is essential and should be continuous.

Health Services

As with education and training, it will be necessary to increase the output of the present health services and to improve their quality, not only to meet the needs of the present population but of the increased numbers in the next decades. This planning applies to health centers and to hospitals, and also to the various ministerial units.

Latin America presents a somewhat discordant situation in that the possibility does exist for caring for a greater number of patients and accomplishing more preventive activities with the institutions and facilities available at present. At the same time, there is a deficiency, if we are not content with minimum standards, in relation to the problems and to the population to be served. However, it appears reasonable first to increase the output of existing institutions through better organization and administration of their services as well as through the training of staff. Following that, construction requirements should be determined.

Tables 9 and 10 and Figure 12 show the numbers of hospitals and beds in North and Latin America. The disparity between Latin America and the United States and Canada is evident. In 1962 Latin America had 3.2 beds per 1,000 population as compared to 9.2 in North America. This difference between the two regions, although smaller, persists in the comparison of the number of beds in general hospitals, with ratios of 2.1 and 4.4 per 1,000, respectively. Moreover, considerable variation is observed between the countries in avail-

TABLE 9.

Number of hospitals by type in the three regions of the Americas, 1962.

Type	Total	North America	Middle America	South America
Total	17,821	8,404	2,728	6,689[a]
General—Total	15,484	7,000	2,548	5,936
General	14,223	6,845	2,012	5,366
Maternity	924	86	451	387
Pediatrics	279	65	44	170
Other	58	4	41	13
Tuberculosis	556	264	44	248
Leprosy	81	3	16	62
Mental diseases	909	615	59	235
Other	778	522	61	195

[a] Includes 13 hospitals in Peru which furnished no information.

ability of hospital beds. Ratios vary from 6 to 0.6 per 1,000 population. In 10 of the 22 Latin American countries there are fewer than 3 per 1,000. The situation is worse when the geographic distribution of hospitals within countries is analyzed. Data from 16 countries show that in large urban areas, that is, in capitals and in cities of over 500,000 population, there are 5.8 beds per 1,000, or two and one half times the

TABLE 10.

Number of hospital beds per 1,000 population by type in three regions of the Americas, 1962.

Type of hospital	North America		Middle America		South America	
	Number	Rate	Number	Rate	Number	Rate
Total	1,887,158	9.2	192,927	2.7	521,823[a]	3.5
General hospitals	898,230	4.4	128,094	1.8	335,588	2.3
Mental diseases	851,401	4.2	32,573	0.5	76,398	0.5
Tuberculosis	58,516	0.3	11,638	0.2	46,559	0.3
Others	79,011	0.4	20,622	0.3	55,907	0.4

[a] Includes 7,371 beds in Bolivia not distributed by type of hospital.

ratio in the rest of these same countries where 77% of the people live.

These data appear to indicate a need for new institutions for medical care. For a reasonable estimate two factors

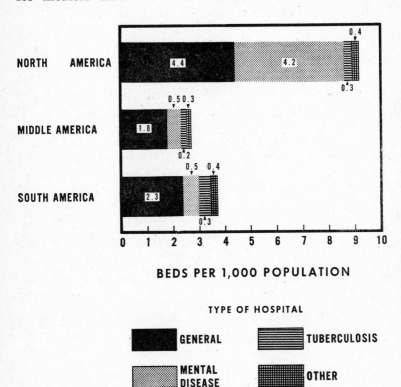

BEDS PER 1,000 POPULATION

TYPE OF HOSPITAL

GENERAL   TUBERCULOSIS

MENTAL DISEASE   OTHER

Figure 12. Hospital beds per 1,000 population by type of hospital in the three regions of the Americas, around 1962.

should be considered: (a) the expected increase in population to be served; and, (b) the ratio of hospital beds to population which is required to provide adequate medical care. With respect to this latter factor there is no optimal index, for many interrelated conditions affect it within each country. Among these are the size and structure of the population, the causes of illness for which hospital treatment is required, the existing organizational structure for providing medical care, health manpower, the geographic distribution of the population, the utilization of existing services, the demand for hospital care in relation to social and cultural characteristics, and the economy of the country.

With respect to the first factor, the expected increase of the population between 1965 and 1980 in Latin America may be 53%, producing a population of 374,000,000 in 1980. To maintain the present ratio of 3.2 beds per 1,000 will require 1,200,000 beds, or 420,000 more than are available today. In other words, in each of the next 15 years, 28,000 beds must be added, distributed proportionally in the countries. The present average cost of construction and equipment per bed varies between 6 and 10 thousand dollars. This serves to emphasize even more strongly both the advantages and advisability of improving the quality and quantity of services the existing hospitals provide. In some countries much has been achieved in recent years. Between 1958 and 1963 the number of hospital beds in Mexico increased by 45%, from 58,226 to 84,680. In approximately the same period, from 1957 to 1962, in Venezuela the numbers increased from 21,406 to 27,463, or 28%.

In most Latin American countries, except for the hospitals, the functions of protection, promotion and restoration of health are carried out principally in health centers or similar outpatient units. In 20 countries, with a population of approximately 196 millions, the number of these units was 11,618 in the period 1963-64. The "coverage" of the area and population with units is not precisely known. On the average there may be one unit for each 17,000 persons, if both urban and rural areas are included. If this relationship is applicable to the total population of Latin America in 1965, there are approximately 14,000 health centers or other outpatient centers. In 1980, when the population reaches 374,000,000, 22,000 local units will be needed to maintain the same average number in relation to population. To reach this number will require the construction of an additional 8,000 in the next 15 years, or 530 yearly. With the "coverage" lower than the minimum needs it is therefore essential to intensify even more the organization of these basic services. There is evidence of progress in reports of health ministries, but much remains to be done.

With respect to equipment, instruments, and supplies, distribution is uneven, but it is clear that with an adequate administration more could be accomplished with what exists. On the other hand, for certain specialized functions modern equipment is lacking and regulations imposed on foreign trade delay the import of parts to replace those no longer usable.

Instruments to Carry on Health Activities

By instruments we mean the combination of resources to carry out certain activities within the limits set by technical and economic factors. Among those of general character are planning, organization and administration of services, education and training, and scientific research.

The Alliance for Progress and its legal document, the Charter of Punta del Este, have emphasized the value of planning and programming as a method of accomplishing economic and social development. The governments have agreed to formulate programs corresponding to each of the objectives of the Charter in such a way as to bring about simultaneous growth of the economy and distribution of national income according to the greatest needs, among them health. In the last three years activities have been directed to training of planners and the formulation of an ordered presentation of problems and resources to facilitate the decisions of executives as to the priorities and investments, and on their application to countries and areas of Latin America. The Pan American Sanitary Bureau, in collaboration with the Inter-American Institute of Economic and Social Planning, has organized courses in health planning. Graduates from them are today participating in their own countries in the formulation of health plans.

As Prebisch very emphatically said "there is not going to be any easy way out for Latin America. Planning means a strictly methodical although not a strait-jacket approach to development problems, and an unremitting discipline in state action. It consists in a series of acts of foresight, of anticipation of future needs, of rationally relating the method of meeting those needs to the scanty resources available."[12] To insist that a plan is not an end in itself but only a step in a continuous activity, we wish to indicate that when the plan is being prepared, the health programs in operation in the country should not be interrupted, particularly those whose benefits for the people and for the economy are obvious. For this reason, they will without doubt be included in the national plan. The perspective of the total program will improve as knowledge is gained of the true output of the resources (operational research) which permits their assignment to specific objectives in a more precise manner.

The entire methodology of planning leads to assigning a value to the diseases and to the actions to avoid and limit them, as well as to establishing the goals which will be reached—within each priority—with available resources. It is a process of rating, of evaluation. Note that we refer to the actions of health and not to health itself, which by its inherent place in human life has no price. Planning is thus transformed into a system which is in reality a language permitting understanding and comparisons of health actions with other activities of socio-economic importance which make up development. It is hoped that the ministries of health will formulate their plans, carry them out and, through periodic evaluation, readjust the goals for each problem, making better use of the limited resources. Thus, continuing efforts will be taken to improve the organization and administration of services and the statistical information in Latin America.

In effect, these latter constitute another basic instrument for carrying out the health program. The concepts of integrating preventive and curative actions, of regionalizing the health structure, and of continuing education are the basis of a policy of organization and administration of health services. Even though widely accepted, they have not been put into practice to a significant degree in Latin America. This should have been done, since it is the course of common sense. This effort should include a substantial improvement in administrative practices in the services whose present weakness prevents their obtaining the results which could be expected from the resources at their disposal.

Referring to education and training—another instrument —we observe substantial progress in the preparation of professionals and auxiliaries, and in the programs which should be carried on to serve a growing population and economy.

The Advisory Committee on Medical Research of the Pan American Health Organization, in analyzing its functions, stated

> The immediate purpose of supporting research in Latin America is to solve problems related to health in a manner which will promote human welfare. . . The long-range goal is to promote upgrading of the community in its most human aspects through the cultivation of science. Indeed science, if understood properly as a form of culture, is a means of eventually providing the whole community with an objective awareness of the proper context of man; it gives a holistic view of the universe, in keeping with man's intellectual nature; it will eventually provide a basis for mutual understanding; and it is in any case a proper basis on which to build education.[13]

This is an excellent definition of the purposes of scientific research and the reason why it is another of the essential elements of the health program.

General Considerations

An analysis of present health conditions in the Americas yields both positive and negative findings. The problems and their relation to development are better understood. However, the acute competition for national and foreign funds has made programming indispensable, requiring more precise knowledge of the magnitude and extent of the problems. Techniques and methods to solve them are modern; however, they do not benefit all the people, and health services are not easily accessible to extensive rural areas.

In quantity as in quality there has been great progress in the preparation of professionals and auxiliaries; however, their number remains below the needs at present and those projected on the basis of population growth. Their distribution, like that of health services, is concentrated heavily in urban centers.

Agreement exists on the value of integrating preventive and curative actions within a single organization which serves the family as a unit; however, in practice this policy is seldom observed, and services of medical care function independently or uncoordinated with preventive health services. This leads to duplication of activities, wasteful expenditures, and poor utilization of the scarce resources available. Institutes of social security and ministries of health do not coordinate adequately to care for more patients with the same investment.

The importance of public administration to technical activities has been pointed out; however, the administrative practices in the health organizations are weak, as is reflected in the output of the resources to fulfill the objectives of each program. "Certainly it can be said that in no respect has public health been more rudely shaken by our population dilemma than in the area of organization and administration. It must, in its own interest, find a solution. But how much more exciting it is to indulge in the hope that whatever solution it does find may by some circumstance serve as a prototype for dealing with the organizational aspects of society's total needs."[14]

Motivation of individuals and communities to cooperate in projects for the common good has been considered essential in view of the results of repeated trials; however, voluntary collaboration has not been systematically organized for health objectives, either at the community or institutional level.

Funds for prevention and cure of diseases and promotion of health in Latin America are far below those needed, as revealed by vital and health statistics, in spite of the progress made in this century. The percentage of governmental funds expended on health varies between 2 and 13%, a difference which is explained in part by the inclusion in some countries of the cost of social services. The formulation of national health plans synthesized in program budgets will allow, on the one hand, a better ordered investment and, on the other, a more precise knowledge of distribution of the funds. However, it is evident that even with better organization and administration of the services, present investments are not sufficient progressively to reduce the incidence of the principal health problems and comply with the objectives of the Charter of Punta del Este.

We have tried to present the problems, resources, and objectives of health in relation to the population trends in Latin America. Our concept is ecological in the sense of considering all vital phenomena as the expression of the active interrelation of man and his environment in search of equilibrium and harmony. Health and disease in each person, as in the communities, reveals his capacity to adapt to the variations of his environment, many of which have been and are produced by man. As the physical and biological aggressions of the environment diminish, and simultaneously the reactive capacity of man improves, influences of a psychological, cultural, and social nature on the development of health problems become more evident. If their origin lies in multiple causes rooted in the structure of society, the solutions, including those which are specific by nature, cannot be isolated and independent. Therefore, we interpret health as a component of development and the latter the result of the increase of the economy and of the structural changes which lead to a sustained level of human well-being.

"Public health has been accused of being aloof from the population question. The charge is made that since it is responsible for the problem, it should assume greater responsibility for its solution. Even when the problem is reduced to one bare essential, i.e., the widening of the gap between natality and mortality, nothing could be more deceptive than to assert that public health must take the sole or even the main responsibility for it. To do so would be to ignore the

fact that the marked upswing in population growth ante-
dates the modern public health movement by more than a
century."[14]

In effect, in countries such as some in Western Europe
where vital statistics have been registered since the 17th century, mortality rates started to decrease long before sanitation was improved and scientific medicine was introduced.
This took place in the middle of the 19th century. It is possible that better living conditions and nutrition had an effect
on the reduction of mortality. We do not want to deny that
in the course of this century the techniques of medical care
and prevention of disease derived from research have produced notable progress. However, it could have been greater
in a healthier environment, with human beings better nour-
ished, less ignorant, and with an income to satisfy basic
needs. The contributions of modern medicine to welfare are
multiplied in those societies with an efficient economic intra-
structure and in which harmonious development takes place.

The present situation in Latin America with respect to the
quantity and quality of health problems reveals substantial
progress. At the same time there is a much larger fund of
knowledge which is not applied and which could prevent
many diseases and deaths. We do not believe, therefore, that
the growth of population in this century can be attributed
exclusively to preventive and curative activities and, on the
contrary, believe that it is necessary to intensify them within
a rationally developed program of total development. This
course follows moral commands and social obligations. This
discussion is not merely academic but has practical implications which could be reflected in a decreasing investment in
health in societies in which the disequilibrium between
needs and income is growing.

Whatever the causes, it is evident that in most Latin
American countries mortality rates, general and specific,
have decreased in varying degree during this century, while
birth rates have remained high with only slight modifications. Consequently, the population has increased but

the economy has not grown sufficiently to satisfy the requirements of progress and social welfare. Under these circumstances efforts should be strengthened to accelerate development, as agreed in the Charter of Punta del Este, through structural reforms and a planned schedule of investments to increase national income and to distribute it for economic and social objectives. We believe that the "population dilemma" does not mean a choice between development and limitation of births. They are not mutually exclusive. On the contrary, if births can be limited, development is fostered. On the other hand, there is no doubt that there are today large gaps in our knowledge of the biology of human reproduction and on the medical aspects of fertility control. A statement of the problems to be solved appears in the World Health Organization's document #A18/PB/4, "Programme Activities in the Health Aspects of World Population Which Might be Developed by WHO." These include, among others, comparative studies on the biology of reproduction, the biology of gonads and gametes, fertilization and gestation, biochemistry of the sex steroids and neuroendocrines, and immunological and pharmacological aspects of reproduction. Additional problems for investigation are the relation of the reproductive function in man with environmental and ethnical variations; the effects of labor on the fetus; the physiology of lactation; the biochemical aspects of spermatogenesis; the mechanism of action of sex hormones and analogous substances, especially that of the orally active progestogens; the biochemistry and microbiology of the female genital tract, with special reference to implantation and feedback. With respect to the implications for health of population dynamics, studies are needed on various contraceptive methods, medico-social factors of fertility, the interrelation between population trends and health services, and the future trends of mortality and fertility and their effect on population changes. Of equal significance are the prospective investigations on the various factors which influence human reproduction in selected communities.

The WHO document referred to above served as the base for Resolution WHA 18.49 of the Eighteenth World Health Assembly in May 1965 which, in giving its approval, also recognized that it is not the responsibility of WHO to endorse or promote any particular population policy and that "it is a matter for national administrations to decide whether and to what extent they should support the provision of information and services to their people on the health aspects of human reproduction."

On requesting the Director General to proceed to develop the proposed program, the Assembly specified that with respect to consultation service it should be understood that "such services are related, within the responsibilities of WHO, to technical advice on the health aspects of human reproduction and should not involve operational activities."

The number of children has been limited for many centuries by various methods arising from the customs and culture[15] of families and societies in different periods. The decision to limit children has been made by each family, for no national policy has existed to exert an influence on population dynamics. The only exception is that certain practices have been forbidden, for example, abortion, with very specific limitations. Today the possibility of establishing such a national policy, and the responsibility of the governments and voluntary organizations is being discussed, and to this the recent resolution of the World Health Assembly refers. The large gaps in knowledge about the complex process of human reproduction have been pointed out, leading to the need for research in the biological, psychological, economic, and cultural implications in order to facilitate the decisions of each society. We think that these studies, especially the applications which are derived from them, should be carried out through the health services. By the nature of their responsibilities within the social structure they come in closer contact with individuals, families, and communities. They are able, therefore, to induce the subtle and indispensable process of motivation which leads to conscious and lasting decisions. It is obvious that education—understood as the capacity to form judgements—is essential for such motivation, as well as to give to those who need it the opportunity to explain their problems and to understand the solutions which are offered.

FOOTNOTES

1. Doc. CECE/III-70, *OAS Official Documents,* September 1960.
2. Doc. ES-RE-Doc. 145 Rev. 3, *OAS Official Documents,* August 1961.
3. Lancelot Hogben, "The Place of Genetics in a Contemporary Curriculum of Medical Studies," *J. Med. Educ., 33:* 421-6, 1958.
4. *Health Conditions in the Americas 1961-1962,* Scientific Publications No. 104, Pan American Sanitary Bureau, Washington, D.C., 1964.
5. Seminar on the Role of the General Health Services in Malaria Eradication, PASB Doc. SSEM/20, Cuernavaca, Mexico, March 4-13, 1965. Idem-Pocos de Caldas, Brazil, June 26-July 4, 1964, Final Report, Doc. SSEM/20, PASB.
6. *Fourth Annual Report 1964,* Social Progress Trust Fund, Inter-American Development Bank, p. 108.
7. La Malnutrición y los Hábitos Alimentarios, Informe de Una Conferencia Internacional y Interprofessional, Sc. Pub. No. 91, PASB, Washington, D.C., 1963.
8. Doc. ES-RE-Doc. 145, Rev. 3, Resolution A2, p. 36, OAS, Official Records, Ser. H/XI, August 1961.
9. Task Force on Health at the Ministerial Level, Official Document No. 51, PAHO, Washington, D.C., 1964, p. 35.
10. PAHO Official Document, No. 55, Part II, 1964, p. 55.
11. IA-ECOSOC, Final Report of the Third Annual Meeting of the Inter-American Economic and Social Council at the Expert Level, IA-ECOSOC/728, December 1964.
12. United Nations Economic and Social Council, Doc. E/CN-12/680, 1963, p. 16.
13. Advisory Committee on Medical Research, Pan American Health Organization, Report of the First Meeting, 1962, Doc. Res. 1/19.
14. James A. Crabtree, "Some Public Health Implications of the Population Problem." Presented at Symposium: Research Issues in Public Health and Population Change, Graduate School of Public Health, University of Pittsburgh, June 2-5, 1964.
15. "Culture is used here in its anthropological sense as the way of life of a people—their social, economic and political organization, and their characteristic patterns of thought, emotion and interpersonal relations." (Report to the Director-General of the Scientific Group on Mental Health Research, Geneva, April 6-10, 1964, Doc. WHO MHO/PA/75.64.)

8. The Catholic Church and Family Planning—Current Perspectives

FATHER GUSTAVO PÉREZ RAMÍREZ

Not since the Reformation has such an upheaval been produced as is evident in the Catholic Church today. Nor have we seen a process of such rapid and unexpected (although no less desired) change as the one we are experiencing at the present.[1]

The Church of Christ has undertaken this titanic effort in its search for renewal and the necessary *aggiornamento*. It is a process of renewal and profound revision, founded in the belief that the truth will make us free. The concepts of natural law, authority, religious liberty, the place of the Church in the world, the hierarchy, the laity, evangelization, and the service are all being carefully examined. Stereotypes which have been irrationally created, are now confronted with the findings of science—from theology to physics and biology—in a demand for a reinterpretation of the "Message of Salvation," which meets the needs of a world in the process of change.

Family planning is one of these areas of study. There are great expectations on the part of those nations whose development is seen to be retarded by the "demographic explosion," as well as by those individuals who feel the need to integrate the teachings of Christ with the realities of the modern world.

The progress of the natural sciences, combined with the successes of new and better hygienic conditions, has drastically reduced the death rate, prolonged life expectancy, and accelerated the rate of growth of the human population to the point where it is obvious that it cannot continue to grow indefinitely.

Luckily, man is endowed with reason and subject to the command to work. His scientific spirit has led him into the depths of social anthropology, physiology, biochemistry, social psychology, sociology, and other sciences. In this way, he has been better able to understand himself and to delve deeply into the secrets of natural law. For its part, theology, faced with these facts and scientific discoveries, has been clarifying its postulates and ethical norms, following a steady line of development, interrupted at times by historical circumstances.

I shall first briefly consider the Latin American problem of family planning and the use of contraceptives. Then I will deal with the debates of the Council and the attempts made by the Church, as an organized institution, to combine demands of day-to-day existence with general lines of doctrine appropriate to Her mission.

The Problem of Family Planning

It is the task of the sociologist to observe social events, to relate these events to a specific culture, and to analyze the value and behavior systems of various cultures. Thus, we will examine the population problem in Latin America in its double perspective, structural on the one hand and ethno-cultural on the other.

Structural Conditioning

In a traditional, pre-technical society, as a result of its very organization, the birth of a child had social implications quite different from those of today. The family was the unit of production and it performed many varied tasks. Grandparents and other relatives lived together, facilitating education and the carrying-out of household tasks. The high mortality rate, especially among infants, demanded a higher birth rate as the inevitable means of survival of the human race. Under these circumstances a much higher birth rate was required so that the family might have an adequate number of surviving children. Today, however, practically every birth means a child who will reach maturity. Moreover, the demands of education are greater in modern society, as are the difficulties of employment, housing, etc.

At the national and international level the problem is no less important. Here, the problem of adequate distribution of limited resources is made even more difficult by currently excessive fertility. When we arrive at the already visible limits, aside from the drastic methods of war or destruction, the most reasonable alternative may be to limit births, in accordance with the ethical requirements of human nature and religious values.

It is worth recalling at this point how the theories of Malthus burst into the middle of the Industrial Revolution, when scientific knowledge was advancing and urbanization growing. All these factors affected the consideration of the population problem.

Meanwhile, Latin America was unaware of these happenings because Spain for a long time remained outside of the Industrial Revolution. Moreover, until recent decades, Latin America has been a traditional, agrarian society without sufficient awareness of the problem of rapid population expansion. Instead, she has perceived the obsolete nature of the agrarian structure and for the present postpones a confrontation with the population problem. Nevertheless, the problem will continue inexorably to make itself felt, even in those societies where there is the most perfect distribution of resources and riches.

The Cultural Frame of Reference

As we have just observed, the cultural background of Latin America is Malthusian. There are cultural values, not sufficiently taken into account in the studies of population, which touch on the question of demography. For example, the generally high death rate, especially of infants, has been considered a matter of fate—inevitable and without remedy. The cult of the dead and the pomp of funerals in Latin America is not motivated solely by elements of prestige and religiosity. They reveal the importance attributed to death, the acceptance of its inevitability and the instability of life, the supremacy of nature as something which imposes itself fatalistically. The concept of the supremacy of nature, joined to reason, only came to be expounded in Kantian and Hegelian philosophies which were outside the Latin American cultural background.

The Cultural Ethos and Catholic Morality

We must also consider other cultural features of an ethical character, features which belong to the Latin American system of values but whose influence on the population problem has not been measured. For example, while the complex of *machismo* uses the number of children and free sexual conduct as an affirmation of masculinity, it also sets up an idealization and false mystification of woman. Further, it contains a mixture of Arabic elements, such as the disgrace of sterility. This perhaps explains the double standard which has traditionally governed the sexual conduct of man and woman: the former permissive and the latter restrictive.

The Gnostic-Manichean dualism adds to this picture a note of de-humanization by reducing human sexuality to simple reproduction, something almost morally contemptible and virtually equivalent to animal sexuality.

The Catholic ethical frame of reference contains a traditional, simplistic ethos which has its origin in the western Christian world. This ethos recognizes few of the advances of science and maintains the status quo because of the defensive attitude of the Church since the Reformation. Only the inevitable laws of recurrence and regularity of nature were perceived, and to these were attached a sacred and intangible character.

Until the thirteenth century there was a great effort at doctrinal elaboration. The fourteenth, fifteenth, and sixteenth centuries saw the flourishing of "*Summas* for the use of confessors" as easy guides for the confessional. The juridical element dominated, without much preoccupation to relate moral facts to the over-all pattern of Christian doctrine.

The line of *practico-practicum* led to the crises of the seventeenth and eighteenth centuries. The very approach of these authors of casuistry, involved in a search for minimal standards for the confessional, led many into *laxity*. Their excesses provoked a reaction of strictness culminating in Jansenism, which has done so much harm in Latin America and other Catholic regions. Errors persist in spite of the teachings of St. Alphonsus, the Thomistic renewal, and the contemporary movement of a morality of response and compromise.[2]

It is only within the framework of the recent doctrinal and moral renewal that the serious problems of sexual morality are finally being studied in the light of scientific advances. Thus, some years ago, faced with the discoveries of Ogino and Knaus, the Church accepted the rhythm method. The introduction of this innovation was by no means smooth. In one Latin American country, all reference to the Ogino-Knaus method was removed from the early editions of Pius XI's Encyclical, *Casti Connubii,* which did not prevent the method from spreading rapidly.

Faced with this evolution, we cannot ignore, at the level of practical conduct, a divorce of religion and science, of the Church and the world, of a naturalistic physical ethic and an ethic with more scientific elements. On the level of practical decisions we find conduct which generally deviates from the traditional and effective norms of the morality of the sexual act and its ends. The confessional bears witness to the drama, which culminates in uneasy, anguished, traumaticized, or rebellious consciences. This phenomenon and its dimensions have not been studied sufficiently in sociological perspective.

In a sociological analysis of the etiology of actions at variance with the norm, it is necessary to understand motivation and its relation to conduct. The theoretical elaboration of Professor Kingsley Davis on the sociology of deviance or anomaly provides the framework for studying this problem within a sociology of Catholicism in Latin America.

One reckons from the fundamental premise that conscious motives or desires and conduct may or may not be congruent. Further, either of them may be normal or deviant.

Professor Davis presents a double-entry illustration in which he makes a cross-tabulation of these possibilities in order to show the interrelations of conformity and deviation with motive and conduct.[3]

Motivation or Desire	*Conduct*	
	Conformity	Violation
Conformity	(1)	(2)
	+ +	+ −
Violation	(3)	(4)
	− +	− −

(1) refers to those whose conduct accords with a desire to conform to the norm. This is the case of Catholics who reject the use of contraceptives, basing their conduct on the existing laws of the Church. Their number may be smaller than has been supposed, as is becoming evident from recent investigations. We will give an example of this later on.

(4) refers to the rebels or innovators who are both motivated to and who in fact do violate the norms. With regard to the use of contraceptives, statistics indicate that, while there are violations of the norms, this does not necessarily imply abandonment of the faith or of religious practices such as the reception of Communion. This might be the group innovators who take a position ahead of religious authorities, when they can justify their conduct.

As Professor Davis explains in a paper entitled *Values, Population and the Supernatural,* "Reflection on history leaves the impression that the reproductive folkways and mores of the common man have varied more in relation to the conditions of his life than with reference to religious or philosophical doctrine. Although contraception has become a western folkway, no major religion advocated its use prior to its popular adoption."

In (2) and (3) complications arise in the relation between deviant motivation and conduct. As indicated in (2), deviant conduct is not necessarily preceded by deviant motivations or desires. For example, we can have the best intentions on the part of a devout married couple who sincerely desire to be faithful to the norms of the Church with regard to the use of contraceptives but who, in practice, violate ecclesiastical laws, not necessarily solely because of "human frailty." Causes for such deviant behavior other than deviant desires should be sought. For example, the absence of a profound adherence to the Church and of a feeling of belonging to Her may contribute to making compliance with the norms even more difficult. In effect, greater pressure from the norms of primary groups such as the family is experienced, along with a tendency, in case of conflict, for the norms of secondary or less intimate groups to prevail.

Finally, (3) illustrates motives for actions at variance with the norm, and desires which are not always translated into deviant behavior. This is the case of innumerable Catholics who still manage to adapt their conduct to the present-day norms of the Church, but who feel the need to integrate the exigencies of modern life (urbanization, education for their children, national survival) with their moral dedication to Christ and the promise of eternal life.

Among the important questions which arise is, "How can we prevent conformist motivation from resulting in deviant behavior?" Certainly there are inhibitions to deviant behavior other than norms, the fear of punishment, or social control. But the problem is more complex than it appears. The solution requires a serene dialogue—an objective confrontation with scientific findings, an unlimited fidelity to the truth, and an interdisciplinary revision of the norms and the facts on which they are based.

An intensive and persuasive exposition of values can only be justified in a stable, cohesive, and integrated society. Repression, intransigence, and the rejection of dialogue as means of guaranteeing conformity lead to collapse, rather than social change, as Professor Davis so rightly points out.

The study carried out by the Centro Latino Americano de Demografía, (CELADE), of Santiago, Chile, simultaneously in Bogotá, Buenos Aires, Caracas, Mexico City, Panama City, Rio de Janeiro and San José throws some light on the abnormal life which some Latin American Catholics lead because of their use of contraceptives.[4] Preliminary data for three cities show the distribution of married women who use contraceptives in relation to the frequency of their attendance at religious services.

TABLE 1.

Per cent of married women who have used contraceptives, according to frequency of church attendance, in three Latin American cities.

Attendance at church	Panama	Rio de Janeiro	San José
Once a week or more	59	58	65
Once or twice a month	64	47	54
A few times per year	—	51	53
Once a year	58	60	62
Once in years	—	64	78
Never	50	58	72

These figures clearly show the degree of deviation from the norms of the Catholic Church by married women who call themselves Catholic. It is significant that the majority of Church-goers *use* contraceptives.

The observed deviation from the norms is confirmed and made even more evident in the following Table:

TABLE 2.

Per cent of married Catholic women who have used contraceptives, according to frequency of receiving Communion, in three Latin American cities.

Frequency of Communion	Caracas	Bogotá	Mexico City
Once or more per month	57	40	35
Less than once per month	64	38	35
Never	55	50	40

Source: Tables 1 & 2, C. Miró and F. Rath, "Preliminary Findings of Comparative Fertility Surveys in Three Latin American Countries," *The Milbank Memorial Fund Quarterly*, Vol. XLIII, 1965, Annex, Table 14.

THE POSITION OF THE CHURCH

The traditional doctrine regarding conjugal morality teaches that the sexual act is legitimate only within matrimony, and provided that nothing artificial prevents conception. This means that artificial contraception—not periodic abstinence—is immoral. Furthermore, His Holiness Pius XI, in his Encyclical *Casti Connubii,* repudiated contraception as "intrinsically and gravely immoral."[5]

Some theologians, among them several Jesuits,[6] hold that this celebrated paragraph is of an infallible character, *ex cathedra.* They cite as a basis for the condemnation of contraception the principle of natural law—according to which the procreative end inherent in the conjugal act should be respected at all times.[7] The situation became even more complicated with Pius XII's declaration according to which the repudiation of contraception is "as valid today as it was yesterday and as it will be tomorrow and always." On the other hand, in the light of Paul VI's declaration of June 1964 concerning control of births, it might be argued that previous Pontifical declarations were not infallible. At the same time that he declared Pius XII's norms to be valid, he implied that they were not immutable, since he added, "consequently, these norms should be considered valid *at least until we feel obliged in conscience to change them.*"[8] He further stated that, "The question is being subjected to as broad and profound a study as possible, as serious and honest as should be the case in a matter of such importance." His Holiness added that he soon hoped to present the conclusions from this study, which is being carried out by many outstanding experts, "in the most appropriate form and to the end that it should obtain." Elsewhere, in his speech of March 27, 1965, His Holiness Paul VI exhorted the members of the Commission on birth control as follows:

> We strongly urge you not to lose sight of the urgency of this situation which turns to the Church and Her supreme authority for very clear guidance. . . We cannot leave the conscience of the faithful exposed to uncertainty which all too frequently today impedes the development of married life according to God's plan. Moreover, aside from such urgent questions for married couples, there are also economic and social problems which the Church cannot ignore."[9]

We must also bear in mind the warning of one of the best-known contemporary moral theologians, Father Häring: "In the field of morality many problems appear in a different light with the passage of time. At times a long struggle is needed to elaborate all the necessary distinctions with sufficient clarity."[10] This brings to mind the case of ecclesiastical prohibition of interest on loans. The Council of Vienna in the fourteenth century reached the point of threatening with chains and prison those theologians who dared justify interest on loans. Only after a long series of discussions only a few decades ago, did His Holiness Pius XI, in the context of a new economic structure, clearly justify the morality of reasonable interest rates. "Something similar has taken place in the case of conjugal morality," comments Father Häring. We hope that this time the process will be much shorter, considering the fact that there is greater clarity with regard to the philosophical-theological reflections and the scientific findings. An anguished and almost unanimous cry on the part of Christianity is asking for "very clear indications on behalf of the Church," as His Holiness Paul VI expressed it.

The encyclical, *Casti Connubii,* published thirty-five years ago, "at the time constituted a milestone on the road to a more positive spirituality of marriage; but the formulations concerning abuses were framed with a backward glance at an era which had not yet come to a close, rather than in anticipation of what was to become an increasingly general attitude and social structure."[11]

One promising fact is that the Vatican Council has included discussion of this matter in Schema XIII, which specifically deals with the relations of the Church to the world, and which establishes dialogue with the world as the fundamental basis for solving a problem directly concerning the community of nations.[12]

In 1964, shortly before the third Session of the Council adjourned, the problem of population and the use of contraceptives was debated. The interventions of Cardinals Suenans of Belguim, Leger of Canada, Alfrink of Holland, and Patriarch Maximus of Antioch are known to all. "I pray that this Council without fear and reticence, " pleaded Cardinal Leger, "will clearly proclaim the two ends of marriage (human-conjugal love and procreation) to be equally good and holy. Once this is done, the moralists, doctors, psychologists, and other experts can better determine the rights and responsibilities with regard to fertility in particular cases." Patriarch Maximus, for his part, referred to the believers who "find themselves forced to live in violation of the law of the Church, separated from the Sacraments, in constant anguish because of the inability of finding a viable solution between two contradictory imperatives: conscience and a normal married life." In addition, he noted the other aspect of the population problem at the level of society, that is, the demographic pressure in certain countries "which stands in the way of any attempt to raise standards of living and condemns hundreds of millions of human beings to an arid misery without hope."

Considering, then, the transactions of the conciliar debates and the writings of the most outstanding theologians and scientists who have spoken out in favor of "Responsible Parenthood," we may make the observations which follow.

Revision of the Concepts of Natural Law

The basis of the problem and of its practical solution lies in the concept of natural law. Any formulation of natural law ought to be the fruit of consideration of the rights and responsibilities of man, in which natural law is viewed as oriented toward the perfection of human nature in its totality and toward the respect of the individual and of human life. God has endowed man with the intelligence and will to participate in the creative process. The common good is the guide for the solution of problems which arise from man's intervention in nature. Thus, there can be no conflict between natural law based on a respect of human values, and a control of human fertility oriented to the general welfare of man.

We should note that "nature" has a double meaning which may cause difficulties. In the first place, "nature" refers to the intrinsic principle of operation or essence. It also refers to the principle of what happens in the majority of instances (*ut in pluribus*). Thus, in the case of a sterile woman, the conjugal act occurs *ut in pluribus,* without the lack of conception changing the specific nature of the act. Applying this distinction to natural law, it is clear that those "primary" principles which concern humanity cannot change without man's changing in essence. The "secondary" principles of natural law refer to the most rational manner of following the inclinations of human nature. And here there exist possibilities for variety and change, provided they be uniquely natural, according to the majority of cases (*ut in pluribus*).

Advances in Anthropological, Sociological and Psychological Concepts

New anthropological concepts also offer valid perspectives for the acceptance of "Responsible Parenthood." Man is viewed as an indivisible entity, composed of body and soul, in contrast with the dualistic concept which tries to minimize the body. Thus, human sexuality differs from that of animals since human conjugal love, which involves both body and soul, is a true end in marriage as something good in itself having its own requirements and laws."[13] Human sexuality cannot be explained exclusively in terms of procreation. The sexual relationship between husband and wife embraces all of the human personality, and therefore, is an essential element in the attainment of its unity.

Many Catholic scientists, in the light of modern psychology and the growing personalization of human relations, are studying the possible contributions of emotional and physical elements to the development of unity in marriage, where the spouses are not merely procreators, but individuals expressing mutual love as an end in itself. The process of social change has profoundly influenced not only value and behavior systems but also man's relation to man, his roles, as well as the fundamental institutions of society. Thus, the process of formation and dissolution of the family has been substantially altered, as was mentioned at the beginning of this work.

The attitude of dialogue with the world as posited in Schema XIII opens up a new perspective for sociological analysis. His Holiness Paul VI let it be understood in this way when he expressed the goals of the Council. "The Church must understand Herself, renew Herself . . . and initiate dialogue with the modern world. Without sociological analysis and a concretizing of sociological conditions these goals cannot be achieved."

New Findings in the Fields of Physiology and Bio-Chemistry

The meaning of sexuality has also been greatly clarified through a better understanding of the physiology of reproduction. Today it is known that sperm production has a continuous and prolific character, that female fertility is discontinuous and extremely limited, and female sexual conduct is not controlled by periodic hormonal secretions. Consequently, since the sexual act is not even physiologically necessarily bound to procreation, fertility cannot be the direct end which gives meaning to each individual act. The obligation of fecundity, therefore, does not depend on the physiological reality of each act but rather on the ensemble of acts and circumstances—both physiological and psychological—which constitute the whole of married life. Given the ends of marriage, this methodical arrangment of nature is very logical, producing a child not as the result of an independent act but rather through another relation of man and wife, a relation which is the married state. Cardinal Leger expressed it in his presentation in the Council, "It would be good to connect the responsibility of fecundity less with each act and more with the very state of matrimony."

New perspectives for the solution of the problem have also been opened up with the era of progesterones and the 19-Nor-estoroides begun somewhat more than a decade ago, although still in the process of experimentation and evaluation. Present investigations concentrate fundamentally on checking the function of steroid derivatives whose action has been considered the equivalent of natural progesterins, endowed with an androgenic action. Setting aside the specifics of the functioning of the *steroids*, we should note that in no circumstances are we dealing with sterilization.

In itself, then, the use of anti-ovulants would not be bad

and would be justified by the end for which they are employed. Another point worth noting is that "the closer look at life which modern biology provides indicates that a biological action is ordinarily multifunctional, and that the inhibition of a function which is not needed is the typical means of achieving the integrated control required by living things."[14] This multifunctioning is quite evident in the case of the sex act, which satisfies various physiological demands aside from procreation and which also performs a psychological function. It follows, biologically, that contraception does not violate natural law, since it is characteristic of biological systems to inhibit a phase of a multifunctional activity when the other phases are not needed. Thus, during pregnancy, certain hormones inhibit further ovulation, thereby eliminating the possibility of another pregnancy. A similar process occurs during lactation.

All of these new foci and discoveries permit a greater clarity in the attitudes to be adopted by Catholic theology. For example, theologians agree on the therapeutic use of progesterins and there are even those who look for their justification purely on the grounds that regulation of birth is, in itelf, a moral good.[15]

Advances in Exegetical and Theological Interpretations of Matrimony

The previously mentioned pronouncements of the Council Fathers in favor of a revision of the Church's position with regard to the problem of births have been based primarily on a new and more profound exegesis of the Biblical texts.

Someone has commented that the Church's pro-birth attitude may have been the result of the Church Fathers quoting the "increase and multiply" verses of Genesis (Gen. 1.28,IX.1) as an affirmation of the essential goodness of procreation in response to the Gnostic heresies which condemned procreation as the imprisoning of souls in evil bodies. Professor Janssens of the Theology Faculty of the University of Louvain shows how the spurious interpreta-

tion which St. Augustine makes of the doctrine of matrimony in Genesis and the Pauline Epistles would be the root
of a matrimonial ethic imbued with Neo-Platonism and
Manichean Agnosticism.[16]

While we are more accustomed to the "increase and multiply" verses in Genesis dealing with the origin of marriage,
we tend to forget the probably older passage in Chapter 2 of
Genesis where the marital union is described in psychological terms: "Wherefore a man shall leave father and mother,
and shall cleave to his wife, and they shall be two in one
flesh." (Gen. 2, 20-24.)

The Apostle St. Paul in his Epistle to the Ephesians attributes to conjugal love the highest religious sense possible for a
human relationship and he cites Genesis 2, clearly referring
to conjugal love (Eph. 5, 25-33), "Husbands, love your wives,
just as Christ also loved the Church, and delivered Himself
up for Her . . ." It is clear that conjugal love is spiritual but
it is distinct from all other love because of the sexual attraction between people of opposite sex. For this reason, Professor Janssens, in clarifying the specific character of marital
love, insists that *eros* should be included in *agape,* or the
love between husband and wife.

While for St. Paul husband and wife have a full right to
each other's body, St. Augustine seems to restrict the rights
to the exclusive goal of procreation. The common interpretation is that for him all sexual pleasure and desire would be
intrinsically bad—only the goal of procreation and the in-
tention of preserving the fidelity of the spouses could give
goodness to the act. Only centuries later was it admitted that
there is no sin in sexual relations where there is neither the
need for nor the hope of procreating. Until then, sexual relations between husband and wife were prohibited once she
had conceived, because the goal of the act was considered to
have been accomplished.[17]

In the context of social change such as is occurring in
Latin America, one must combine the patterns and social re-
lations of daily obligations with those which may guide the
Church as an organized institution. In this way the Church

can contribute to the mobilization of her leaders and members so that they may be more effective in carrying out their roles, related in so many ways to the solution of the Latin American crisis. It is a dynamic and complex task, including everything from standards to practical decisions. This multiple action touches upon:

The cultural frame of reference, by means of a confrontation of traditional values with new scientific findings, implying resolution of the conflicts which exist between the traditional and the new. As a part of this process, standards of interpretation are required which will permit the assimilation of new values: standards which are flexible in the use of means, dynamic with regard to the ordering of ends, and ever aware of the implications of the decisions made. We should also mention the advisability of resolving all types of incongruities—especially those of a cultural nature; for example, to bring up-to-date the doctrine on matrimony as it appears in the present rituals and manuals.

The socialization process, since values and norms are accepted thoughtlessly without the required interiorization or cathexis of values of which Parsons speaks. This socialization process begins in the family, and neurotic families cannot solve the crises of the continent. For its part, education will fulfill its function by giving a positive assessment to sex and by creating a sense of altruism and responsibility. Preaching is another important channel for socialization. Unfortunately, it often appears imbued with an exaggerated pro-natalist mentality and a Gnostic-Manichean dualism. Equally important is the socialization of the opinion and religious leaders in general, with respect to sociological perspectives and scientific advances in family planning.

Adaption of the goals and pastoral counseling, to those Christians who come to the confessional with a need for achieving an interpenetration of the realities of the world and the teachings of Christ. An international group of Catholic scientists expounded the human meaning of this problem in a recent private document. They referred to the drama of millions of well-intentioned couples who find great difficulties in reconciling, within the framework of existing directives, the different ends of marriage: procreation, education of children, and mutual love. In innumerable cases, their difficulties are leading to conflict, perversion of conscience, abandonment of the Church, and a loss of harmony between the spouses.

We share this unrest and the hopes of all those who wish a resolution of the conflict between religious norms and social realities.

FOOTNOTES

1. I have given this complex study a sociological orientation, analyzing those facts which must be kept in mind in an objective study of the demographic question in Latin America. Among these facts I shall mention the doctrinal position of the Catholic Church and the efforts for exegetical and theological interpretation which are taking place within the Council. I do not intend to treat issues which fall solely within the competence of ecclesiastical magisterium, especially since the Holy See has set up a Commission, composed of more than 50 experts, to consider the problem in a scientific and interdisciplinary framework.

2. Bernard Häring, *La Loi du Christ,* vol. I, pp. 48-92, "Perspectives sur L'Histoire de la Théologie Morale." J. Ferin, L. Janssens, "Canonigo, Morale Conjugale et Progestogenes," *Ephemerides Theologicae Lovanieses,* vol. XXII. Louvain, 1963, pp. 787-826.

3. J. Blake, K. Davis, "Norms, Values and Sanctions" in *Handbook of Modern Sociology,* Rob. E. L. Faris (ed.), Chicago: Rand-McNally, 1964, p. 468 ff.

4. Leon C. Tabah, "Plan de recherches de sept enquêtes comparatives sur la fécondité en Amérique Latine," *Population,* Paris No. 1, 1964, pp. 95-126.

5. Encyclical *Casti Connubii,* Acta Apostolicae Sedis, XXII, 21-XII, 1930.

6. Capello, Vermeersch, Creusen, Zalba, Cartechini, etc.

7. Ford, S. J., Kelly, S. J. "Will the Church's Teaching on Birth Control Change?" *The Catholic World,* Vol. 198, No. 1184, Nov. 1963, pp. 87-93. The article begins with the following affirmation which sums up the article: "In the Catholic Church, the repudiation of contraception is unquestionably irrevocable."

8. L'Osservatore Romano, June 24, 1965.

9. L'Osservatore Romano, March 27, 1965.

10. Bernard Häring, "Responsible Parenthood, Morality as Growth," *The Commonweal,* Special issue on Responsible Parenthood, Vol. LXXX, No. 11, June 5, 1964, p. 327.

11. *Ibid.,* p. 327.

12. Schema XIII, chapter IV, paragraph 21, "On the Dignity of Marriage and the Family."

13. *Intervention,* Cardinal Leger in Conciliar debate, Oct. 29, 1964.

14. Julian Pleasants, "The Lessons of Biology," *Contraception and Holiness,* Collins 1965, pp. 82 ff. Doctor Pleasants, trained in chemistry and theology, is a researcher for Lobound Laboratory of Notre Dame University.

15. O. P. Van der Marck, taken from Louis Dupré, "From Augustine to Janssens," *The Commonweal,* Vol. LXXX, No. 11, 1964, p. 340.

16. J. Ferin, L. Janssens, "Canonigo, Morale Conjugale et Progesto-genes," *Ephemerides Theologicae Lovanieses,* Vol. XXII, Louvain, 1963, pp. 787-826.

17. John Noone, *Contraception: Its Treatment by Catholic Theologians and Canonists,* Harvard University Press, 1965.

9. Perspectives of Family Planning Programs in Latin America

RAMIRO DELGADO GARCÍA*

Other papers in this book consider the dramatic consequences that the high rates of natural population increase
are having on the well-being of most Latin American countries. If these consequences continue, standards of living may
drop to a level where social unrest will lead to bloody revo-
lutions with their sequelae of death, hunger, and misery. In
our opinion, the main positive answer to this possibility is
the decline of birth rates through the deliberate use of effective methods of family planning. Economic development and
changes in the social structure are other important factors,
but the demographic problem is inescapable, on a world, national, family, and individual level. While parents have
much more to do with determining the birth rate than do
governments, favorable governmental policies are nonethe-
less necessary to facilitate effective means of family regulation. Further, because of technical and social obstacles, the
problem is difficult both to face and to study. The present
paper tries to analyze some of the factors involved in the possible success of national family planning programs in Latin
America.

FERTILITY SURVEYS

For the first time, an effort to study the reproductive history of Latin American couples is being carried out systematically. The Latin American Demographic Center (CELADE),

* The views expressed in this paper are the writer's and do not
necessarily reflect those of the Institutions he represents.

with the collaboration of the United Nations and Cornell University, is gathering data about the attitudes, use, and knowledge of family planning and contraception through surveys in different areas of Latin America. The preliminary results deserve careful attention because they reveal important aspects of the population problems on the continent.[1,2]

TABLE 1.

Latin America.

Average number of pregnancies, live births, stillbirths, and miscarriages in seven selected cities.

	Pregnancies	Live births	Stillbirths	Miscarriages	
				Average	Percentage
Bogotá	4.54	3.99	0.04	0.40	9%
Buenos Aires	2.49	2.03	0.04	0.40	16%
Caracas	4.35	3.76	0.04	0.52	12%
Mexico City	4.89	4.17	0.08	0.58	12%
Panama City	3.88	3.46	0.06	0.38	10%
Rio de Janerio	3.63	2.99	0.08	0.51	14%
San José	4.46	3.82	0.06	0.53	12%

Source: Program of Comparative Fertility Surveys, CELADE, 1964. Based on IBM cards supplied by the countries, which are still subject to some internal checks.

At the present stage, 2,000 women were interviewed in each of seven Latin American capitals. While what happens in capital cities does not necessarily represent the national situation, it indicates an important trend. Generally, the results of this study agree with those reported elsewhere in Latin America.

Table 1 summarizes the reproductive performance of frequently-pregnant women interviewed in seven cities. The low rate of abortion (9-16%) could partly reflect under-reporting. In Santiago, Armijo and Monreal found an abortion rate of 31%, which is considerably higher than any of the rates obtained in the CELADE survey.[3] This shows the importance of conducting specific and more carefully controlled studies on abortion. While the seriousness of the abortion problem is evident in assessing maternal death rates, cost of hospital care, social impact on the family, etc., its actual prevalence

TABLE 2.

Latin America.

Gross reproduction rates in seven selected cities.

	G.R.R., estimated from survey[1]	National G.R.R.[2]	Ratio of national to city G.R.R.
Bogotá	2.38	—	—
Buenos Aires	0.97	1.40	1.44
Caracas	2.12	3.10	1.46
Mexico City	2.56	3.10	1.21
Panama City	1.92	2.70	1.41
Rio de Janeiro	1.67	—	—
San José	2.10	3.50	1.67

[1] A curve was fitted to plotted values of average number of live births by age from which specific rates were computed by differentiation. From these G.R.R.s, values were calculated.

[2] United Nations. "Conditions and Trends of Fertility in the World." Population Bulletin No. 7, Table 5.1. Values quoted are for 1960 or years around it. No recent data were available for Brazil & Colombia.

Source: Program of Comparative Fertility Surveys, CELADE, 1964.

seems quite difficult to establish. Thus, Armijo's results show several discrepancies from those obtained by Dr. Mariano Requena in Santiago.[4] Other studies on abortion have been reported by Drs. Françoise Hall in Lima,[5] Iris Rosada in Montevideo,[6] and Francisco Villadiego in Cali.[7]

Table 2 compares the Gross Reproduction Rates (G.R.R.)

TABLE 3.

Latin America.

Average number of live births by level of education in seven selected cities.

	Bogotá	Buenos Aires	Caracas	Mexico City	Panama City	Rio de Janeiro	San José
All women	3.16	1.49	2.97	3.28	2.74	2.25	2.98
No education	4.12	2.50	4.27	4.53	4.00	3.33	3.89
1–3 primary grades	3.36	1.55	3.82	4.16	4.18	2.93	3.73
4 & more primary grades	3.17	1.90	2.97	3.83	3.73	2.46	3.74
Complete primary education	3.23	1.74	2.61	3.14	3.14	2.17	2.83
1–3 secondary grades	2.89	1.46	1.88	2.20	2.67	1.63	2.26
4 & more secondary grades	2.52	1.35	2.16	1.85	2.14	1.43	1.91
Complete secondary education	2.52	1.07	1.71	1.82	1.65	1.38	2.00
Less than 5 years of university education	0.68	1.12	0.68	1.41	1.09	1.05	1.59
5 and more years of university education	1.89	1.03	1.31	1.89	1.22	1.21	1.18
Not specified	2.00	1.23	6.00	—	3.00	2.00	—

Source: Program of Comparative Fertility Surveys, CELADE, 1964.

of the capital cities with the country as a whole. It is interesting to note that the discrepancy between the capital and the nation is larger in Buenos Aires than in Mexico, possibly expressing greater population pressure in the highly urbanized countries, which are rapidly passing through the demographic transition.

Table 3 suggests that, as in other parts of the world, the level of education in Latin America has an important influence on fertility. The strong negative correlation be-

TABLE 4.

Latin America.

Percentage of Catholic women who have ever used contraceptives, by educational level, in seven selected cities.

	Bogotá	Buenos Aires*	Caracas	Mexico City	Panama* City	Rio de Janeiro	San José
Women in legal or common law marriage	39.4	77.6	59.9	36.2	59.7	55.8	65.0
No education	14.6	52.0	38.1	11.0	35.0	40.0	48.3
Some primary education	28.2	74.8	52.5	27.7	46.3	45.5	54.1
Complete primary education	39.7	81.3	71.7	42.9	56.2	60.0	68.4
Some secondary education	59.5	73.9	77.6	54.4	65.0	69.1	78.5
Complete secondary education	74.0	83.4	64.7	63.8	66.7	72.7	50.1
Some university education	70.0	73.5	76.2	50.9	62.7	71.0	77.6

Source: Program of Comparative Fertility Surveys, CELADE, 1964.
* Refers to all women.

tween these two factors is very clear in all seven cities. It may imply that better educated people attach greater value to life, being aware that from the moment of conception all humans must have a chance to strive for health, happiness, and better opportunities. The importance of education for human dignity lies not only in the struggle against illiteracy as a component of freedom, but in the specific benefits derived from visualizing the family in its relation to national development, in a new appreciation of the family quality, rather than quantity, and in sufficient understanding of the human body and reproduction to make family planning effective according to the individual conscience.

Table 4 reveals that the proportion of Catholic women who declared they had ever tried to control their fertility rises with increasing levels of education. The lowest percent-

TABLE 5.

Latin America.

Percentage of Catholic women who declared knowing or having ever used a contraceptive method, by method, in five selected cities.

Method of contraception*	Use					Knowledge				
	Bogotá	Caracas	Mexico City	Rio de Janeiro	San José	Bogotá	Caracas	Mexico City	Rio de Janeiro	San José
Douche	12.3	24.5	14.5	23.0	17.2	56.4	79.2	60.0	81.4	72.0
Sterlization	1.0	5.9	1.8	6.1	5.9	36.1	80.2	50.4	63.2	72.0
Diaphragm	2.0	4.4	3.4	3.5	3.8	23.5	47.2	37.2	42.6	44.0
Jelly	6.6	2.0	3.8	5.4	4.6	46.2	23.6	23.2	29.4	27.6
Rhythm	18.5	18.2	14.9	16.0	21.3	48.6	59.8	47.0	62.0	70.8
Condom	10.5	30.6	8.9	12.4	36.9	39.7	78.9	43.1	62.2	87.7
Coitus interruptus	16.4	22.1	7.1	5.4	23.9	38.8	63.4	32.4	39.9	62.0
Pills	2.4	1.2	6.1	4.1	1.8	4.9	3.9	20.2	6.8	3.5

Source: Program of Comparative Fertility Surveys, CELADE, 1964.
* Methods are listed here in the same order in which they were included in the questionnaire.

ages of users were found in Bogotá and Mexico City among women with no education. These areas also have the highest average number of live births per married woman (3.95 and 4.16, respectively). A significant proportion of these women practiced contraception prior to their third pregnancy. It is clear that a substantial and increasing number of Catholics are using contraception in Latin America. The experience is

TABLE 6.

Percentage of 448 women reporting knowledge of specified contraceptive methods, Quinta Normal, Santiago, Chile, 1962–63.

None	7.1
Intra-uterine device	56.5
Diaphragm	30.4
Vaginal suppositories	29.2
Oral pills	11.6
Condoms	9.8
Vaginal douches	9.6
Rhythm	3.6
Ligation of fallopian tubes	3.4
Aspirin	2.5
Contraceptive jelly	2.5
Others	0.9
No answer	2.2

Source: B. Mariano Requena, "Studies of Family Planning in the Quinta Normal District of Santiago," *The Milbank Memorial Fund Quarterly*, Vol. XLIII, 1965, p. 81.

tion, 58% gave lack of information as their main reason for not doing so, and 25% stated fear of illness. Thus, over 80% showed ignorance of the nature of contraception. On the other hand, less than 4% cited religious reasons for not practicing birth control.

A sample survey conducted in Lima, Peru, showed the condom to be one of the most popular methods of contraception in all three socio-economic groups considered. Over 86% of the women at the upper and middle socio-economic levels knew of at least one "reliable" method of contraception (condom, vaginal tablets, diaphragm, oral anti-ovulation pills, etc.). Whereas only 62% of lower-class women had information about these methods and scarcely 35% had ever used one, 45% of the middle- and 57% of the upper-class women had done so.

TABLE 8.

Percentage of women reporting use of specified contraceptive methods, by socio-economic level, Lima, Peru, 1964.

Method of contraception	Socio-economic level		
	Upper	Middle	Lower
Rhythm	28.6	22.1	14.9
Douching	0.0	15.1	23.9
Coitus interruptus	3.6	4.7	20.9
Condom	28.6	32.6	22.4
Vaginal tablets or suppositories	0.0	2.3	1.5
Diaphragm	10.7	2.3	0.0
Oral pills	10.7	11.6	6.0
Other	17.9	9.3	10.4

Source: M. Francoise Hall, "Family Planning in Lima, Peru," *The Milbank Memorial Fund Quarterly*, Vol. XLIII, 1965, p. 109.

In summary, the fertility surveys thus far show a sizeable proportion of women who strongly feel the need for family limitation—generally about 80%. The lack of sexual education and the scarcity of family planning programs throughout the continent are the biggest obstacles to the limitation of family size.

similar in other Catholic countries: the birth rates of
Spain, and Portugal have fallen below those of the U
States through a wider resort to contraception.

Table 5 shows that many Catholic women know and
used contraceptive methods not sanctioned by their C
Many women resort to the less effective methods (do
jellies, *coitus interruptus*). The anti-ovulation pill do
yet appear to be very popular.

Local family planning surveys have been conducted
eral areas of Latin America. Table 6 refers to a study

TABLE 7.

*Percentage of 200 women who reported use of specified contraceptive
methods in Candelaria, Colombia, 1965.*

Coitus interruptus	33.0
Condom	21.0
Oral pills	9.0
Rhythm	7.0
Vaginal douches	20.0
Vaginal tablets (Aspirin)	10.0

Source: Alfredo Aguirre, "Epidemiological basis of infant mortality
published).

district of Santiago where intra-uterine devices seem
known extensively, along with the diaphragm and oral
However, it would seem that knowledge of family pla
methods is not enough, since 82% of the women did n
any contraceptive method.[8]

A sample of 200 women representing 20% of tho:
posed to the risk of conception in the locality of Cande
state of Valle, Colombia, gives a notion of the use of c
ceptive methods in a more rural setting. In Table 7 v
that a third of the couples were using *coitus interru*
21% the condom, and 20% vaginal douches. Anti-ovul
pills were taken by 7% of the women, a surprising
considering the high price of the product and the lo
come of the users. But here, as in many other such area
contraceptive methods most used are the least effective.
of interest that of the 114 women *not* practicing contr

CHARACTERISTICS OF FAMILY PLANNING PROGRAMS

There is no basic common feature of family planning programs throughout Latin America. Each country is trying to adapt to its own particular circumstances, organizing private clinics or research units in particular cities. No government is yet directly sponsoring these programs, which are, in general, led by the medical profession. Several countries have legal restrictions limiting the sale or distribution of contraceptives. The Catholic Church favors family planning in Latin America, provided the methods used are "natural," and that the aim be the regulation of family size within the general context of responsible parenthood. Furthermore, if we consider that the average educational level in Latin America is quite low, and that the present social organization does not encourage communication between the different classes, the conclusion is that the organization of national family planning programs in Latin America is still a thing of the future.

On the other hand, five national ministries of health have adopted a favorable attitude toward population studies and programs. The National Health Service of Chile is supporting the National Committee (Association) of Family Protection.[9] The Family Welfare Society of Guatemala has been officially recognized and is providing contraceptive services through the American Hospital in the city of Guatemala. The Demographic Association of El Salvador, The Center for Population and Development Studies of Peru, and the Population Division of the Ministry of Health and Social Assistance of Venezuela are working in close collaboration with their respective governments in a careful evaluation of socio-economic and demographic problems. By means of census analysis and special surveys of abortion and sexual attitudes, the seriousness of the population problem is being assessed. There are also demographic divisions in the National Planning Offices of Ecuador, El Salvador, Nicaragua, Paraguay, Peru, Venezuela, and Chile. Moreover, the Latin American Demographic Center (CELADE), created in 1957 under the auspices of the United Nations, has promoted am-

222   *Ramiro Delgado García*

bitious demographic research and training programs in Latin America.

Thus, there is hope that in future the traditional Latin American indifference toward population problems will be replaced by a positive policy favoring direct action and allowing private institutions to provide services in family planning.

SCOPE OF EXISTING FAMILY PLANNING ORGANIZATIONS

Active organizations giving limited contraceptive services (mostly to the urban communities) are present in Argentina, Barbados, Brazil, Chile, Colombia, Costa Rica, Ecuador, El Salvador, Guatemala, Haiti, Honduras, Jamaica, Mexico, Peru, Puerto Rico, Uruguay, and Venezuela. But only in Chile and Colombia are these organizations well coordinated and attempting to cover the entire country, although Honduras is now making similar plans.

Chilean Activities in Family Planning

The objectives of the Chilean Committee (Association) of Family Protection are the promotion of responsible and voluntary parenthood by providing equal opportunities for knowledge and means to the low-income groups; prevention of abortion and undesired pregnancy; and promotion of studies and research leading to national population growth commensurate with national resources.

In January 1964, the Committee was legally constituted as a private agency, and immediately began an evaluation of local health programs. In August 1965, the National Health Service, recognizing the important role of such activities, appointed a seven-member commission charged with making recommendations concerning the possible incorporation of family planning services into the regular program of the National Health Service.

Represented in the Association are such prestigious institutions as the University of Chile medical faculty, through the Departments of Obstetrics, Gynecology, and Preventive Medicine; The School of Public Health (Department of

TABLE 9.

Distribution of contraceptives according to type, Santiago, early 1965.

Type of contraceptive	Number	Percent
Intra-uterine devices	8,521	56.4
Gestagens	4,288	28.5
Rhythm	1,902	12.6
Spermicides	302	2.1
Diaphragm-jelly	81	0.4
Total	15,094	100.0

M.C.H.); The Catholic University medical faculty, through its Department of Obstetrics; The National Health Service; the Medical College of Physicians; the Colleges of Nursing and Midwifery; and the Chilean Society of Public Health, Obstetrics and Gynecology.

Prior to 1964, one or two hospital departments were providing contraceptive advice as part of routine gynecological service. In 1964, the Committee began to expand clinical facilities in Santiago and throughout the country. In Santiago alone, 14,002 patients were given contraceptives and a total of 45,297 consultations held in 1964. During the first half of 1965, contraceptives were prescribed to 15,094 couples. Contraceptives are usually free, and couples are generally allowed to select the method.

Teaching activities began in 1965, and since June of that year the first training program for Latin American physicians has been in operation, covering the principles of population dynamics, prevention of abortion, and birth control methods. This one-month course is sponsored by the International Planned Parenthood Federation, Western Hemisphere Region and, with the financial aid of the Public Welfare Fund, is being coordinated by the Department of Obstetrics, Barros Luco Hospital. The CELADE and the School of Public Health collaborate actively. Twenty-one physicians coming from Brazil, Argentina, Peru, Dominican Republic, Ecuador, Colombia, Venezuela, and Honduras completed this training before the end of the year.

Subjects related to demography, family planning, and abortion prevention have also been incorporated into the undergraduate curriculum of several schools (medicine, nursing, midwifery, etc.), and The School of Public Health of the University of Chile is instituting a Department of Demography and Population Dynamics. The first course is being offered to public health physicians in 1966.

In the way of research, six teams, each headed by a professor of the medical faculty, are conducting research on the prevention of abortion and acceptability of birth control methods. For example, one team from the Department of Obstetrics is studying an extensive program of contraceptives in a marginal urban development in order to evaluate the reduction of induced abortion, the effects upon birth rates, and the acceptance of intra-uterine devices by the population.

Colombian Activities in Family Planning

The first Assembly for the study of Colombian Demographic Problems was held in Bogotá in May 1964, under the auspices of the Colombian Association of Medical Schools, and with representation from the leading universities, the Ministry of Health, the National Planning Office, and the National Department of Statistics. Two organizations were created at this Assembly: the Division of Population Studies, which derives its membership from institutions, and the Colombian Association for the Scientific Study of Population, whose members are private citizens.

The Division of Population Studies sponsors and coordinates eight interdisciplinary population committees located in the six principal cities of the country and belonging to a medical school or university. The activities of the committees are locally supervised and usually directed by a full-time executive secretary. Four research areas have been given priority: fertility, family planning, abortion, and social demographic analysis. Fourteen research programs were launched in 1965, involving nearly 100 physicians, economists, sociologists, biostatisticians, social workers, nurses, midwives, and lawyers. A minimum of 20% of the cost of the projects is covered by the respective university or institution, and the rest is provided by national or international agencies and private citizens.

The Division of Population Studies furnishes information to the participating institutions, spreads general population news throughout the nation, coordinates activities with governmental offices, organizes national and international training programs, plans and promotes courses, seminars, and assemblies on population, publishes and distributes informative material, studies and coordinates the various research programs submitted for its consideration, finances and supervises the development of the different projects, and attempts to focus the attention of the community on the increasing population problems of the country. In 1965 it awarded 27 fellowships for study abroad in demography, family planning, communication, and the physiology of reproduction: 16 to physicians; 5 to economists; 3 to sociologists; 2 to social workers; and 1 to a priest. Additionally, ten Colombian doctors took a special one-month seminar in Chile on the Physiology of Reproduction and Family Planning.

Twice a year the Division organizes a three-day seminar on Demography. At the first seminar, 31 different projects were submitted for consideration, of which 12 were selected for financial support by the Division. The second seminar, held in October 1965, covered such topics as population pressure in Colombia, the relations between migration, urbanization, fertility, and communication and motivation in family planning. Foreign consultants to the seminar included Doctors J. Mayone Stycos (Cornell University and The Population Council), Donald J. Bogue (Chicago University), Alvaro Lopez (Princeton University), Walter Mentens (University of Montreal), and Lyle Saunders (Ford Foundation). Among the 70 participants and 15 observers were three representatives from Bolivia, Ecuador, and Peru, and nine Catholic priests. An obvious consequence of these preliminary steps will be the organization of an important number of family planning services in the principal areas of the country as normal components of the regular programs on maternal and child care.

In the universities various biomedical research projects are being developed and oriented toward the physiology of reproduction. The programs are usually carried out in the basic sciences laboratories and in the Departments of Endocrinology and Obstetrics and Gynecology of the Schools of Medicine. At the hospital level, some research is being conducted on abortion and contraceptive techniques.

The active population programs sponsored by the universities have given high status to the subject of family planning, which has become a respectable topic for open discussion in intellectual circles. Some politicians are even including the population issue in their platforms, a gratifying result of the campaign to educate the community leaders.

Conclusions

Several trends encourage us to foresee success for the future organization of extensive family planning programs throughout Latin America:

1. The increasingly felt needs of many couples in all social strata for effective methods of family regulation. The religious warnings, the frequent failures after using unreliable methods of contraception, and the economic limitations of the lower income groups are causing many couples to ask anxiously for modern contraceptives.

2. The interest of the universities and other institutions of higher education in conducting scientific research in the population field. Special credit in triggering this interest should be given to the medical profession, the first to become acquainted with the social problems caused by large families. The schools of medicine are deeply involved in research programs related to the physiology of reproduction and family planning. Young scientists are being trained in demography, communications, sampling techniques, social anthropology, etc.— fields completely ignored only a few years ago.

3. The concern of many governments for the social implications of population pressure. Some Latin American countries have created official population centers, in coordination with the planning offices, to study the situation.

4. Scientific research has developed more effective contraceptive products, which have the additional advantage of being used without relation to the sexual act.

5. The improvement of communication techniques, permitting a public awakening to the advantages of family planning.

FOOTNOTES

1. C. Miró and F. Rath, "Preliminary findings of Comparative Fertility Surveys in Three Latin American Countries," *The Milbank Memorial Fund Quarterly*, Vol. XLIII, 1965, pp. 36-61.

2. C. Miró, "Some Misconceptions Disproved: A Program of Comparative Fertility Surveys in Latin America," Conference of The Population Council on Family Planning, Geneva, August 1965.

3. R. Armijo and T. Monreal, "Epidemiology of Provoked Abortion in Santiago, Chile," Fourth Conference of the International Planned Parenthood Federation, Puerto Rico, April 1964.

4. M. Requena, "Epidemiology of Induced Abortion in Santiago, Chile: Social and Economic Correlates," *Demography*, Vol. 2, 1965, pp. 33-49.

5. F. Hall, "Family Planning in Lima, Peru," *The Milbank Memorial Fund Quarterly*, Vol. 43, 1965, pp. 100-112.

6. I. Rosada, "La Situación del Aborto Voluntario en el Uruguay: Posibles Soluciones," Fourth Conference of the International Planned Parenthood Federation, Puerto Rico, April 1964.

7. F. Villadiego and G. Llanos, "Prevalencia del Aborto en Cali," Second Seminar on Demography, La Ceja, Colombia, 1965.

8. M. Requena, "Studies of Family Planning in the Quinta Normal District of Santiago," *The Milbank Memorial Fund Quarterly*, Vol. XLIII, 1965, pp. 69-94.

9. H. Romero, "Experience with the Family Planning Program in Chile: Achievements and Problems," The Population Council Conference on Family Planning, Geneva, August 1965.

10. Demography and the Study of Population Problems in Latin America

J. MAYONE STYCOS

Latin America, with the most acute problem of population growth of any cultural region in the world today, has evinced the least concern about population problems. When the United Nations General Assembly voted on a resolution in 1962 to "give technical assistance, as requested by Governments, for national projects and programs dealing with problems of population" only Chile and Costa Rica voted in favor. Close to two-thirds of the Latin nations voted in opposition, and a quarter abstained. By way of contrast, only 8% of the Asian nations and a third of the African, European or North American nations opposed the legislation. The General Assembly then passed a revised resolution requesting the Secretary General to conduct an inquiry on population problems and economic development among the member governments. An extensive questionnaire was sent out, but by the time of the Secretary General's report in November 1964, only six Latin American nations had replied. Of these, Bolivia was uncommitted on the question of the relation of population growth and economic development, Colombia and Guatemala merely observed that economic development has been too slow for the population growth rate, and Venezuela ". . . views population growth, on the whole, as a positive factor in the development of the economy."[1] There seemed to be little reason for revising the conclusions of an earlier United Nations report which stated that "most of the countries look on the prospect of a population much larger than the present as a challenge, but not as a burden."[2]

The Latin position on population (or its absence) has usually been explained by reference to the political or religious power of the Catholic Church. While undoubtedly of some influence, especially in inhibiting public discussion of the topic, the Church has thus far had few battles to fight on the demographic issue because Latin intellectuals generally have not believed in the existence of a population problem—for reasons which have nothing to do with religion. Marxists have regarded the emergence of excess population as impossible in an efficient socialist state, and have labeled the population problem an imperialist smoke-screen to divert attention from the need for more basic social and economic reforms; nationalists have viewed the peopling of Latin America's open spaces as a kind of manifest destiny which would bring power to the small, weak nations of the Western Hemisphere. The concept of people as power is well illustrated in the writings of N. Viera Altamirano, editor of El Salvador's *El Diario de Hoy,* who maintains that Latin America needs two billion more inhabitants to reach an optimal level,[3] as well as by a Brazilian Minister of Health when he made the following statement:

> . . . in underdeveloped countries such as Brazil, where over 50% of the energy utilized in production is muscular in nature, population size constitutes a real element of power which is the most important means of national progress. Therefore, anything which increases population growth is beneficial for us.[4]

But the Marxist and nationalist positions are minority ones in Latin America. Indifference to the question of population has been more characteristic. This indifference is the product of Latin America's demographic history, combined with the virtual absence of Latin American demographic analysis.

DEMOGRAPHIC HISTORY OF LATIN AMERICA

Latin Americans have long lived in a psychological atmosphere of *underpopulation.* The Spanish and Portuguese settlers were acutely conscious of their small numbers *vis-à-vis*

the Indians, who were often reluctant to work for the colon-
izers. At various periods and places different schemes were
devised for obtaining a labor force sufficient to work the
mines, the plantations, and the haciendas: the *encomienda*
and *mita* systems, and slavery, were efforts at providing
cheap manpower, generally for rural pursuits. Later, a number of Latin American countries encouraged massive European immigration, just as did the United States and Canada.
While the problem of scarce labor has been replaced by that
of unemployment and underemployment in Latin America,
the mystique of the rural frontier and of boundless areas of
untapped land and resources lives on.

In any event, neither population size nor rate of natural
increase has been remarkable until recently. As late as 1920,
the total population of the 20 republics of Latin America
was less than the present population of Indonesia. With only
about nine persons for every square kilometer, Latin America
today has a population density half that of the United States
and one-tenth that of Europe. Finally, as late as the period
1925-35 only two countries had annual growth rates as high
as 2.5%, whereas in the decade ahead (1965-75) 16 nations
will fall in this category, with four of them growing at 3.5%
or more.[5] The novelty of current rates of growth and the
failure to distinguish problems of absolute size or density
from problems of growth account for much of the indifference.

Data and Demographers

Latin America, so European in many aspects, lagged far
behind Europe in developing a tradition of gathering systematic data via censuses and vital statistics. Only eight republics took population censuses between 1925 and 1934,
and 13 in the 1935-44 period.[6] While virtually all nations
took a census during the past ten years, Uruguay's recent
census was its first in over half a century.

Data based on the registration of vital events are even
more deficient. For example, only five of the 20 republics are
considered to have reasonably complete registration of

deaths, and these countries (Argentina, Chile, Costa Rica, El Salvador, and Mexico) account for only one-third of Latin America's population. Some of the reasons for the poor quality of birth and death registration are cited by Gaete-Darbó:

> Registration is carried out by a large number of officials who work on a notably autonomous basis, separated from one another, with no possibility of consulting each other and with little advice or control; the statistical training of registration officials is practically nil . . . it is virtually sufficient to know how to read and write (in most countries) . . . in no country does training cover statistical work or scientific administration; registration of data depends partly on the registrar, partly on the community, and partly on the medical and paramedical group, . . . which makes it more complex, with errors in registration more difficult to discover and correct.[7]

As scarce as are good demographic statistics in Latin America, demographers to analyze them are even scarcer. "Despite the fact that most countries now take periodic censuses," notes one observer, "analysis of these data leave much to be desired."[8] "Relatively few articles which appear in internationally-read journals are written by Latin American scholars," writes another commentator. Even the official journal of the Inter-American Statistical Association, *Estadística*, ". . . has had to fill its pages with translations because of the lack of original material."[9] As one measure of the professional contributions of Latin American demographers, we may look at the national origins of contributors to the World Population Conferences (Table 1). At the first conference, held in Rome in 1954, 13 Brazilians presented papers, but the other 19 Latin American republics were represented by only a dozen contributors—only one more than the Netherlands delegation, and well under the number of readers of papers for either Japan or India. A decade later, at the Belgrade Conference, the number of Latin American contributors of papers had declined from 25 to 21 and the proportion of Latin American contributors from seven to four per cent. (These figures do not include contributions of Latins working in international organizations. At the 1965 meeting,

232 *J. Mayone Stycos*

there were contributions on Latin America by six members
of the United Nations Latin American Demographic Center
and four members of CEPAL.)

TABLE 1.

Place of origin of contributors of papers to World Population Conferences 1954 and 1965.
(in per cent)

Origin	1954	1965
Latin America	7	4
Africa	4	4
Asia	8	17
North America[a]	25	22
Eastern Europe (including USSR)	2	18
Western Europe and Oceania	44	21
International Organizations[b]	10	14
Total	100	100
Number of contributors	(359)	(547)

[a] Includes English-speaking Caribbean and Puerto Rico.
[b] Since it was often difficult to establish the national origins of members of
nternational organizations, they were given a separate classification.

Another measure of the size of the profession is provided by
data on membership in the International Union for the
Scientific Study of Population. In 1964 Africa had 19 members, Asia 78, the United States and Canada 143, and Europe
279. Latin America had only 49, of which Argentina, Brazil,
and Chile accounted for 31. Japan and the Netherlands each
had almost twice as many members as Mexico and Central
America combined, while Japan and India together had six
more members than all of Spanish-speaking Latin America.[10]

The situation with respect to training shows Latin Americans similarly disadvantaged. Most fellowships for the graduate study of demography are given by the Population Council. As shown below, as many fellowships have gone to Ko-
reans in the past ten years as to citizens of the 20 Latin
American republics.

But Population Council fellowships are normally for
study in the United States or Europe. What about training
in Latin America itself? The principal facility at the present

TABLE 2.

Demographic fellowships, The Population Council, 1953–64.

Africa	18
Asia (Total)	109
India	44
Pakistan	13
Japan	14
Korea	9
Latin America	9

Source: Data in *The Population Council Newsletter*, March 1965.

time is the Centro Latinoamericano de Demografía (CE-LADE) in Santiago, Chile. Organized by the United Nations in 1957, the Center has offered instruction in technical aspects of demography to about 15 students per year. There is general agreement among experts that the quality of instruction is very high, that staff and students are extremely hard working, that administration is efficient, and that morale is high. However, the impact of this institution on *national* development of demography in Latin America has been disappointing. Of the 89 students trained between 1958 and 1963 few came from or have risen to positions of influence in government or universities. Indeed, because of the quality and background of the students and the brief period of training, "Only a rather small group," according to CELADE's director, "will eventually be demographers. . . ."[11] Only four graduates are now engaged in full-time teaching, although a dozen more may teach a course or two.

The absence of demographic teaching or research in Latin American universities is a key to the problem. CELADE cannot train people for positions which do not exist, nor can it attract high-quality academic students if they have never heard of demography. It has had to rely largely on governmental nominations of middle-level civil servants from official statistical bureaus. In the meantime few inroads have been made in the Latin American universities, the great majority of which offer not a single course in demography.

Even in Brazil where, because of the efforts of G. Mortara,

a relatively distinguished tradition in demography has been established, Mortara can speak of the ". . . contempt for demography in the organization of university programs." He notes wrily that in the faculties of statistical sciences there is only one course in demographic statistics and in the faculties of philosophy and economics, "a half-course," and concludes that true development of scientific research in demography requires ". . . a modification in higher education which would grant this discipline the place it merits among the course materials of economic, social and administrative sciences."[12]

It may seem strange that this demographic desert should exist in the universities of Latin America where, unlike most underdeveloped regions, academic institutions have been well entrenched for one or two centuries. Further, sociology and economics, the disciplines most intimately associated with demography in the United States and Europe, have long been recognized disciplines in Latin American universities. Sociology, the study of which began in the nineteenth century, now has "hundreds of professional chairs," and chairs of economics are even more numerous. Actually, the absence of demographic work in the universities is largely due to the peculiar development of the social sciences in Latin America, where sociology was early established along non-empirical, humanistic, and literary lines, strongly under the dominance of the powerful schools of law; and where economics was more allied to accounting and business administration than to science. While the scientifically inclined tended to enter technological professions such as medicine and engineering, "sociology" tended to be such an amorphous discipline that "lawyers, literary men, and even physicians were called 'sociologists'."[13] Indeed, the early acceptance and institutionalization of "sociology" has impeded its progress as a modern discipline in Latin America, and scientifically oriented schools or departments emerged in Latin American institutions only in the 1950's. Even now, however, only a minimal amount of demography is provided in the newer institutes,[14] partly because the field has been viewed as more appropriate for government technicians in the census bureaus or statistical services. At the moment, the only possibility for academic demographic study at the graduate level in a Latin American national institution is provided at the Centro de Estudios Demográficos y Económicos of the Colegio de México.

Of the three problems we have discussed, indifference to population questions, shortage of reliable data, and scarcity of demographers, the greatest strides toward solutions thus far have been taken with respect to data. The improvements have come from census data rather than vital statistics. Including Peru, which took a census in 1940, 16 countries which took censuses in 1950 took them again in the early 1960's. For the first time for most of these countries, a reasonably accurate measure of decennial population growth was provided, and provided during a period of especially high rates of growth. The improvement of data had some influence in dispelling indifference toward population problems, for population growth had exceeded and economic gains had fallen short of expectations. The combined impact on the new government bureaucracies dedicated to economic and social development, if not profound, was at least perceptible. In 1964, by Presidential decree, Peru established a Population Center, and in the same year Venezuela created a Population Department in the Ministry of Health. The new concern even led the Organization of American States to such unprecedented actions as a 1964 symposium on Population Problems, held at the OAS General Secretariat and chaired by Alberto Lleras, and the appointment in 1965 of a special committee to consider demographic problems. The Directing Council of the demographically conservative Pan American Health Organization recommended recently in its Resolution 31 that the PAHO undertake studies " . . . on population dynamics and population growth, dealing with medical demography, epidemiology, and human reproduction as related to socio-economic development. . . ."

It will be much longer before such concerns eventuate in an increase in trained personnel, and, so far as I know, only a few universities in Chile and Colombia have taken any concrete steps in this direction.

Clearly, one of the highest priorities at the present time is the encouragement of university teaching and research in demography. The most hopeful recent developments are the PAHO efforts at stimulating training programs in "medical demography" for schools of public health, and the 1966 Conference on "Demography and the Universities" sponsored by the Council on Higher Education of the American Republics (CHEAR), The Population Council, and the University of San Carlos in Guatemala.

POPULAR CONCERN FOR POPULATION CONTROL

For policies and programs leading to the solution of population problems, the attitudes, knowledge, and skills of the educated elite in Latin America are most relevant. But in order for such programs to function successfully, the cooperation of the general public is required. This is especially true with respect to fertility which, unlike mortality, can only be affected by the behavior of individual couples. In this connection, then, we shall review the evidence with respect to the receptivity of the general Latin American public to possible programs of fertility control.

Population control of *some* kind is not new to Latin America, and exists to a varying degree in all countries. Fertility in Argentina began to decline as long ago as the late nineteenth century, and Chile showed a marked decline in the late 1920's.[15] It is not unlikely that Uruguayan fertility also saw early declines. Further, it is the case that in nearly every Latin American country today, there is a close association between the degree of urbanization of its provinces or departments and the average fertility rates of those provinces.[16] Finally, within the major cities of Latin America there are marked fertility differentials by education or social class. In most countries those groups with lower fertility are too few in number to affect national averages, but the differentials are there and we can learn something from them.

The three principal methods for limiting fertility in Latin America are increased age at marriage, induced abortion, and contraception.

Age at Marriage

One of the principal ways in which European countries brought pre-industrial fertility rates down to modern levels was by delayed marriage. While Argentina and Chile show ages at marriage similar to those of European countries, (about 40% of the females aged 20-24 married), virtually all other countries have over half the women in this age group married.[17] Moreover, there are undoubtedly important differences among social classes. For example, a survey of women in Lima disclosed that the mean age at first legal or consenting union was 22.4 for the highest of four social classes, and 19.1 for the lowest.[18] This might suggest that as education and economic development increase, the disadvantaged nations and classes will approximate the later ages of marriage of the economically advanced nations and classes. On the other hand, if education, urbanization, and economic development produce a shift from consensual union to marriage, fertility could be affected positively. Studies in the West Indies indicate that consensual unions are much less stable and consequently much less fertile than legal marriages.[19] Very little is known about the relationship of mating patterns to fertility for most of Latin America, and this subject should be assigned a high priority for research.

Abortion

Induced abortion is an age-old and probably universal method for controlling family size. In Japan and in the communist countries of Eastern Europe, medically supervised abortions are among the commonest means of family planning, the annual number of abortions exceeding the number of births in some nations. Western countries have tended to regard this technique as abhorrent, sinful, and criminal. Mainly for these reasons, our knowledge of its incidence in

Western societies is very poor, but some authorities believe it had a great deal to do with the decline of fertility in Western Europe.

In Latin America, physicians associated with the maternity services of hospitals have long been aware of the high incidence, because of the number of women hospitalized for complications due to induced abortion. The whole topic, however, was officially ignored. Diagnostic classifications in hospital records were often vague, the topic was rarely discussed at medical conferences, and each country tended to regard the problem as unique. A small bombshell was dropped in 1962, however, when Drs. Armijo and Monreal of Chile presented a paper on the epidemiology of abortion in Santiago to the Seventh Pan American Congress of Social Medicine.[20] Participants were startled to hear this problem discussed openly and frankly, and even more suprised to discover that other countries shared their "unique" problems.

The Armijo-Monreal paper was the first in a Chilean series based on household probability samples involving interviews with nearly 3,800 women aged 20-50 in the cities of Santiago, Concepción, and Antofagasta. The study disclosed a startling incidence—just under one out of every four women interviewed admitted at least one induced abortion, ranging from 15% in Concepción to 27% in Antofagasta. Of the aborting women, a quarter had already had three or more abortions.[21] It was also found that a third of the Santiago abortions resulted in hospitalization—ranging from over half of those performed by the women themselves, to less than a quarter of those performed by doctors or midwives.[22] These results were publicized around the same time that other investigators were assessing the costs to the national health service of hospitalizing abortion cases. It was found that approximately 184,000 hospital "bed-days" were expended on abortion cases in a single year (1960); that 42% of the general admissions to emergency services were abortion cases; and that abortion represented over a third of the surgical treatments given in the obstetrical services of the hospitals surveyed.[23]

The addition of economic to the moral and health considerations produced even greater concern, and a number of investigations were initiated or announced in other countries. Preliminary results parallel the Chilean. Thus, in Buenos Aires intensive interviewing was carried out among the 600 female patients aged 35-49 who attended non-obstetrical or psychiatric clinics of the Guillermo Rawson Hospital in 1964. Over 25% of all pregnancies were found to have been terminated in induced abortions.[24] In a representative sample of households in Rio de Janeiro in 1963, of the 1,585 married or mated women aged 20-25 who had had at least one live birth, 10% had also had at least one induced abortion.[25] The lowest reported incidence thus far comes from Lima, where a survey was confined to younger women, aged 20-39. Less than 5% of the pregnancies of these women had resulted in an induced abortion, according to their own admission.[26] More impressive data have been reported for other countries, ranging from three provoked abortions for every live birth in Uruguay,[27] to 15% of all pregnancies in Guatemala.[28] Whatever the precise figures, there is little doubt that abortion rates in Latin American cities are higher than anyone suspected.

20-30% of pregnancies or more!

It should not be thought that the higher rates reported are primarily due to pregnancies stemming from promiscuous relations. The Brazilian incidence data are based only on married women, and over three-quarters of the Argentine abortions occurred to married women. In the Santiago study, 85% of the induced abortions occurred to married women, who constituted 71% of the entire sample.[29]

Of greater interest here than the medical or social problems occasioned by these rates are the implications for popular motivations concerning limitation of family size. If so many women are willing to adopt measures which are not only illegal and irreligious but painful and dangerous, the desire to control fertility can be assumed to be fairly intense.

This would suggest that the climate is ripe for the acceptance of contraceptive methods for the control of fertility.

Contraception

Results from the CELADE surveys discussed in Delgado's paper show interesting differences among cities, but on the whole confirm findings from earlier studies in the Caribbean, Peru, and Chile. Most women do not regard a large family as ideal, and if they could choose the number of children for themselves, would have three or four. Furthermore, the majority of the women have already tried some method of contraception.[30]

TABLE 3.

Preliminary data from CELADE sample surveys conducted among married women, 20–50, in six Latin American cities.

	Preferred number of children	Per cent who have practiced contraception
Bogotá	3.6	40
Caracas	3.5	59
Mexico City	4.2	38
Panama City	3.5	60
Rio de Janeiro	2.7	58
San José	3.6	65

Although Rio de Janeiro seems somewhat unusual in terms of small family ideals, let us use this city as an example for more detailed analysis, since further data are available. The woman interviewed had averaged only 2.3 live births at the time of interview, but when asked if they wanted any more, eight out of every ten replied negatively. The differences by social class are especially interesting. Women with university training have the largest ideal family size (2.9) and those who have not gone beyond primary school the smallest (2.5). "Of women in the highest status category, 23.4% regarded one or two children as the ideal. On the other hand, as many as 42.6% of women in the lowest category wanted only this number of children."[31] However, class differences in fertility itself are exactly the reverse. Women with no education have had 3.3 births, those with some university training just over one. Thus, the lower classes, who want the fewest children, in fact have the most.

The author found this same pattern of relationships in Peru, both in Lima and in the provincial city of Chimbote. It was also found that the lower classes were much more sensitive than the upper classes to the economic liabilities of additional children.[32] Why then do the lower classes have more? Probably because they marry earlier, practice less contraception, and practice it less effectively. Perhaps, too, ignorance of modern contraceptive techniques, and disenchantment or failure with methods such as *coitus interruptus* or rhythm may lead many women into abortion. In Rio de Janeiro, women who had aborted were more likely than others to have practiced contraception, and the lower the social class the more likely was this method to have been *coitus interruptus,* the safe period, or folk techniques. In the Buenos Aires study, about half the abortions had been preceded by contraceptive practice, and in 83% of these cases *coitus interruptus* was the method employed.[33] In Peru, although the incidence of over-all contraceptive practice declined from about two-thirds of the upper class women to just over a third of the lower class, the use of *coitus interruptus* and douche increased from 4% of the upper to 44% of the lower class users.[34]

CONCLUSIONS

The traditional indifference of Latin American intellectuals to population problems is understandable in the light of Latin America's demographic history, its relatively poor demographic statistics, and the scarcity of demographers. Data have improved markedly in the past two decades, however, with pronounced effects on attitudes of the elite toward population problems. Technical skills have developed more slowly, and the faculties of social science and medicine in Latin American universities have not yet responded to the great need for training and research programs.

On the other hand, the general public, while probably indifferent to population problems in general, shows considerable interest in family planning, at least as indicated by urban studies of contraception, abortion, and attitudes toward family size. Solution of Latin America's population problems requires attacking the problem at various levels and in various ways, from providing more information about modern contraception to those who desire it, to alerting intellectuals to the significance of national and regional population growth. At whatever level, more professionally trained people is the first requirement.

FOOTNOTES

1. United Nations Economic and Social Council, *Inquiry Among Governments on Problems Resulting from the Interaction of Economic Development and Population Changes,* 64-26191, November 1964.

2. El Tiempo (Bogotá), reporting on the publication of the U.N. *World Social Situation for 1963,* April 10, 1963.

3. J. M. Stycos, "Opinions of Latin American Intellectuals Toward Population and Birth Control," *Annals of the American Academy of Political and Social Science,* July 1965.

4. Wilson Fadul, speech to the World Health Organization, Geneva, 1964.

5. Arthur Corwin, *Contemporary Mexican Attitudes Toward Population, Poverty and Public Opinion,* University of Florida Press, 1963, p. 42.

6. Giorgio Mortara, "Appraisal of Census Data for Latin America," *Milbank Memorial Fund Quarterly,* Vol. XLII, No. 2, Part 2, April 1964.

7. A. Gaete-Darbó, "Appraisal of Vital Statistics in Latin America," *Milbank Memorial Fund Quarterly,* Vol. XLII, No. 2, Part 2, April 1964.

8. Waldermiro Bazanella, "Areas de Prioridad en la Investigación Social en América Latina," in *Ciencias Políticas y Sociales,* Vol. 26, October 1961, p. 520.

9. Nathan Keyfitz, "Assessment of Teaching and Training Program in the Universities of Latin America," *Milbank Memorial Fund Quarterly,* Vol. XLII, No. 2, Part 2, April 1964, pp. 236-37.

10. Figures taken from *Le Démographe,* October 1964.

11. Carmen Miró, "Principles and Practices of Teaching and Training in CELADE," *Milbank Memorial Fund Quarterly,* Vol. XLII, No. 2, Part 2, April 1964, p. 219.

12. G. Mortara, "Demographic Studies in Brazil," in P. Hauser and O. D. Duncan, *The Study of Population,* Chicago, Chicago University Press, 1959.

13. Orlando Fals Borda, "Desarrollo y Perspectivas de la Sociología Rural en Colombia y la América Latina," *Memorias del Primer Congreso Nacional de Sociología,* Bogotá, Editorial Iqeuima, 1963.

14. For discussions of courses available see E. Dieulefait, "The Teaching of Demography in Latin America," *The University Teaching of Demography*, UNESCO, 1957.

15. For estimates of general fertility rates in earlier decades see K. Davis, "The Place of Latin America in World Demographic History," *Milbank Memorial Fund Quarterly*, Vol. XLII, No. 2, Part 2, April 1964.

16. J. M. Stycos, "Needed Research on Latin American Fertility: Urbanization and Fertility," *Milbank Memorial Fund Quarterly*, Vol. XLIII, No. 4, Oct. 1965.

17. K. Davis, "The Place of Latin America in World Demographic History," *op. cit.*, Table 9, p. 39.

18. J. M. Stycos, unpublished survey data.

19. J. M. Stycos and K. W. Back, *The Control of Human Fertility in Jamaica*, Ithaca, Cornell University Press, 1964; and J. Blake, *Family Structure in Jamaica*, Free Press of Glencoe, Inc., 1961.

20. R. Armijo and T. Monreal, "Epidemiología del Aborto en Santiago," *Revista Conferencia Medico Panamericano*, Vol. 10, August 1963.

21. R. Armijo and T. Monreal, "The Problem of Induced Abortion in Chile," *Milbank Memorial Fund Quarterly*, Vol. XLIII, No. 4, Oct. 1965.

22. R. Armijo and T. Monreal, "Factores Asociados a las Complicaciones del Aborto Provocado," *Revista Chilena de Obstetricia y Ginecología*, Vol. 91, April 1963.

23. S. Plaza and H. Briones, "Demanda de Recursos de Atención Médica del Aborto Complicado," Congreso Médico Social Panamericano, Santiago, Chile, 1962, mimeographed.

24. Nydia Gomes Ferrarotti and Carmen Garcia Varela, "Investigaciones Sobre Incidencia del Aborto Criminal," unpublished paper, 1964; and "Encuesta Sobre el Aborto y sus Variables, Incluyendo Métodos de Planificación 'de Familia,'" *Revista de la Sociedad de Obstetricia y Ginecología de Buenos Aires*, No. 611, December 1964.

25. B. Hutchinson, "Induced Abortion in Brazilian Married Women," *América Latina*, Vol. 7, No. 4, October-December, 1964.

26. M. F. Hall, "Birth Control in Lima, Peru: Attitudes and Practices," *Milbank Memorial Fund Quarterly* Vol. XLIII, No. 4, October 1965.

27. I. Rosada, "La Situación del Aborto Voluntario en el Uruguay, Posibles Soluciones," Fourth Conference of the Western Hemisphere Region, International Planned Parenthood Federation, San Juan, P.R., April 1964, mimeographed.

28. Roberto Santiso, "Contraceptives as a Means of Combating Illegal Abortions," Fourth Conference of the International Planned Parenthood Federation, Western Hemisphere Region, San Juan, P.R., April 1964, mimeographed.

29. R. Armijo and T. Monreal, "Epidemiología del Aborto provocado en Santiago," *op. cit.*, p. 38.

30. C. Miró and F. Rath, "Preliminary Findings of Comparative Fertility Surveys in Three Latin American Countries," *Milbank Memorial Fund Quarterly*, Vol. XLIII, No. 4, Oct. 1965.

31. B. Hutchinson, *op. cit.*, p. 32.

244   *J. Mayone Stycos*

32. J. M. Stycos, "Social Class and Preferred Family Size in Peru," *American Journal of Sociology*, July 1965.

33. Armijo and Monreal found such a low incidence of *coitus interruptus* in Chile that the possibility of faulty interviewing techniques must be entertained.

34. M. F. Hall, *op. cit.*, Table 2.

Sponsors of the Pan-American Assembly on Population

The American Assembly

The American Assembly was established by Dwight D. Eisenhower at Columbia University in 1950. It holds non-partisan Assemblies of American leaders and publishes authoritative books to illuminate issues concerning United States policy. The Assembly seeks to provide information, stimulate discussion, and evoke independent conclusions in matters of vital public interest. An affiliate of Columbia University, the Assembly is a national, educational institution incorporated under the State of New York.

All Assemblies follow the same procedure. A group of men and women representing a broad range of experience, competence, and leadership meet in small groups for several days to discuss the Assembly topic and consider policy alternatives. At the close of these informal sessions, participants adopt in plenary session a final report of findings and recommendations.

Universidad del Valle

Since its founding twenty years ago, the Universidad del Valle, in Cali, Colombia, has stimulated fundamental changes in the university structure of the country. It has achieved university autonomy, departmentalized its faculties, undertaken studies of community problems, and established a general studies curriculum as a prerequisite for advanced education. Its School of Medicine is a center in Latin America for the training of general physicians and specialists.

245

Association of Colombian Medical Schools

The Association of Colombian Medical Schools is a non-profit organization established in 1959, consisting of the nation's seven medical schools as founding members: the School of Arts and Sciences of the University of the Andes, the Superior School of Public Health, the Colombian Hospital Association, the National Nutrition Institute, and the Military Hospital, as affiliate members; and of medical school professors as individual members. The fundamental purpose of the organization is the advancement of medical education and research.

The Population Council

The Population Council was established in 1952 for the purpose of advancing knowledge in the field of population, conducting research, training, and technical consultation, as well as offering assistance in the medical and social sciences. As a private, non-profit foundation, it is not connected with any government, and has relations with no political, religious, or commercial group. Its staff is composed primarily of medical and social scientists.

Notes on the Contributors

CARMEN A. MIRÓ is the Director of the Latin American Demographic Center and a Vice President of the International Union for the Scientific Study of Population. She is a member of the Inter-American Statistical Institute and the Population Association of America, and is a Fellow of the American Statistical Association. Her articles have appeared in several journals.

ARTUR HEHL NEIVA is Professor of Demography, School for Sociology and Political Science, Pontifical Catholic University, Rio de Janeiro. He is Executive Secretary of the United States Educational Commission (Fulbright Commission) in Brazil. Professor Neiva is a Fellow of the Brazilian Institute for History and Geography and the International Union for the Scientific Study of Population. His publications include several studies of migration, especially in Brazil, and elsewhere in Latin America.

GEORGE W. ROBERTS is Professor of Demography, Department of Sociology, University of the West Indies, Kingston, Jamaica. He is a Vice President of the International Union for the Scientific Study of Population. Among his publications are *The Population of Jamaica*, 1957, and (with D. O. Mills) *Study of External Migration Affecting Jamaica*, 1958.

FRANK W. NOTESTEIN is President of The Population Council. He is a former Professor of Demography and Director of the Office of Population Research, Princeton University, and served as the first Director (Consultant-Director) of the Population Division of the Bureau of Social Affairs of the United Nations. Dr. Notestein is a past president of the Population Association of America, a member of the American

Statistical Association, the American Association for the Advancement of Science, and the International Union for the Scientific Study of Population.

OCTAVIO CABELLO has been a United Nations statistician since 1949 and currently serves as a regional adviser on housing problems and programs with the Economic Commission for Latin America. He is the author of numerous publications dealing with statistics, demography, public health and housing.

JORGE V. ARÉVALO is on the staff of the Latin American Demographic Center. He is a former Chief of the Statistics Division of the National Education Council in Argentina, and is currently a member of the International Union for the Scientific Study of Population and of the Population Association of America.

ABRAHAM HORWITZ, a Chilean, is Director of the Pan American Sanitary Bureau, operating arm of the Pan American Health Organization and Regional Office for the Americas of the World Health Organization. He has written numerous articles on infectious diseases, health and preventive medicine education, epidemiology, and public health administration.

MARY H. BURKE is chronic disease statistician of the Pan American Sanitary Bureau. Under her responsibility the publications of this office include *Health Conditions in the Americas* and *Reported Cases of Notifiable Diseases in the Americas*. She was previously associated with the United States Public Health Service and the Veterans' Administration.

REV. GUSTAVO PÉREZ RAMÍREZ, a Roman Catholic priest, is Director and founder of the Colombian Institute for Social Development, Secretary of the Latin American Secretariat of The International Federation of Institutes for Social and Socio-Religious Research, and a former President of the Colombian Association of Sociology. His publications include

The Colombian Peasant Farmer; a Structural Problem (1962), and *The Church in Colombia, Ecclesiastical Structures* (1961).

RAMIRO DELGADO GARCÍA is President of the Interdisciplinary Committee, Division of Population Studies, Colombian Association of Medical Schools, and Vice President of the Colombian Association for the Scientific Study of Population. Dr. Delgado is also Executive Secretary of the University Committee for Population Research and Chairman of the Department of Morphology, Universidad del Valle.

J. MAYONE STYCOS is Professor of Sociology and Director of the International Population Program at Cornell University. He is also a consultant on Latin America to The Population Council and an Assistant Editor of *Demography*. Dr. Stycos is the author of *Family and Fertility in Puerto Rico* and co-author of *The Family and Population Control* and the *Control of Human Fertility in Jamaica*.